AYRSHIRE AND THE

To Betty,
Jack and Inez,
fellow-expatriates,
and to
Gillian and Stephen

AYRSHIRE AND THE REFORMATION

People and Change, 1490–1600

Margaret H.B. Sanderson

TUCKWELL PRESS

First published in 1997 by
Tuckwell Press Ltd
The Mill House
Phantassie
East Linton
East Lothian EH40 3DG
Scotland

Copyright © Margaret H.B. Sanderson 1997

All rights reserved
ISBN 1 898410 91 7

British Library Cataloguing-in-Publication Data
A Catalogue record for this book
is available on request from the
British Library

The right of Margaret H.B. Sanderson to be identified
as the author of this work has been asserted
by her in accordance with
the Copyright, Design and Patent Act 1988

Typeset by Hewer Text Composition Services, Edinburgh

Printed and bound in Great Britain by
Short Run Press Ltd, Exeter

Contents

Preface	vii
Abbreviations	xi
Illustrations	xiii
Map	xiv
1. Ayrshire and Beyond	1
2. The People's Church: Before 1560	11
3. The Cure of Souls	23
4. The Lollards' Legacy	36
5. Towards Reform	48
6. A Receptacle of God's Servants	64
7. The Work of Reformation	84
8. Faithful Workmen	105
9. The People's Church: After 1560	120
Notes	145
Appendix: Revised *Fasti* of Ministers, Exhorters and Readers in Ayrshire, 1559–1600	159
Bibliography	177
Index	185

Preface

The historiography of the Scottish Reformation has been transformed since David Hay Fleming's classic account was published in 1910, in which he chronicled in documented detail what he saw as the spiritual bankruptcy of the old kirk and the nation's spontaneous welcome of the new. Since then historians have been re-assembling the pieces of sixteenth-century Scottish religious life scattered during his work of demolition. Their many-sided work of reconstruction has enriched our understanding of the revolution that took place and has created a wide field for exploration: the continuities and Anglo-Scottish protestant links, expounded by the first of the revisionists, Gordon Donaldson, 400 years after the events themselves; the nature and functions of the pre-Reformation church organisation, and its role in society; the contribution of many of its staff to contemporary European scholarship; the European links of early Scottish protestantism; the political context of the 1559–60 revolution, and the relationship of protestantism and ideas of national identity; the provision of a reformed resident parish ministry; attempts to realise the Reformers' ideals in the field of education; the continuity of Scottish culture, if in different forms and for different purposes, in the visual arts, music and literature despite the upheaval.

There is always the danger, of course, that in revising we might swing too far in the opposite direction. In this, we would-be objective historians are as much the children of our times as our openly partisan predecessors. It is all too easy to concentrate on the context of the Reformation at the expense of the content. However, the growing number of studies of the Reformation in the localities – of which Ian Cowan published an interim survey in his Historical Association pamphlet, *Regional Aspects of the Scottish Reformation* (1978) – should save us from simply replacing the old assumptions with new assertions, or exchanging a Reformation waiting to happen for one that never was, or at best arrived late.

In her own paper, '"Princes" and the Regions in the Scottish Reformation' (*Church, Politics and Society, 1408–1929*, ed. N. Macdougall, Edinburgh, 1983, 65–84), Jenny Wormald remarked that 'local reformation studies have scarcely begun in Scotland', adding that Ian Cowan's pamphlet and Michael Lynch's *Edinburgh and the Reformation* (Edinburgh, 1981), the first such study to appear in book form, 'whet the appetite for more'. Before then articles had appeared on the Reformation in such localities as Dumfries, Galloway, Ayrshire, St Andrews, and Orkney and Shetland, and others have followed on Dunkeld, Dunblane, Dundee, St Andrews, Perth, Monifeith, Aberdeen and the Highlands, largely due to the longstanding support given to historical studies by local publishing societies. Details of these papers appear in the Reformation bibliography compiled by James Kirk (*RSCHS*, xxiii, 1987). However, the only other study to appear in book form so far is Frank Bardgett's *Scotland Reformed: The Reformation in Angus and the Mearns* (Edinburgh, 1989). It is hoped that the work done by Ian Flett on radical Dundee, Allan White on conservative Aberdeen, and Mary Verschuur on Perth, whose Reformation most closely of Scottish towns resembled the pattern in some European cities, will yet be published in book form.

The value of these local studies is twofold. They show that Scotland had not one but a variety of Reformations which, when we are at last able to compare them should help to make the nationwide picture much clearer. They also reveal that a balanced picture is emerging from the work of revision, a picture which includes both political influences and theological schism; a church which attracted much contemporary criticism, but was a less than monolithic structure, not all of whose office-bearers contributed to its loss of credibility on the eve of Reformation; the long timescale over which the movement for reform matured, as well as the vulnerability of the Lords of the Congregation right up to their moment of victory, which they achieved with considerable political skill; the personal links and social networks which strengthen the impression of underground but persistent religious dissent, emergent in the privy kirks of the later 1550s; the vital role of the laity alongside religious leadership; an appreciation of the extent to which the new kirk was staffed as well as understaffed in its early years; the creation of a new protestant spirituality and the presence of catholic recusancy.

Ayrshire made a distinctive contribution over a long period to the growth of religious dissent in Scotland and the final acceptance of protestantism. This study, which incorporates a complete revision of a much earlier short article (*RSCHS*, xvii, (1970), 81–98), places the changing religious life of sixteenth century Ayrshire in its national and international, social and political contexts, while keeping at the heart of the discussion those questions that were being asked about traditional belief and practice. It is relevant to the current debate on the origins and progress of the protestant Reformation in Britain. At the same time it is the story of real people in real parishes who lived through changing times.

I am grateful to Sheena Andrew, Reference Librarian at the Carnegie Library, Ayr, for working photocopies of Ayr burgh and Alloway barony court books and to Andrew Broom for photography. My thanks are due to the following for permission to reproduce items from their collections, records and publications as illustrations: The Ayrshire Archaeological and Natural History Society and Dr John Strawhorn, the Carnegie Library, Ayr, Historic Scotland, the Keeper of the Records of Scotland, the Kirk Session of

Preface

Galston, the Royal Commission on the Ancient and Historical Monuments of Scotland and the National Monuments Record of Scotland Archive, and the Scottish Text Society. Finally, two Ayrshire schoolteachers, Miss Mary Kerr and Mr Andrew Borland, first kindled my enthusiasm for history, social and religious, and I am glad to have this opportunity of repaying some of my debt to their memory.

Margaret H.B. Sanderson,
1997

Abbreviations Used

These include Scottish Record Office document references and abbreviations used in the Appendix. Full details of short titles used will be found in the Bibliography.

AANHS Ayrshire Archaeological and Natural History Society publications
Adm. Admitted (of a minister's appointment)
B. Burgh records (SRO)
CC Commissary Court records (SRO)
CH Church records (SRO)
CS Court of Session records (SRO)
D. Died
dem. demitted (office)
DI Diligence records (SRO)
E. Exchequer records (SRO)
Edin. Tests. Edinburgh Testaments (SRO)
GD Gifts and Deposits – private archives (SRO)
Glasgow Tests. Glasgow Testaments (SRO)
Gr. Granted
JC Justiciary Court records (SRO)
Mun. Muniments – family papers
NLS National Library of Scotland
NP Notarial records (SRO)
Pars. Parson
Pres. Presented
RD Register of Deeds (SRO)
Reg.Pres.Ben. Register of Presentations to Benefices (SRO)
RMS *Register of the Great Seal of Scotland*
RPC *Register of the Privy Council of Scotland*
RSCHS *Records of the Scottish Church History Society*
RSS *Register of the Privy Seal of Scotland*
RSS Register of the Privy Seal of Scotland; unprinted (SRO)
s. son
SC Sheriff Court Records (SRO)
SRO Scottish Record Office
SRS Scottish Record Society

TDGNHAS *Transactions of the Dumfries and Galloway Natural History and Antiquarian Society*
Trans.   Translated; to or from a parish appointment
vic.   Vicar or vicarage
wid.   Widow
wit.   witness

Note on spelling and terminology

Original spelling has been retained in all quotations from contemporary sources. Modern English equivalents, as well as explanations of legal terms, are given in brackets. To avoid confusion, the spelling 'Cunningham' is used for the surname, 'Cunninghame' for the locality.

Illustrations

1. Symington parish church
2. The New Testament in Scots
3. The Tower of Bar
4. Dean Castle
5. Abbey Green, Kilwinnning
6. Galston Baptismal Register
7. Monkredding House
8. Crossraguel Abbey

The Parishes of Sixteenth-Century Ayrshire.
(By permission of the Ayrshire Archaeological and Natural History Society)

CHAPTER ONE

Ayrshire and Beyond

Ayrshire has been aptly described as 'a great natural amphitheatre facing westwards towards the sea'.[1] Seated in imagination on the upper terraces of the eastern uplands and looking down on the sixteenth-century scene, a few natural features would be familiar to us, such as the wonderful sunset behind the islands of the Firth of Clyde and the courses of the rivers some of which formed the internal boundaries of the sheriffdom. The two royal burghs of Irvine and Ayr would be immediately identifiable on their coastal sites, if much smaller, all the more visible because of the absence of the many towns of modern Ayrshire which in the sixteenth century were only village-sized or did not exist at all. Today's farms with their neatly hedged fields converging on a single farmstead would be replaced with a patchwork of settlements seemingly scattered across the arable land and surrounded by far more moorland and undrained moss than today. The traffic would be moving unbelievably slowly to our eyes, at human and animal pace. We would notice, looking from left to right, that there were more people around the centre of the 'stage' than at the extremities, which is still true after 400 years.

The characteristics of the three ancient bailiaries into which sixteenth-century Ayrshire was divided from south to north, Carrick, Kyle and Cunninghame, varied geographically and demographically. Carrick, stretching from the river Doon southwards, was essentially a pastoral country which shared its landscape with Galloway; 'a barren country but for bestial' was how an English observer described it in the 1560s.[2] It contained only eight of the sheriffdom's 43 parishes although it was as large in area as Kyle to the north which had 20 parishes. The population of Carrick was concentrated along the rivers Doon, Stinchar and Girvan whose valleys were peppered with lairds' houses and in the baronies of Crossraguel and Monkland belonging to the abbeys of Crossraguel and Melrose respectively. The small town of Maybole was created a burgh of barony for the earl of Cassillis in 1516. The impression of the English observer already quoted was that the Kennedy lairds, such as Bargany and Blairquhan, were 'nothing inferior in living to the earl of Cassillis except that he is their chief and of a surname', something that was less true of the cadets of the earls of Glencairn and Eglinton in Cunninghame. If the evidence of testamentary inventories is taken as a guide, the Carrick lairds seem on the whole to have been richer in cattle, sheep and horses and even in the value of household goods and the amount of net estate than their counterparts in Kyle and Cunninghame.

It is tempting to speculate that the very nature of the land in Carrick may have bred a conservative race. There were no royal burghs to act as reminders of authority other than that of the feudal lords, although to be sure these could often dominate the politics of a royal burgh. The most populous districts of Carrick lay too far south and west for easy access to those roads that led to the political heartland of Scotland so familiar to the inhabitants of Kyle and Cunninghame, although the people of Carrick used them nevertheless. Any elements of conservatism would be reinforced by the fact that the monopoly of social and military power lay firmly in the hands of the earls of Cassillis and their Kennedy kinsmen. The only important ecclesiastical institutions apart from the parish churches (and including some of these), the abbey of Crossraguel and the collegiate church of Maybole, were part of the Kennedy hegemony.

Kyle was a contrast in many ways. At its northern and southern coastal extremities it held Ayrshire's two royal burghs Irvine and Ayr where the relatives of many landed families great and small were long established in the merchant and craft communities and in the public affairs of the burghs. Kyle's 20 parishes were more fertile and more populous than those of Carrick, especially along the coast and its immediate hinterland and in the valleys of the rivers Irvine and Ayr. 'The country is plenteous in corn, bestial and fish', noted the English observer, 'populous of men . . .' In this fertile region tenants' holdings were often small; in the barony of Monkton, for example, 30 acres of the 'acredales' were held among 32 tenants in mid-century. The barony of Kylesmure on the upper reaches of the river Ayr, centred on the clachan of Mauchline which itself stood on an important eastward route out of Ayrshire, was systematically feued by Melrose abbey in the 1550s to scores of tenants who had previously held by quasi-heritable life-leases.[3]

A notable feature of Kyle society was the large number of families who, although long in possession, were not cadets of noble houses – the Reids, Airds, Gibbs, Lockharts, Farquhars, Shaws, Fullartons and Wallaces, to name only a few. The most notable cadets, the Campbells, were by then socially and economically independent of their ancestral chiefs the earls of Argyll. In the realm of public affairs, however, they often acted together; in 1536 no fewer than 38 lairds and others from Ayrshire were named in letters of protection to the earl of Argyll and his dependants.[4] The frequently used collective designation 'gentlemen of Kyle' was an appropriate one, for the lords of parliament Lord Ochiltree and Lord Cathcart, who came to Ayrshire from Clydesdale and Renfrewshire respectively, were the only noblemen in Kyle. Apart from the Trinitarian monastery of Fail, which became largely secularised in the 1540s, neither of the abbeys who had tenants in Kyle, Melrose and Paisley, was on the spot and therefore much of the day-to-day running of their estates was delegated to local lairds. The surviving accounts of Melrose's chamberlain at Mauchline in Kylesmure contain references to the presence of Campbell of Loudoun who combined his hereditary roles of abbey bailie and sheriff of Ayr with considerable effect.[5]

The society of Cunninghame in the north was more baronial. The bailiary was too small to hold comfortably the two earls Eglinton and Glencairn and Lord Boyd, the first two constantly at feud, the third not without 'unfriends' in his own country. A large number of Cunninghame lairds were cadets of the houses of Glencairn, Eglinton and Boyd. Their ranks were filled out by branches of the Crawfords, by descendants of the medieval baronage such as the Blairs of Blair and lesser families who also took their surnames from the land, such as the Dunlops of Dunlop.

Agriculturally the bailiary of Cunninghame had a productive arable coastal plain and pasture on the uplands lying towards Renfrewshire. This mixed pattern is reflected in the kind of rents paid to Kilwinning abbey by its tenants on the baronies of Kilwinning and Beith and in the teinds which it drew from 11 Cunninghame parishes, which included quantities of wheat, butter and cheese. The widespread payment of feu-duty in cash on the Kilwinning lands from mid-sixteenth century also suggests a measure of prosperity which nevertheless has to be seen against a background of rising grain prices and the fact that Cunninghame appears to have been highly populated. There were 15 parishes in this the smallest of the Ayrshire bailiaries.

Tucked away almost in the south-west corner of Scotland with its face to the western seas and its back to the political heartland, sixteenth-century Ayrshire may suggest an inward-looking region. Admittedly, it could be difficult to get from Ayrshire to where national institutions normally did their business. The earl of Cassillis once blamed the considerable mileage for his failure to obey a summons to attend the court of session in Edinburgh, and the convention of royal burghs meeting in St Andrews was sympathetic when Ayr's commissioner George Cochrane arrived a day late, explaining that his delay on the last lap had been due to 'the stay of the passage at the Queensferrie'. Yet, travel problems notwithstanding, Ayrshire faced outwards. Well-established contacts linked Ayrshire society with national events and institutions and with the social, commercial and cultural life not only of neighbouring regions but of more distant parts of Scotland and beyond.

In an age when travellers readily turned to the seaways a number of natural landing places on the Ayrshire coast, some of which were upgraded to minor customs posts in the seventeenth century, probably afforded facilities for a good deal of passenger traffic in small boats: places such as Ballantrae, Dunure, Girvan, Maidens, Saltcoats and Portencross.[6] The islands of the Clyde estuary, Kintyre, parts of Argyll, Ireland and the Isle of Man provided an accessible trading area for the Ayrshire burghs of Irvine and Ayr as well as for Dumbarton, Glasgow and Renfrew. At the end of the sixteenth century Irvine constructed a harbour at Troon to relieve the effects of the perennial problem of silting at Irvine harbour itself. The Ayrshire merchants bought up fish, hides, wool, plaids and salt from and sold everyday commodities to the communities of the islands, Argyll and Ireland.

Business recorded in merchants' testaments and notaries' protocol books reveals the social and trading networks of the region. Lairds, freeholders and tenants in the offshore communities bought and borrowed from mainland merchants, boys from Kintyre, Arran and Bute went to Irvine and Ayr to be apprenticed or attend school, small travelling merchants acted as middlemen between the island weavers and the burgh merchants who bought plaids. Merchants in inland Ayrshire towns such as Kilmarnock traded through merchant-factors in Irvine and Ayr who made purchases for them in Ireland, the islands and Kintyre. Trade with Ireland expanded in the early seventeenth century, facilitated by contacts with the growing Scottish community in Ulster which included many expatriate Ayrshire people.

Activity in home waters, however, was only the first stage in a trading enterprise which had Europe as its ultimate market. Hides bought from Irish and Ayrshire farmers found their way to French and Flemish ports, some of them having been initially transported across Scotland to be exported by middlemen Edinburgh merchants. Other goods were exported from nearer home; the 300 hides put into the hands of an Irvine merchant by John Ritchie of Kilmarnock were destined for Flanders where Ritchie's son-in-law was his factor.[7] Thus the cattle-rearing farmers of Ireland and Ayrshire were linked by a commercial chain to the markets of northern Europe. The herring for which the Ayr and Irvine merchants bargained with the fishermen of the western waters were taken by shipmasters to the French ports of La Rochelle and Bordeaux where the 'free money' realised from their sale was spent mainly on wine. The handling of foreign currency was all in the day's business, done through Edinburgh money-changers. Sometimes a Scottish shipmaster would be entrusted with payments due from several merchants to European creditors, as when William Tran took sums to a Portuguese merchant from four fellow-merchants of Irvine.[8]

Some Ayrshire traders went personally to Europe either as merchant-shipmasters or to accompany their own share of a cargo. Some died abroad having made a will before leaving home. Taking the hazardous western route to Europe meant running the gauntlet of English shipping in the Irish Sea and English Channel. Cargoes were divided between ships in order to minimise the risk of loss at sea or were sometimes carried in foreign vessels. The latter were not uncommon in Clyde waters. Most of them seem to have had a happier landfall than the Breton skipper whose ship ran aground at Goldberry on the coast of Cunninghame opposite the island of Meikle Cumbrae in September 1559. In spite of trusting to the 'auld amitie' between the two countries, somewhat strained in the autumn of 1559, the skipper found his briefly abandoned ship ransacked and the cargo and ship's boat carried off by local inhabitants.

If seaborne trade widened the horizons of Ayrshire society, so too did overland links. By early-modern standards the sheriffdom had a fair number of well-used long-distance routes: the highway that ran north and south along the populous coastal strip and those ancient thoroughfares that found their way along rivers, across moorland and through the encircling uplands towards Galloway, into Lanarkshire and on to the Lothians and Edinburgh, up into Renfrewshire to Paisley and Glasgow, or across the Clyde into the Lennox and on to Stirling.

Two destinations were particularly important: Glasgow the archbishop's burgh and Edinburgh the centre of political life and economic opportunity. Glasgow was on the mental horizon of many Ayrshire dwellers; in 1558 a Cunninghame laird and his creditor agreed to conclude their business 'before the fair of Glasgow', an event which was described by Bishop Leslie as 'the maist renowned mercat in the west, honorable and celebrate'. Until the deepening of the river Clyde Glasgow was virtually an inland port whose merchants depended on downriver outlets, notably Irvine until that harbour became too difficult, after which Port Glasgow was developed. Yet the compact little city which leapt from 11th place in the taxable league of Scottish burghs in 1535 to 5th place in 1591, having survived the dislocations of the Reformation, had two sources of drawing power not shared by other western burghs. One was its university where the students included many from Ayrshire and the other was the archbishop's consistorial court to which in pre-Reformation times lay men and women were obliged to come for many reasons affecting their everyday lives.

The cathedral itself, the other churches, friaries, chapels, hospitals, the archbishop's household and the administrative and judicial activities of the church courts created a huge ecclesiastical establishment. In addition to the work which this generated for an army of officials, clerks and servants, these institutions were also a market for merchants and suppliers of all kinds, many of them from Glasgow's hinterland and Ayrshire. Lead for Archbishop Robert Blackadder's building operations in 1507 was supplied by an Ayr merchant, Thomas Tait, who held property in Glasgow.[10] A number of Ayrshire nobles and lairds had lodgings in the city, many more took temporary accommodation. Apart from social reasons it was convenient to have a base from which to attend the notoriously slow proceedings of the consistory or to do business at the booths of writers and notaries.

The court of the archbishop's Official dealt with cases from the entire archdiocese and with appeal cases from the suffragan sees of Galloway, Argyll and the Isles. The scope of the court's jurisdiction included many matters of personal concern to the laity: business relating to testaments and executory, marriage and the rights of widows and of children under age, and all kinds of disputes arising from contracts and agreements since these were looked upon as having been undertaken on the moral basis of an oath or promise. The consistory might be the place to put pressure on parties to a dispute in an attempt to reach a settlement, or people might even be called upon to retract statements made in anger. A good deal of routine business such as the recording of deeds could be dealt with by the consistory clerks as in any other law court. Serious cases such as accusations of heresy or crimes against or by the clergy might be heard before the archbishop himself in chapter.

For many people of the south-west Glasgow was associated not only with trading activity, with opportunity to study and qualify for a professional career at the university or with the extension of their familiar social circle gained by periodic sojourns in the city, but with the sanctions of the church. For most early-sixteenth century people contact with the church was made at their local accessible parish church with their parish priest, who was likely to be a man from their own community. Yet, the episcopal judicial machine turning over at the heart of Glasgow was a reminder of those stages in life, whether anticipated or unforeseen, when ordinary people came face to face with the wider jurisdiction and ultimate authority (and associated with these the monetary demands) of the church which with the secular authority jointly ordered their lives.

Contact with Edinburgh was quite a different experience. Commissioners to parliament, representatives at the convention of royal burghs which often met in Edinburgh, burgh officials on legal business or 'keeping the exchequer', litigious lairds and tenant-farmers pursuing actions in the civil courts or called there as defendants and witnesses might find themselves in the capital for weeks at a time. The registers of decrees of the lords of council and of the court of session from the late fifteenth century onwards contain many cases involving Ayrshire people great and small, men and women, a good number of whom attended the courts in person.

Living in Edinburgh even for short spells inevitably spun a web of involvement with the inhabitants. In the crowded burgh it was customary to rent lodgings. Permanent town houses were mostly maintained by magnates from the Edinburgh hinterland and eastern Scotland, a well-known exception being the lodging of the earls of Eglinton which that family occupied for many generations.[11] Many a visitor went home leaving debt behind and a bond to that effect in the hands of an Edinburgh merchant or lawyer. When he died in 1578 Sir Hugh Kennedy of Girvanmains owed a year and a half's chamber rent to the merchant and moneylender Janet Fockhart.[12] Ayrshire merchants who bought from Edinburgh wholesalers or used the latter as factors often kept running accounts, as did Ayrshire landed families who often found themselves in the capital. In 1557 Alexander 4th earl of Glencairn, who owed £500 to Mr John Preston for merchandise and lent money, assigned Preston his pension of 1000 francs from the French government. Preston agreed to meet the expense of collecting the money in Paris and bringing it home in a Scottish ship. Should the French royal treasurer demur at handing it over, Glencairn promised to pay the debt to Preston personally in Edinburgh.[13] Travelling around the country as Glencairn did during the years of political confrontation which led to the Reformation crisis of 1559–60 must have played havoc with many a lord's financial resources.

Debts thus contracted were often for outright loans, for which a number of Ayrshire men turned to the Edinburgh lawyers, especially the advocates. One of these who knew Ayrshire well was Mr John Moscrope, Edinburgh's procurator-fiscal who also acted as procurator for Ayr, for which he was rewarded with a fee and occasional gifts of barrels of west-coast herring. Individuals who did business with him included Sir Matthew Campbell of Loudoun, sheriff of Ayr, who at one time owed him 7000 merks.[14] Moscrope occasionally visited Ayr where he is found witnessing the land transactions of local lairds; he may well have drafted the relevant documents, a service advocates sometimes provided for their clients. A fateful element in borrowing was the fact that security for repayment often took the form of land or rents. If the debtor failed to repay, the land could pass to the creditor. In this way some Edinburgh lawyers and merchants came into possession of Ayrshire territory.

Reinforcing contact with Edinburgh, as indeed with Glasgow, was the fact that Ayrshire people settled there. Between 1583 when the Edinburgh register of apprentices begins and 1625, 62 Ayrshire boys were recorded as having begun apprenticeships to Edinburgh masters some of whom shared their surname and were probably relatives. Seventeen of these apprentices are later found in the burgess register, on average 10 years after they had been entered as apprentices. It is reasonable to suppose that this kind of contact had been established long before the period covered by the existing apprentice and burgess registers. Varied contacts meant that many Ayrshire families were familiar with the life of the capital directly or indirectly, and with its leading figures in the fields of commerce, the law and public life. Conversely, those at the centre of political life were well aware of the power wielded by 'the lords of the westland', some of the most prominent of whom came from Ayrshire.

The political and religious changes of the sixteenth century affected Ayrshire society directly through the participation of many leading families in the events that brought them about. Political alignments during the period were in turn closely associated with patterns of landholding which extended the influence of some magnates beyond Ayrshire, and at the same time brought the influence of families from outside to bear on the Ayrshire scene.

The most remarkable spread of territorial possession by any Ayrshire magnate was that of the Cunningham earls of Glencairn which by the end of the fifteenth century comprised lands in nine sheriffdoms. In the 1540s the anglophile William 3rd earl could arrange to meet the English warden of the west marches at Glencairn in Dumfriesshire, to conduct the English army from Carlisle to Glasgow 'without stroke' and to raise 1000 men of his own surname and friends in addition to 1000 of his allies in Ayrshire and Renfrewshire. He suggested an anchorage for English ships at Ardmore on the Clyde ('one of the best havens in Christendom') looking across to his own castle of Finlayston in Renfrewshire within marching distance of Stirling.[15] Just as important to the Cunninghams as their home baronies of Glencairn and Kilmaurs (in Dumfriesshire and Ayrshire) were their lands and houses in Renfrewshire and the Lennox, that is Finlayston and Kilmaronock which were acquired by marriage soon after 1400. Others also saw them as a power in that region. It made Glencairn the natural choice of the anglophile party as custodian of the strategic castle of Dumbarton – the family had a town house in Dumbarton for good measure. On one occasion Sadler the English ambassador explained to his government that like other lords Glencairn had gone home, '60 miles off in the Highland as they call it here, towards the Isles . . .'[16] Alexander 4th earl lived much and in fact died at the castle of Kilmaronock.[17] The influence of the earls in Renfrewshire and the Lennox was reinforced by the presence of their cadets, Cunningham of Craigans and Cunningham of Drumquhassil, the latter holding land from the earl of Lennox and acting as his bailie. It is not surprising that three generations of the Glencairns were allies of Lennox. They had a less comfortable relationship with the powerful earls of Argyll on whose doorstep their northern territories lay, although they made common cause with the 4th earl and his son, Lord Lorne, once they had openly thrown in their lot with the movement for religious reform and the anglophile party. Possession of the barony of Redhall in Midlothian, granted to the Cunninghams by Robert III in 1399, provided them with a supply base near Edinburgh where the earls of Glencairn took part in public affairs. On several occasions they wadset land in their Midlothian barony to Edinburgh creditors.

If the Cunninghams as landholders fitted into the sphere of Lennox interest on the fringes of the Highlands, at the same time the Lennox Stewarts had a stake in Ayrshire. This lay in their possession of the baronies of Galston and Tarbolton in Kyle in a district where sympathy for Anglo-Scottish rapprochement had a long history. Some prominent anglophile-reformers, including Campbell of Cessnock and Lockhart of Bar, held land from the earls of Lennox. The hegemony of Lennox's dynastic rivals the Hamiltons increased in Ayrshire in the sixteenth century. This was partly achieved through a Hamilton abbacy and commendatorship of Kilwinning abbey by Alexander and Gavin Hamilton and the abbacy of Paisley (which had lands in Kyle) by John Hamilton, who from 1546 was also archbishop of St Andrews. These offices made the dynastically-minded Hamilton clerics superiors of extensive tracts of land in Cunninghame and Kyle, which were filled out by the holdings of Sir James Hamilton of Finnart (transferred to various Ayrshire lairds among others on his fall in 1540) and those of Sir William Hamilton of Sanquhar whose family had held territory in Ayrshire since the late fifteenth century. Sir William, who began his own public career in the royal service, steadily acquired land in Kyle and was several times provost of Ayr.[18]

It was not so much with Lennox that the Hamiltons clashed in Ayrshire as with the Montgomeries of Eglinton whom they persistently tried to deprive of real power as bailies of the Kilwinning abbey lands in Cunninghame, even although these lay on Eglinton's doorstep. When the Hamiltons were forfeited at the end of the civil war it was the Cunninghams of Glencairn who succeeded to the commendatorship and administrative offices of Kilwinning and the territorial patronage that went with them. The earls of Eglinton had to wait until the early seventeenth century to acquire the lordship of Kilwinning as a secular estate. Throughout the sixteenth century the blood feud between the Cunninghams and the Montgomeries defied all attempts to settle it, which meant that Glencairn and Eglinton were likely to take opposite sides on the major political and religious questions of the day. As already mentioned, offshoots of the house of Argyll were to be found in Kyle, particularly in the Irvine valley in the parishes of Galston and Loudoun where the Campbells of Loudoun, Cessnock and Newmilns were settled, and around Mauchline in Kylesmure where the Campbells of Kinzeancleuch were influential.[19] The Campbells of Loudoun as hereditary sheriffs of Ayr were more instinctively on the side of constituted authority than some of the other Campbells and the anglophile party had to work hard at one point to win Sir Hugh Campbell's co-operation, which also required composing his quarrel with the then anglophile earl of Cassillis.[20]

The association of surname and traditional territorial designation can obscure the spread of property interests of even the smallest lairds from Ayrshire as from elsewhere. They did not own but held the land from the crown which had the last word in the matter of its continued possesssion. Forfeiture for political mistakes or for supporting others who made them, escheat (confiscation of goods) for all kinds of legal and political misdemeanours and the apprising (confiscation) of land for unpaid debt could all lead to the loss of one's landed inheritance and with it the rents on which landed families depended for survival. The effects of these calamities on family fortunes are not always easy to document but they must have been widespread.

Also widespread must have been the complication of inter-family relations, the interference of outsiders in a family's affairs and the aggravation of feuds and quarrels which resulted from the crown's exploitation of its ability to forfeit and escheat. By selling its own right to escheats, to the wardship of lands of which the heir was under age (along with the right to settle the heir's marriage and to claim the 'relief' payment when he or she did succeed), its right to the fines due to the crown for an heir's failure to enter him or herself to the property when he or she came of age, and to annex the property of forfeited persons, the crown created a market in property rights. In addition it granted hundreds of charters of apprised lands to creditors and others. Property thus acquired need not be in the grantee's own locality; in this way land apprised from the laird of Grimmet in Carrick was granted to William Wood of Bonnyton in Angus (1530), the earl of Eglinton acquired parts of Langside in Lanarkshire apprised from Lord Cathcart (1531), and Mure of Caldwell on the border of Ayrshire and Renfrewshire bought the escheat of Thomas Kirkpatrick of Closeburn in Dumfriesshire who supported the earls of Lennox and Glencairn against the governor Arran (1544).[21] Property of this kind need not be acquired for good but might be sold on, perhaps to one of the purchaser's own creditors. Sometimes the original proprietor might buy it back.

People heard of these opportunities to acquire property by means of personal contact, including contact with those close to the crown, and by being themselves part of the great feudal network along which the early-warning sounds of political and financial collapse reverberated. In this network the resources of moveable and heritable property were jointly exploited in the vital business of survival which so preoccupied families great and small in early-modern Scotland. It was a business that often led people into relationships with others outside their home territory, for in a sense its very vulnerability made early-modern society an open one. And if word of material opportunities could travel along the social network, so too could new ideas, and news of developments in church and state.

CHAPTER TWO

The People's Church: Before 1560

The medieval church is sometimes portrayed as a churchman's church, as the all-powerful dispenser of spiritual grace to the faithful on its own terms, protected by its own law and clerical privilege. Over-concentration on the power of the ecclesiastical organisation, however, can create the impression of a homogeneous body of officials on the one hand and an unprivileged mass of recipients on the other. At local level especially the people saw the church as existing to serve them. From their standpoint it was an essential service which like all essential services, then and since, they both depended on and felt free to criticise. More than that, they contributed to its maintenance and character. The involvement of the people in the church's affairs affected the quality of its service, the appointment of its personnel at all levels, the sufficiency or otherwise of its material endowments for spiritual purposes, the discharge of its temporal responsibilities and the extent of its social commitment.

There was no social gulf between the personnel of the church and the laity. Its management and executive ranks were staffed by members of landed families great and small, the familiar parish priest probably belonged to the rural community whom he served, the chaplains in the burgh churches were usually from burgess stock. Clerics shared and where possible were expected to advance the interests of their families whose influence may have been a lot more constant than that of ecclesiastical superiors.

Family influence in the making of church appointments was strong. A look at the names of the higher clergy of the archdiocese of Glasgow between 1520 and 1560 shows that out of a total of 72 appointments only 59 individuals were involved and that almost three out of every four appointments were given to men from families members of whom already held or had held offices in the diocesan establishment. This suggests not only a good deal of ladder climbing by ecclesiastical careerists but an extensive exercise of patronage (in the common if not legal sense) by churchmen at the top of the ladder. In the early 1550s members of the Hamilton family held in the west of Scotland alone the abbeys of Kilwinning and Paisley, the provostry of the collegiate church of Hamilton, the deanery of Glasgow cathedral (exchanged for Kilwinning abbey), the subdeanery and subchantorship of Glasgow, the office of commissary of Rutherglen (held by three successive Hamiltons) and that of the commissary of Glasgow and Clydesdale, with a very large number of parsonages and vicarages, a clear reflection of the Hamilton family's territorial hegemony.

Officially the Scottish church itself controlled appointments, although in doing so it increasingly had to fend off the encroachments of the papacy and the crown.[1] In real terms, however, those heads of monasteries, members of cathedral chapters and other religious institutions who nominated the appointees often acted in the interests of the family to which they belonged and which could bring pressure to bear in the matter of selection. Quintin Kennedy, a secular cleric, succeeded his uncle William as abbot of Crossraguel in 1547. After the Reformation the earl of Cassillis, head of the house of Kennedy, persistently obstructed the administration of the abbey's affairs by the crown-nominated commendator Alan Stewart. The Kennedys' power was acknowledged in the preamble to a lease of the abbey revenues which Cassillis obtained from Mary and Darnley: 'their Majesteis understandis that the Abbay of Corsraguell hes evir bene disponit to the freindis of the hous of Cassillis at the sute [request] of the erlis thereof for the tyme'.[2]

Although the ancient right to present a priest to a parish living, known as the right of advowson, was still conveyed with land in the formal clauses of charters, it had long been eroded. Patronage of parish churches had mostly passed to major ecclesiastical institutions so that by the sixteenth century only a handful of parish churches remained in lay patronage. One of them, Cumnock, was in Ayrshire, in the patronage of the Dunbars of Cumnock. Even although that family's main territorial power-base had been transferred to their adopted country of Moray, the Cumnock revenues, annexed to a canonry of Glasgow cathedral, were held by Mr John Dunbar from the 1540s to the 1570s. In spite of the official absence of lay patronage at parish level the recurrence of the local surnames of Montgomerie, Cunningham, Crawford, Blair, Reid, Wallace, Boyd and Kennedy among the holders of Ayrshire parsonages and vicarages before the Reformation and among the ministers, exhorters and readers after it speaks for itself.

Even where a parish had been appropriated to a monastery, family influence might operate. In 1554 the Hamilton commendator of Kilwinning abbey was doubtless behind the presentation of Mr Thomas Hamilton to the appropriated parish of Kilmarnock in succession to Mr Robert Hamilton.[3] The vicarage of Stewarton, on the other hand, although also appropriated to Kilwinning, was held with only a short intermission by five members of the Montgomerie family covering most of the sixteenth century; in 1527 it actually passed from father to son.[4] In 1548 the vicarage of West Kilbride passed from Mr James to Mr Archibald Crawford.[5] In 1568, again showing that the Reformation did not always break this family tradition, sir Alan Porterfield, vicar of Ardrossan who declined to take office in the reformed church, resigned his vicarage in favour of his kinsman Mr John Porterfield who later became minister at Ayr.[6] Paid deputies carried out the parochial duties of these pre-Reformation clerics, so that their vicarages were regarded by them simply as pieces of property, hence the family interest in securing them for relatives.

The minor office of parish clerk, the parish priest's assistant, which carried its own emoluments, was also subject to lay influence.[7] The parishioners were often the patrons of the office, and all those who possessed land in the parish, men and women, were entitled to vote at the election of the nominee. Records of elections are often to be found in the protocol books of the notaries who conducted them. In 1524, for example, 173 landholding householders of Mauchline parish called at the manse to record their votes in the election of the parish clerk Adam Reid.[8] The presence of a candidate (often the sole nominee) while the notary recorded votes orally often gave rise to allegations of intimidation. Since the major landholders in the parish had the last word, competition between local families for possession of the parish clerkship sometimes led to disputes and even to violence, as when the Mures and the Cunninghams fought over the clerkship at Stewarton kirk in 1508.

At the induction of Adam Reid as clerk at Mauchline kirk on 6 November 1524 following his election just mentioned it was Sir Hugh Campbell of Loudoun, sheriff of Ayr, who handed Reid the holy water stoup as the symbol of his office, having previously asked the assembled parishioners whether the election was against their wishes, at which 'they all remained silent'. Few were likely to resist the wishes of Campbell of Loudoun, but two people did protest, David Lundy, who had been nominated by Melrose abbey (the patron), and John Liddell, one of the Melrose monks who spoke up on his behalf, protesting that Lundy had been forcibly prevented from being elected and that Adam Reid had been nominated because he was Sir Hugh Campbell's servant.[9] Apart from registering their protest nothing was done and Reid continued in office.[10]

In St Quivox parish in 1522 the Wallace family forced the nomination and election of Ninian Wallace as parish clerk after extracting a resignation of the office from sir John McTere, chaplain, who later swore before Abbot Robert Shaw of Paisley (as patron) that he had done so only for 'fear and dread of death'.[11] The Wallaces also held the parish clerkship of Barnweil, where John Riddell resigned in favour of Paul Wallace the laird of Craigie's natural son in 1508, and that of Symington where in 1500 Hugh Wallace the laird of Craigie's brother resigned to his nephew William.[12]

In rural parishes the clerk's fee and the offerings he received might be quite small. The job included making the responses at mass, looking after the altar vessels and keeping the church clean, carrying the holy water stoup round the parish to 'asperse' the people in their homes and providing the holy water required at certain ceremonies. On the face of it the small income from fees and offerings seems unlikely to have appealed to even the younger sons of lairds, or to have caused such competition between families. The appeal may have lain elsewhere than in the emoluments from which most clerks from landed families were prepared to pay a deputy to carry out the actual duties. In fact, the clerk was a privileged person. In most rural parishes he was simply a tonsured clerk – that is having the minimum of clerical character needed to claim privilege and immunity from the secular law courts. If summoned before the latter the clerk could be repledged to the bishop's court. The landed parish clerk thus had the best of both worlds; he was a tonsured cleric but he behaved like a layman, able to take part in his family's private wars with the likelihood of impunity from the civil law. Some clerks were even married. Here, at the point where the local community had a voice in choosing a minister of the church, the line between cleric and layman was at its thinnest.

Patronage was firmly in the hands of the lay founders of collegiate churches, chapels and chaplainries at altars within churches. The collegiate churches of which over 40 were founded between the mid-fifteenth and mid-sixteenth centuries were private chapels on an elaborate scale. Their purpose was to make more lavish provision than could be made at an altar or chapel within a church, for masses for the soul of the founder and his family. Equipped with their own song schools, collegiate churches could often achieve a more dignified ceremonial and higher standard of music than was to be found in most rural parish churches.[13] Their main concern, however, was with the welfare in the next world of the souls of the founder, his family, their ancestors and descendants. The church was staffed by a 'college' of priests, called prebendaries as in a secular cathedral, each prebend endowed from the founder's land, each individual prebendary appointed by him and his descendants. The rules for conduct of the services and the personal and professional lives of the clergy were written into the founding charter. For example, it was usually stipulated that unlike the beneficed parochial clergy those attached to a collegiate church should be personally resident, in an attempt to ensure a higher combined standard of professional ability and personal commitment and, above all, that the patron's family received the service they required. The collegiate church was the characteristic lay endowment of the late middle ages, a modern alternative to the endowment of the monasteries by earlier generations. As an expression of belief in the efficacy of masses for the dead it gave a landed family the opportunity to provide for this spiritual service on its own terms.

Rural chapels, some of which reinforced the parish system in remote areas, might also carry the right of lay patronage for those who were the descendants of the founders or on whose land the chapel was built. In this way the Blairs of Adamton were the patrons of the chapel of Our Lady of Kyle in Monkton parish, a famous place of pilgrimage; the earls of Eglinton held the patronage of the chapel of St Wissan at Kilwinning and that of the Virgin Mary at Lainshaw near Stewarton; and the Campbells of Cessnock became patrons of the chapel of St Ninian at Lanfine in Galston parish which had formerly been in the possession of the earls of Lennox. Sir William Hamilton of Sanquhar, who acquired the lands of the chapel and hospital of St Leonard near Ayr, engineered the presentation of two successive members of his family to the office of preceptor. Such chaplainries helped to maintain those clerical members of landed families who are often designated the 'servants' of landed men: clerics whose writing skills, legal knowledge and teaching ability were in demand by their lay relatives and their children. Those skills were also provided by those private chaplains who carried out their duties in the secular environment of the lairds' households, as well as officiating in their private chapels. Sir John Campbell, a chaplain, and other 'servants' of the earl of Cassillis described how they had been set upon in an Ayr street by the men and servants of Kennedy of Blairquhan.[14] The chaplain insisted that his group had not fought back; perhaps some stability was to be gained by leavening one's following with the occasional chaplain. The presence of sir William Cathcart, private chaplain to Alan Cathcart of Waterhead, at the choosing of legal tutors for the lairds' daughters is more typical of the private chaplain's involvement in a family's affairs.[15] The extra-parochial service of private chapels was sometimes resented by the parish clergy, especially if the chaplain was the servant of an influential layman. As the vicar of Straiton put it, '. . . the seculars look sharply after the doings of churchmen as churchmen do after the doings of seculars'.

Chaplains at altars in burgh churches more than any other clergy had the character of employees of the secular authority, hired and fired by the magistrates whose representatives handed them their equipment – altar vessels, vestments and service books – on appointment; 'the haill . . . consale of Ayr present . . . hes consentit and grantit to gif sir George Thomson chaplain the chaplainry of St Nicholas altar . . . siclyke as umquhile Mr Stevin Adamson chaplain had befoir, and to mak service thairfor as the said Mr Stevin did . . . and ordains the dean of guild to passe with certane nechtbouris and gif him possessioun of the samin togidder with the vestmentis bukis and challeis . . .'[16] By mid-sixteenth century all eight altars in St John's kirk, Ayr, and most of those in St Mary's kirk, Irvine, were in the patronage of the magistrates.

The doctrine of purgatory and belief in the efficacy of prayers for the dead multiplied the number of such altars, with their dedications to numerous saints and popular forms of devotion, constantly adding to the number of masses to be said at each. In practical terms the altar chaplain had several employers: the family of the founder of the altarage or chaplainry for whom prayers were said on stated occasions according to the terms of the endowment; those who since the original foundation had endowed an 'obit' at the altar for themselves and their families, which required prayers to be said on the anniversary of death; and the magistrates who appointed the chaplains and laid down the rules governing their service. The archbishop of Glasgow might confirm their presentations – at Ayr the magistrates gave Mr Stevin Adamson just mentioned his travelling expenses to Glasgow and the cost of obtaining episcopal institution in office – but from day to day the authority of the magistrates dominated the chaplains' working lives.

The terms of a burgh chaplain's appointment might be extremely detailed, loaded with duties and restrictions. Remuneration, partly from the burgh's common purse, was on the whole small, in the region of £5 to £13 at Ayr which was on a level with that of the more poorly paid parish curates.[17] The most common method of paying burgh chaplains and choristers was to earmark a ground annual from burgh property so that very many burgh properties were burdened with annuals payable to altarages. Annuals due to the altars of Saints Ninian and Katherine, St Nicholas, and Saints Peter and Paul in Irvine burgh kirk involved the properties of 54 burgesses in the High Street, Kirkgate, Seagate and Sandgate.[18] Those payable to the choristers of St John's kirk, Ayr were due from 65 tenements and crofts.[19] Payment was sometimes difficult to obtain and was often in arrears. The chaplain often went round himself collecting his annuals when they fell due but sometimes the chaplains as a body would pay someone to collect on their behalf. Poor remuneration caused many chaplains to acquire more than one altarage and many practised as notaries.

Chaplains were not always given long-term appointments. At Ayr, Thomas Andrew was appointed in 1538 for three years with a fee of £4 from the common purse, 5 merks from the glovers' incorporation and a merk from an annual bequeathed to his altar. In May 1542 there was a wages dispute between the Ayr chaplains and the town council when the latter decided that the treasurer should 'not gif ony money of the common purss to ony chaplain of the queire of Aire in tyme cuming . . . howbeit thai had augmentatiounis befoir, becaus the bailies . . . has utheris thair common warkis on hand mair necessair to be done to wair [spend] these guidis upoun, and alsua hes certane causis and faltis to lay to the saidis chaplainis chargis'.[20]

The spiritual service of masses for the dead would be accompanied by visible ceremonies which commemorated the more prosperous members of the community. In a charter of 1506 Rankin Brown, an Irvine burgess, left substantial annualrents to the curate and chaplains of the burgh kirk in return for masses: to the chaplains of the altars of St Mary the Virgin, to whom the church was dedicated, St Peter, St Katherine, St Convall, the local dedication of the Virgin Mary of the Bank and to two chaplains observing two weekday masses at the altars of St Salvator and St Thomas the Martyr 'in the aisle which the grantor built in the nave'. The private masses were to be said in this aisle on every second weekday 'with procession and solemn chant'. On these occasions prayers were to be said for King James IV and Queen Margaret, their progenitors and successors, and for the soul of the grantor, his father, mother, three wives, his daughter and 'for the good estate and happy government of the bailies and community of the said burgh present and to come'. Brown's own obit, accompanied by placebo and dirige (vespers and matins for the dead) was to said at the altar of St Salvator. The foundation charter was witnessed by the bailies.[21] As a memorial, apart from their religious significance, these commemorative services must have been just as compelling as the modern memorial window or plaque in preserving the memory of a prominent burgess and his family. For the poor who were always present and could not afford to found such a commemoration, the founders of altarages often made provision for distribution of alms after the service. Andrew McCormyll, vicar of Straiton, who as a celebrant was no doubt familiar with the scramble that could ensue at the end of such a service, stipulated when founding his own obit at Ayr that the dean of guild should be present to see that distribution of the alms was fairly carried out, receiving 12d for performing this duty but nothing if he did not turn up; which was one way of having the last word over the burgh officials.[22]

In addition to lay influence in clerical appointments to all ranks and in the practical provision for spiritual services, there was in the immediately pre-Reformation period a huge area of lay involvement in the management of the church's property and the administration of its temporal affairs. Abbeys and priories were the largest property-owning ecclesiastical corporations. Legally speaking, they consisted of the abbot, or prior, and the convent, that is the monks, in the case of female religious houses, the prioress and the nuns. However, in the sixteenth century the appointment of new-style monastic superiors — external, non-elected appointees most of whom had never been monks — opened up a divergence of priorities between superior and convent in the management of the property. We have only to read about the behaviour of James Stewart, the royal commendator of Melrose, towards the monks there to see this kind of situation at its worst. When the Melrose monks protested at the commendator's failure to use money, raised by feuing the barony of Kylesmure, for necessary repairs to the abbey as he had promised, Stewart threatened them and almost assaulted the elderly subprior.[23]

Almost all commendators were technically clerics and some at least were concerned about the wellbeing of their monasteries.[24] Nevertheless, their appointments were largely in the interests of the great landed families and had been brought about by a combination of royal and baronial pressure on the papal system of presentations. This and the fact that many commendators brought great church estates within the scope of their families' territorial power gave a secular character to their management of them. This state of affairs qualifies the old belief that the Scottish lords supported the Reformation in order to get their hands on the church's property. The fact is that many families were entrenched in their possession of church estates before the Reformation, through the device of commendatorships; they included the Flemings at Whithorn, the Humes at Jedburgh, the Kerrs at Newbattle, the Stewarts at Inchcolm, the Colvilles at Culross and the Erskines at Dryburgh and Inchmahome. Many lords refused to support the First Book of Discipline, which called for the endowment of the new church from the revenues of the old, because it would deprive them of what they already held. John Knox remarked bitterly of John, 6th Lord Erskine, former commendator of Dryburgh who sidestepped into a secular career at the Reformation, that 'if the poor, the schools and the ministry of the kirk had their own, his kitchen would lack two parts and more of that which he unjustly now possesses'. Even where the heads of monasteries were practising churchmen, nepotism could keep estates within a family's hegemony, as indeed was also the case with the lands of the bishoprics. Three successive Chisholms were bishops of Dunblane. The succession of Beatons and their close relatives at Glasgow, Arbroath, Melrose, Dunfermline and St Andrews was nepotism in the literal sense – nephews following uncles; Quintin Kennedy, as we saw, followed his uncle at Crossraguel; in the decade before the Reformation the commendators of Kinloss, Deer, Culross and Paisley abbeys made arrangements for relatives to follow them in office. The Hamiltons through commendatorships held ecclesiastical estates across the country, Kilwinning, Paisley and Arbroath, as well as the lands of the archbishopric of St Andrews north and south of Forth.

Many monastic superiors were absentee landlords who held offices in the central government or civil law courts or acted as diplomats abroad. The daily running of their estates was left to officials – bailie, chamberlain and justiciar – who in turn often acted through deputies. The appointment of nobles or lairds to these offices created a measure of continuous lay participation in the church's affairs. This may have worked well enough in the days when an abbot was primarily the spiritual head of the religious community, glad to hand over the burden of business and the problem of legal and military protection to a powerful layman. However, as monastic estates came to be regarded as personal property by commendators from powerful families, resentment against the interference of a rival landowner (in the person of the bailie or chamberlain) in the running of the estates could lead to friction. Relations could be particularly difficult with the bailie, the chief judicial officer, who presided over the monastery's barony or regality court. People often complained that the bailies pursued private quarrels under cover of officialdom. In Ayrshire the lands of the Campbells of Loudoun, who were bailies of Kylesmure for Melrose, and those of the earls of Eglinton, bailies of Kilwinning abbey, lay next to those of the abbeys concerned. Both bailies had additional sources of temporal power at their disposal, Campbell as sheriff of Ayr and Eglinton as crown coroner of Cunninghame. Campbell's relations with Melrose and the abbey's chamberlain at Mauchline, the administrative centre of Kylesmure, were reasonably good. This may have owed something to the strict terms of his appointment as bailie which highlight some of the areas in which a bailie might behave as if the lands were his own. By agreement with Abbot Robert Beaton of Melrose in 1521 Sir Hugh Campbell of Loudoun promised not to tax the tenants or demand carriage service from them, or lift fines in the barony court or nominate a deputy without the abbot's licence, and not to take his friends hunting or hawking over the farmland. He also promised to evict a tenant if required to do so in spite of any 'freindschip' or bond of manrent between them. He was obliged to pledge his rents, lands and moveables for the honouring of his agreement.[25]

If relations were potentially difficult in Kylesmure, they were actually acrimonious at Kilwinning. The institution in office of the 2nd earl of Eglinton as heir to his grandfather in the hereditary office of bailie came at the end of an almost two-year-long refusal by Abbot Alexander Hamilton to recognise his title. In 1545 the earl asked for formal installation in his office. When the abbot refused, Eglinton took the case to court. Although royal letters authorising the earl's infeftment were granted in December 1545, the abbot did not comply until August 1547. It is not surprising that the 3rd earl made doubly certain of his authority by obtaining a new charter of his office from the commendator Gavin Hamilton soon after the latter was installed in 1552. When the Hamiltons were temporarily disgraced during the Chase-about-Raid in 1565 following their protest at the marriage of Mary and Darnley, the Queen's lieutenant the earl of Lennox authorised Eglinton to take possession of the abbey buildings.[26] The monopoly of power enjoyed by the earl of Cassillis in Carrick prevented a clash of interests over his use of the office of bailie of Crossraguel, although his efforts to maintain control of the bailiary of Glenluce abbey in Galloway brought him into conflict with the laird of Lochinvar who had rival ambitions for the office.

A good working relationship between the monastic superior and the chamberlain, the chief financial officer, was extremely important. In earlier times the office had been held by an ecclesiastic, sometimes a member of the convent, but by the early sixteeth century it was passing increasingly into the hands of laymen. Since the chamberlain handled the income and expenditure, and monitored the setting of the ground to tenants and the regular payment of rents he had to be trusted to act in the superior's interest in the latter's absence. For this reason the chamberlain was often a kinsman of the commendator.[27]

Lay involvement in the management of the church's affairs affected not only that part of the property known as the 'temporality', that is the lands and rents, but also the 'spirituality' or teinds, the tenth of all parish produce which had originally been intended to support the parson and parochial service. These teinds had been relentlessly diverted from the parishes over the centuries by being appropriated to major religious institutions such as monasteries, canonries and other cathedral offices, collegiate churches and university colleges. The holder of the teinds, whether an individual such as a cathedral canon or a corporate body such as an abbey, became the legal parson who then paid a vicar with a smaller share of the teinds to serve 'the cure of souls' in the parish. Before long, however, even these vicarage teinds were effectively removed from local use by being granted to absentee vicars who did not discharge parochial duties. Instead, they paid a deputy, usually with a very small income, to act as parish priest.[28]

Teinds were notoriously difficult to collect by whoever had the right to them. Besides, parishioners were reluctant to pay, as many court actions in the records of the court of session testify. Above all, absentee vicars wanted a convenient salary in cash rather than the cumbersome responsibility of collecting, transporting and marketing grain and other commodities. The widespread practice of leasing church revenues including the teinds was a solution to some of these difficulties. The practice is a comment on the realities of the church's situation in sixteenth-century society. On the one hand it reflects the desire of churchmen to avoid the difficulty of collecting their own incomes, and on the other the readiness of others to exploit the church's difficulties. In this respect the church came into line with those secular authorities who were faced with similar problems: the town council who set the burgh revenues in tack and the crown officials who farmed out the customs.

In Ayrshire as elsewhere the teinds of very many parishes were leased out by the time of the Reformation, usually to local tacksmen. So too were those lands which had been attached to parish kirks. The extent of pluralism and non-residence among Ayrshire vicars made the leasing of teinds and parish kirklands inevitable. We have only to think of the difficulty experienced by the resident reformed ministers in collecting their stipends to realise why their non-resident predecessors resorted to leasing. The tacksman if he was a local landholder was in a better position to put pressure on the parishioners to hand over their teinds than an absentee vicar. If as seems likely the terms of the lease were the outcome of a bargain between benefice-holder and tacksman, it looks as if the latter often got the best of the bargain. At Galston in Kyle, for instance, the vicarage teinds were said to be leased for a sum 'greatly under their real worth'.[29] The vicarage kirklands of Kilmaurs were leased to Cunningham of Robertland for 20 years for a smaller sum than the vicar ought to have received from the petty kirk dues.[30] The fact that many leases were in operation for long periods without increase in the tack-duty must have meant a profit for the tacksmen in a period of rising grain prices. The entire revenues of Irvine parish, for example, were leased for 40 years to the same family for an annual payment of £26 13s 4d.[31] Where tack-duty did rise, this may reflect local competition: in 1534 Crossraguel abbey leased the parsonage teinds of Straiton to Kennedy of Bargany for 5 years for £40, then to his antagonist the earl of Cassillis in 1553 for twice that amount. Cassillis, however, held on to them until 1566 for the same annual payment.[32] A lay middleman might pass on the difficulty of collecting the teinds by subletting them.

It is unnecessary at this point to discuss at length the relations of ecclesiastical landlords and their tenants, but it should be said that important changes in rural economy and landholding may have rendered these relations less personal as time passed. Cash payments or commutations in lieu of labour services such as carriage and harvest work were becoming more common, since absentee monastic superiors preferred a cash income wherever possible. The spread of feu-ferm tenure, which was at its height between 1550 and 1570, helped to speed up the process of commutation, since feuars were usually asked for cash in lieu of labour services and feu-duty itself was largely paid in money in many areas, including the Ayrshire lands of Melrose and Kilwinning abbeys.[33] The many church tenants who became feuars in the middle decades of the century became distanced from their superior legally and, possibly, psychologically. The landlord had less control over a feuar than over a tenant. A feuar as a rule had more rights over the use of the land than a tenant. The feuar's money-payment was in a sense symbolic of his increased independence. Farmer-feuars like those in Kylesmure, who made a feu contract with the commendator in 1555, may have come to think of themselves less as a labour force than as the employers of others. Lairds who feued land from monasteries, land which their families had previously leased, effectively added to their own resources within the territorial sphere of influence of the commendator and his family. At the level of kirklands attached to the parish churches, a good deal of the church's assets returned by means of leases and feus to the representatives of founding families or to the most influential lairds in the vicinity. In this way the lands of the collegiate church of Kilmaurs (which was also the parish church) returned to the Cunninghams, those of Maybole collegiate church to the Kennedys, those of the chapel of Our Lady of Kyle to the patrons the Blairs of Adamton, those of Dreghorn to Mowat of Busbie, Dunlop to Cunningham of Aiket, Girvan to Cathcart of Carlton, Kilbirnie to the Crawfords, Ochiltree to Lord Ochiltree and Perceton to Barclay of Perceton. The lands of the Carmelite Friary of Irvine (actually in Dundonald parish) returned to the founding family the Fullartons.[34] In a sense this was the disendowment of the medieval church at local level in favour of those who had endowed it in the first place.

Medieval churches were busy, even noisy places. Spiritual business was never suspended in the largest of them. Worldly business was also transacted in the parish kirk which, apart from the laird's houses was the largest and most convenient location for the purpose in the community. Notaries set up their tables in it for the transaction of legal business and lay men and women discussed and arranged their everday affairs in its interior and precincts.[35] People claimed the right to enter their parish church and took instruments from notaries against those who tried to prevent them. Altercations frequently occurred. In November 1520, when a debtor's representative was barred from entering Dalmellington kirk to count out redemption money on the high altar as was customary and offered to count it out in the churchyard instead, the creditor Margaret Crawford, widow of William Hepburn of Lowis, refused to accept it. In June 1518 John Campbell of Little Cessnock refused to accept money from a representative of his debtor the earl of Lennox, even when counted out on the altar of Galston kirk, because the earl had failed to send with it a promised letter of tack. A certain amount of business might even be transacted surreptitiously at a time when services were taking place. In April 1529 Bailie George Wallace of Ayr, when attending vespers in St John's kirk, accused a man of 'holding court in the kirk', but withdrew his accusation when it was shown that the man had simply been handing over 15 shillings to another in the presence of two witnesses.

So familiar were these surroundings that in 1552 the provincial council of the Scottish church urged curates to admonish parishioners 'who have fallen into the habit of hearing mass irreverently ... or presume at such times to make mockery or engage in profane bargainings in church porches or churchyards'.[36] Even more disturbing to the council was the prevailing 'neglect of divine mysteries' and the fact that even in populous parishes only a minority 'deign to be present at the sacrifice of the holy mass ... or to attend the preaching of God's word', a phenomenon not confined to Scotland. Even allowing for the provincial council's rhetoric, we are reminded here of those habits of mechanical observance, apathy and open derision which must be put alongside the evidence for popular piety, in order that we should have a balanced view of everyday religious life.

Looked at in this light, the church appears not as an authoritarian institution but as an essential service endowed, maintained and, in some aspects of its performance, regulated by those whom it served. In some respects it was open to exploitation by the users, primarily in the appointment of its personnel and the management of its material resources. Yet, if we can imagine lifting off this external ecclesiastical framework, permeated as it was by lay influence, we should find that the essential working part of the church's organisation remained in place. For there was an inner aspect of this service beyond the influence of the laity: the point at which the mediatory priesthood claimed to dispense divine grace, teaching that there was no salvation outwith the divine ordinances which it was their responsibility to make available. It is time to make contact with this specifically spiritual service by looking at those who actually provided it at parish level.

CHAPTER THREE

The Cure of Souls

In trying to assess the quality of service provided by the working parish priest in pre-Reformation Ayrshire we must first recognise the 'management' and 'workforce' elements in the church's staff structure. It is easy to think of the late-medieval church as a monolithic structure, yet there were differences in the clerical ranks with regard to responsibility, remuneration, educational standards and career prospects. It was not simply that only a minority reached the top of the profession but that many did not begin at the bottom. It was possible with suitable backing and finance to start a clerical career fairly well up the ladder; many beneficed clergy had never been lower than the rank of cathedral canon.

Use of the word 'beneficed' identifies one of the most important divides among the clergy: some were beneficed and some were not, or to put it another way, some were propertied and some were not. A benefice was a piece of property, or at least was regarded as such. It was drawn from the parish teinds which as we saw had long been diverted from parochial uses by being appropriated to the upkeep of ecclesiastical institutions and the clergy who staffed them. The benefice-holders then paid deputies to undertake the parochial 'cure (i.e.care) of souls'. The vicars who were nominally paid to do so (with either a share of the teinds or a money pension) were often themselves absentees who also paid deputies. Mr Andrew Oliphant, a native of Fife who held the Ayrshire vicarage of Ballantrae from 1539 to about 1571, was a full-time diocesan official and secretary to three successive archbishops of St Andrews. The vicarage of Craigie was held from 1548 until well after the Reformation by Mr Thomas Marjoribanks, a civil lawyer from an Edinburgh family, who became king's advocate and clerk register. The beneficed clergy found employment in diocesan administration, the church courts or the universities, the last being largely clerical training schools. Many beneficed clergy entered royal service, receiving appointments in the central administration, diplomatic service and secular law courts.

Given the large number of clerics seeking non-parochial employment, there simply were not enough benefices to go round. In the ecclesiastical property market the buyers exceeded the supply of goods. The situation was aggravated by the endemic practice of pluralism, the holding of more than one benefice at a time. Clerics talked of 'purchasing' their benefices at Rome where agents were employed on a regular basis to present supplications as they were called on behalf of the thousands of applicants who were unable to petition the papal court in person. Rival claimants were bought out with pensions charged on the successful applicants' benefices. Petitioners might apply for the next vacancy in a particular living or for the benefice on the death or resignation of the current holder, or for permission to exchange benefices. Some pluralists like the well-known Mr John Thornton, precentor of Moray, bid for and exchanged benefices for themselves and others in a manner bordering on stockbroking.[1] In the case of prelacies, as major benefices such as bishoprics and abbacies were called, large sums of money were involved which demanded money-lending facilities both at Rome and in Scotland or the services of European bankers.

Some historians have seen this situation as inevitable, given the way the structure of the medieval church developed. They seek to mitigate judgement on the system by pointing out that the phenomena of non-residence, pluralism and appropriation have to be looked at in the context of the times, as the result of compromises made by the papacy in an age of secular initiative and pushing lay patrons, especially royal patrons. However, the papacy itself must bear some of the responsibility for the development of this competitive and venal system. Abuse of the lay power of nomination (as in the case of James V's illegitimate infant sons who held some of the richest abbacies in Scotland) was no more blatant than the abuse of the papal power of dispensation which made such appointments possible. Dispensation, from being an opportunity to treat a case on its merits, had become an opportunity to buy a licence to set aside some rule of the church or article of canon law, such as the dispensation to hold a benefice although under (often well under) the canonical age for ordination, or to postpone ordination itself while nevertheless retaining a benefice.

Hunting for a benefice did not necessarily mean hunting for a job, since that could be delegated to a deputy. It meant hunting for an ecclesiastical income while pursuing the career of one's choice. Lacking sufficient numbers of educated laity, the crown was glad to employ beneficed clerics at little cost and even used benefices in crown patronage to pay crown servants. Perhaps there were too many ecclesiastics doing jobs that laymen could have done had more of them had a higher education. But clerics were still needed in teaching, administration, in legal practice and on the judicial bench, although by the sixteenth century laymen were already making inroads into these areas of employment. Perhaps more younger sons would have taken up these jobs without clerical status and a benefice had they been better paid, crown service being notoriously the worst paid of them all. After all, many so-called clerics were little more than 'exempt laymen',[2] set apart in youth by receiving the tonsure which later qualified them to hold a church living in support of their careers but which did not necessarily bind them to the life of a practising churchman.

Perhaps there were simply too many clerics; it almost looks as if the church was stiffening society with as many of them as possible. A recent study was made of the diocese of Aberdeen where the ratio was one cleric to 32 lay people.[3] A breakdown of the clerics' employments revealed that fewer than half of them had the cure of souls, the rest being employed in administration, teaching and social occupations which could equally well have been done by educated laymen had these been available in greater numbers. It may be asked, did all this comparatively low-paid delegation of work matter so long as the beneficed clergy contributed to the work of the church in other ways and their deputies discharged their duties responsibly? After all, parish revenue might be well spent even outwith the parish. The parochial teinds of Colmonell in Carrick helped to support six choirboys in Glasgow cathedral who were taught grammar 'and other good arts of the school',[4] while the vicars of Colmonell were a succession of cathedral canons and diocesan officials most of whom were almost certainly absentees from the parish.

Nevertheless, the practices of appropriation and delegation of parochial duties reveal a descending scale of values in which ministering to the parishioners was at the bottom. It is admitted even by historians who defend the performance of the medieval church in general that graduate ecclesiastics who had studied law and theology were reluctant to lower their sights and take on parochial duties. It is an indication of the mainly academic thrust of their studies that these were not seen as an appropriate preparation for pastoral work.

The effect of these priorities came home to roost in the decades leading to the Reformation crisis. As early as 1506 the archbishop of Glasgow during a diocesan synod published a statute enjoining residence on all beneficed clergy (except when studying in the city) under a scale of monetary penalties, with the ultimate sanction of deprivation at the end of six months.[5] The provincial council of the Scottish church in 1549 endorsed the dictum of the council of Trent on the subject which remained a matter for concern to the church's leadership. However, like so many seemingly self-denying ordinances of the church in the following decade, that against non-residence had little effect and in any case the way the ecclesiastical machine operated militated against its implementation.

The largely graduate management, the beneficed clergy, controlled policy through provincial councils of the Scottish church when these met, or more often the diocesan synods, and by the participation of prelates in the deliberations of parliament where these affected the interests of the church. They were also the executive, through the diocesan machinery and the visitations of the rural deans who were the deputies of the bishop's archdeacon who had oversight of the clergy. The higher clergy, the prelates, controlled the funds, voting taxes to the crown from church revenue, imposing taxation on the church based on the valuation of church livings, and fixing the amount of curates' salaries. Unlike the working parish priest, a number of them may never have been fully ordained to the priesthood or may have been able to postpone this step for much of their careers although holding a benefice.[6] Professor Hale's analogy is apt: 'The church was coming to resemble a business which secure from competition ploughs its profits into directors' salaries and leaves its sales force slack or despairing'.

Who were the sales force and how were they recruited? Training for the pre-Reformation priesthood was an essentially practical business resembling an apprenticeship. There was no equivalent of the modern seminary. Clerical students having at an early age received the tonsure, the distinguishing mark of the cleric, attended grammar and song school or learned from the parish priest or local schoolmaster. They learned their job by serving in the church. This meant that trainees lived in the community with the priests whom they understudied. There are glimpses in the records of young men in the early stages of their careers, usually witnessing legal transactions which was a common off-duty activity of clerics. William Mure, acolyte, accompanied the curate of Irvine to Ayr tolbooth for this purpose in 1520.[7] Deacons are found witnessing documents drawn up by the clerical notaries whom they served. Living in the community amid the activities of relatives whose influence may have been stronger than that of a clerical mentor often landed young clerics in trouble. In 1511 Humphrey Blair, deacon, was caught up in his family's feud with the Crawfords, being one of those accused of the slaughter of William Crawford, son of the laird of Baidland.[8] Since the canonical age for ordination was 24, a clerical trainee was still unfledged so to speak at an age when other young men in the community might have their own holding and household or have reached the stage of journeyman craftsman. If the trainee went on to be a chaplain, as many did, he might remain in a kind of social and economic dependence on an individual or corporate patron for most of his working life. The effects of his clerical privilege and the remote character of ecclesiastical supervision of the lower clergy may have been some compensation.[9]

The first rung on the ladder after ordination was often a chaplainry; William Mure the acolyte of 1520 just mentioned is found as a chaplain at Irvine in the 1530s. Although the designation, chaplain, can simply mean priest, it usually indicated service at one of the many altars in a large church or at that of a separate chapel. Chaplains are in fact sometimes called altarists, like Thomas Brown, altarist, who witnessed the foundation of an obit in St John's kirk, Ayr in 1498. Chaplain is the occupation in which over a third of pre-Reformation Ayrshire clergy were found in the course of this study: 133 chaplains out of 320 clergy. Of the 133 chaplains, only 9 were graduates, 110 were non-graduates and the educational status of 14 is unclear. Twenty-one were found practising as notaries. Only 17 of the chaplains were later found with higher clerical status having acquired benefices.

These figures should be regarded as giving the general picture only, since they are based on the fortuitous survival of references to individual clergy over a period of some 60 years, from about 1500 to the Reformation. They include the easily identified, largely absentee higher clergy who held Ayrshire benefices as well as the more elusive clergy in the lower ranks. Chaplains' remuneration was variable, being drawn from different sources: fees from the patron, annuals, small bequests and incidental charity. It was as subject to fluctuation as any other revenue. At Ayr, for which we have most information on the subject, chaplains' income rose and fell between the mid-1540s and 1559.[10] Mr Gavin Ros, who was also a busy notary, received a steady fee of £10. Sir Alexander Kerr, who also took charge of the church's books and vestments, enjoyed a rise, from £5 6s 8d to £13 6s 8d. The chorister Nicholas Shearer's fee rose from £4 9s 4d in 1545 to £10 in 1557, but dropped thereafter. These figures can only be compared to the £13 6s 8d minimum salary laid down for parish curates by the provincial council of 1559. Clearly, in the light of their numbers, the variety of their duties, the fact that they went straight from training to a practical job and, it would seem, were likely to stay in that job for a long time if not for life on a fairly modest income, chaplains were the church's workforce. They served its altars, manned church extension chapels in rural areas, acted as choristers, sacrists, organists, teachers, and clerks to a host of ecclesiastical bodies from the diocesan court to local hospitals.

As we have seen, many chaplains were employed by lay patrons, individual and corporate, who used chaplainries in their gift to provide a living for family members or other dependants who in addition to their religious duties often taught their children and conducted their business affairs. Chaplains provided a pool of scribes with a knowledge of the law from which local secular authorities drew administrative personnnel. Sir Adam Wallace, chaplain of Dundonald chapel, acted as clerk of the court of Kylestewart for the bailie, his kinsman John Wallace of Dundonald. Sir Robert Leggat, who may have begun his career as a private chaplain, was clerk to Prestwick burgh court for most of his working life[11]. In roles like these chaplains discharged at local level responsibilities similar to those undertaken by the higher beneficed clergy for government and the central law courts. They were also the churchmen with whom most people were familiar, not only in the church but in many of their daily circumstances. They were characteristic of an age when there was little or no division between the spiritual and secular contexts of life. It has also to be said that circumstances rendered the chaplains very like the members of the community in which they lived and worked, so much so that church councils spent a good deal of time issuing and reissuing those rules that were meant to distinguish kirkmen from their neighbours with whom they had a tendency to identify. An increased amount of responsibility in spiritual matters was carried by a chaplain who took on the cure of souls of the parish, who was usually known as the curate. In the sense that the job of curate carried additional responsibility and a minumum salary, it could be looked upon as promotion for a chaplain. The extent to which the parish teinds had been appropriated elsewhere determined the nature of the cure and the arrangements for payment of the curate.

The distribution of Ayrshire's 43 parish churches (we are discounting for the present the chapels of Crosbie and Kirkbride) reflected that of the population, being thickest in south Cunninghame and north Kyle, more of them in the arable regions than in the pastoral uplands. All Ayrshire parishes had long been appropriated to monasteries, offices in Glasgow cathedral and other major churches. In the north, with the exception of Largs which was appropriated to Paisley abbey and Kilmaurs which was annexed to Kelso, the teinds of all the Cunninghame parishes were appropriated to Kilwinning abbey: West Kilbride, Ardrossan, Stevenston, Kilwinning itself where the nave of the abbey kirk served the parishioners, Dalry,[12] Beith, Kilbirnie, Dunlop, Stewarton, Perceton, Dreghorn, Kilmarnock and Loudoun. Just over the border in the bailiary of Kyle were the royal burgh and parish of Irvine which was also annexed to Kilwinning, and a group of parishes in the ancestral country of the Stewart monarchs (Kylestewart) which their forebears had gifted to Paisley abbey: Craigie, Riccarton, Dundonald, Monkton, Prestwick and St Quivox. Also in Kylestewart were Symington, Barnweil and Galston, all appropriated to the Trinitarian monastery of Fail. In south Kyle (King's Kyle) the churches were wider apart: the major burgh kirk of St John's at Ayr where the teinds supported a canonry in Glasgow cathedral and a living in the Chapel Royal at Stirling; the kirks of Alloway, Coylton, Dalmellington and Dalrymple near the border with Carrick which were also annexed to the Chapel Royal; those of Tarbolton and Cumnock which provided livings for Glasgow cathedral canons; the upland parishes of Ochiltree and Mauchline appropriated to Melrose abbey and Auchinleck appropriated to Paisley. Of the eight parishes of Carrick, five were annexed to Crossraguel abbey: Straiton, Dailly, Kirkoswald, Girvan and Ballantrae. Colmonell was appropriated to Glasgow cathedral, Kirkmichael to Whithorn priory and the teinds of Maybole were divided between the collegiate church of the Virgin Mary and St Anne in Glasgow and the nunnery of North Berwick on the other side of the country.

The more populous north and west of Ayrshire was well-served with parish churches. By contrast people must often have lived at a fair distance from the church and the priest's ministrations in some of the extensive parishes of the south and east. John Mair remarked on this difficulty in Scotland generally: 'sometimes as many as thirty villages though scattered have one parish church between them, so that a village may be anything up to ten miles from it . . . in the neighbouring chapels of the lords, however, they may have a chance to hear divine service because even the meanest lord keeps one household chaplain . . .'[13] There were many chapels in Ayrshire which provided a kind of church extension of quasi-parochial status. Two chapels were dependant on the parish church of Maybole, Auchendrane and

Kirkbride, the latter becoming a separate parish after the Reformation. The chapel of Kildominie served the southern and that of St Donan the northern part of Girvan parish; as late as 1639 the parishioners in the south petitioned for Kildominie to be rebuilt and created a parish kirk as Girvan was too far away. There were two chapels in each of Dailly and Colmonell parishes and in the huge parish of Mauchline, one of which became the parish of Sorn in 1656 and the other that of Muirkirk in 1631. Up in Cunninghame there were two chapels in the parish of West Kilbride and one on the island of Meikle Cumbrae.[14] Crosbie chapel, dependant on Dundonald, was served by a curate and reckoned quasi-parochial both before and after the Reformation.

Paid deputies were probably the norm in the Ayrshire parish churches. In at least 11 parishes, according to the original appropriation settlement or later documentation, there was a formal arrangement for the appointment and payment of a curate, in the person of a chaplain or removeable priest.[15] These 11 churches may therefore be described as official curate-charges, where the curate was directly responsible to the appropriating institution that appointed him, usually a monastery. These curate-charges were Largs, Kilwinning, Loudoun (in Cunninghame), Barnweil, Prestwick, Riccarton, St Quivox, Dalrymple, Auchinleck (in Kyle), Dailly and Kirkoswald (in Carrick). In these parishes, where there was no constant superior ecclesiastical presence, the curates may have had a fairly free hand, and little back-up of course, from day to day.

Under most appropriation settlements, however, it had been common to make arrangements for the appointment of a vicar to take responsibility for the cure of souls. The appointee was know as 'vicar perpetual' and was allowed a share of the 'great teinds' which were drawn from the grain crop. However, in cases where even the vicarage teinds had been appropriated a 'vicar pensioner' was appointed who was paid a pension or salary, with perhaps a share of the 'small teinds', taken from dairy produce, wool, eggs, poultry or young animals. A number of the vicars may in earlier times have been resident in their parishes but by the sixteenth century resident vicars were probably a minority. They were almost certainly a minority in pre-Reformation Ayrshire where most vicars appear to have paid a curate to undertake the parish service. During this study deputising curates were found at work at various times in 20 Ayrshire parishes: West Kilbride, Ardrossan, Beith, Dalry, Stewarton, Dreghorn (in Cunninghame), Irvine, Dundonald, Symington, Ayr, Monkton, Alloway, Ochiltree, Coylton, Mauchline, Galston, Dalmellington, Tarbolton (in Kyle), Maybole and Girvan (in Carrick). These deputising curates must have worked as much on their own initiative from day to day as did colleagues in official curate-charges, although in the case of the deputy his beneficed superior was in the background and might personally intervene.

Deputies might be appointed even where the vicar was a local man. The Montgomerie vicars of Stewarton which the lairds of Hessilhead tended to regard as a family benefice paid a curate, as did another Montgomerie vicar at Dundonald.[16] At Tarbolton in 1524 the vicar-pensioner Ninian Montgomerie leased his benefice for three years to a local chaplain Adam Allanson who promised to serve the cure and to pay the diocesan contributions.[17] Allanson was still lessee-vicar in 1539. At the Reformation, however, the (unnamed) curate of Tarbolton was paid directly by the benefice-holder at the top of the ladder, Mr James Chisholm whose Glasgow canonry was funded from the parsonage teinds of Tarbolton. Chisholm is a clear example of the absentee pluralist parson. His major office was that of archdeacon of Dunblane, where his kinsmen were bishops for three generations. He leased his Tarbolton benefice for £160 a year, from which he paid £7 6s 8d to the vicar-choral who substituted for him in his stall in the choir of Glasgow cathedral and £20 to the curate of Tarbolton.[18] The practices of delegation and paid substitution were well-established in the staff structure of the late-medieval church as in other areas of public life. It may have been more common in the upper than lower ranks, although there is reference to 'sir William Aird, chaplain, serving in the cure under sir James Mitchell, curate of the parish of Mauchline supplying his turn for the time'.[19] Curates were sometimes asked to undertake tasks involving travel, which created temporary work for chaplains.

In the remaining 12 Ayrshire parishes no references to curates at work have yet come to light. In the cases of Perceton, Kilbirnie, Craigie, Cumnock, Colmonell and Ballantrae the known vicars were mostly career clerics who were almost certainly absentees and we can only conclude therefore that references to curates there have so far proved elusive rather than that they did not operate. The vicars of Kirkmichael and Straiton on the eve of the Reformation were non-graduate priests from local families who may have worked in their parishes. This was certainly true of sir John Howie, parish priest and vicar of Kilmaurs, and sir James Mason, parish priest and vicar of Kilmarnock who died in 1537, when he was followed by graduate absentees.

It is noticeable that those curates, like Howie and Mason who later acquired a benefice, nevertheless remained in active parish service. This was also the case with sir James Mitchell, curate and later vicar of Mauchline, sir Robert Leggat, curate of Prestwick and later vicar of Ayr, sir Edmund Henderson, curate of Kilwinning who became vicar of Kilmacormock in Knapdale, and sir Thomas Rolland, curate of Ayr at the beginning of the century who acquired a share of the parsonage teinds and who, although correctly called parson of Ayr on occasion, remained 'curate and principal chorister' in St John's kirk, Ayr.[20] In the same way the parsonage revenues were also granted to the curate of Ayr sir Henry Hunter in 1528. The grant of a benefice to these non-graduate, local, working clerics may have improved their financial circumstances but did not enable them to transfer to the fast stream in terms of career. It would seem that the question of how to get on depended not on whether you had a benefice, or even on whether you were a graduate (there were many non-graduates high up in diocesan service), but on whether you had served as a working parish priest. If you served your apprenticeship, were ordained at the canonical age and took on real spiritual duties in the parish, you were likely to stay there. On the other hand if you purchased a benefice first, settled on a career outwith parish service and got ordained when you chose, you might rise high up in the profession. At least, that was how a number of those at the very top did it. The options described are the extremes, for there were ways and means between. On the whole, however, once a curate always a curate, whereas a chaplain who did not sidestep into parish service might do well in terms of promotion. The two broad categories of 'promoted' and 'unpromoted' staff must have been apparent at the time.

It is paradoxical that the post-Reformation minister, university-trained and often from outwith the parish, is more readily identifiable than the normally locally-born parish priest. Thirty-five named curates have been identified so far, representing 28 Ayrshire parishes. For most parishes only one curate has been identified, but there are four for Ayr, three for Irvine, and two each for Mauchline, Monkton, Riccarton and Symington. On the whole only one or two references turn up to most of the lower clergy but in some cases there are references to service covering several years. Most notable in this respect are the curates, sir Thomas Rolland (1471–1506) and sir Henry Hunter (1507-c. 1530) at Ayr; sir John Mitchell (1541–1560) at Irvine; sir William Tunnock (1524–1533) at Ochiltree; sir Alexander Lumsden (1544–1553) at Stewarton; sir Robert Leggat (1525–1560) at Prestwick; sir John Howie (1540–1560) at Kilmaurs; and, the longest-serving curate traced so far, sir Edmund Henderson (1512–1557) at Kilwinning. Where their social connections can be identified, the curates were usually from tenant families in the rural parishes or from burgess stock in the towns.

Almost all the Ayrshire curates were non-graduates, addressed by the honorific 'sir', which stuck to them after the Reformation since it was a courtesy title, not ecclesiastical. Although ridiculed in contemporary literature as 'sir John Latinless', probably a jibe at their rudimentary education rather than ignorance of the liturgy which they would come to know by heart anyway, all these curates had writing skills and a certain knowledge of the law; many practised as notaries. In terms of accessibility the parish priest was the church in the eyes of most parishioners. It was he who implemented the edicts of the provincial councils and synods and who was first in the parishioners' line of fire when they chose to resist clerical demands, especially those of a fiscal sort. He became involved in the family and legal disputes of the community, often trying to settle them, wrote out and read documents for his mostly illiterate flock and was in turn dependent on their generosity to eke out his meagre income. He officiated at their marriages, baptised their children and sent their souls with the church's blessing into the next world. As John Bossy has described him, he was both a familiar and an almost magical figure, the latter especially when at the altar of the normally small, plain parish kirk he made God present before their eyes in the host at the mass.[21] Like most essential services, his was both appreciated and criticised as he carried out his duties in the sight of the local community.

There are many glimpses of the curates at work. Often, they are carrying out routine procedures such as taking possession of property set aside for obits, or publicly reading dispensations for marriage and calling the couple's banns. On 23 January 1522 when the banns for the marriage of Robert Lindsay, grandson of the laird of Crosbasket, and Janet, daughter of George Ross of Haining, were called in the private chapel of Janet's home, the parish priests of bride and bridegroom took part: sir John Ledhouse, curate of Riccarton, for Janet and sir Gavin Brown, curate of of West Kilbride, for Robert.[22] In contrast to this private occasion, sir Henry Hunter, curate of Ayr, read out the dispensation for the marriage of the son of Thomas Kennedy of Bargany and the daughter of the late Sir Hugh Campbell of Loudoun while the parishioners of Ayr were present at high mass in St John's kirk, and then went on to proclaim their banns of marriage.[23] The dispensation for the marriage of Robert Tinto of Crimpcramp and Giles Ross was read by the curate of Riccarton, sir William Bankhead, immediately before he performed the marriage ceremony.[24] A curate was often involved in drawing up a will and in compiling the inventory of goods and debts which became part of the recorded testament.[25] He also inducted the vicar, or just as likely his proxy, as part of regularising the appointee's entitlement to the fruits of his benefice, and also installed the parish clerk in office.[26]

Curates also had the unenviable task of reading out sentences of excommunication and other censures, which were sometimes defied by those sentenced. In April 1524, in a case the outcome of which is not recorded, sir Henry Hunter, curate of Ayr, was defied by four excommunicate burgesses whom he had ordered to leave the church; they complained that the letters read out were unlawful because the curate had proceeded with them in advance of the date set for their trial before the dean of Glasgow.[27] A more violent scene occurred in Dalry parish church in 1510 when an excommunicate priest, Thomas Brown, who had been brought into the church by John Blair of Blair, was forcibly bundled out by some obliging parishioners after he had defied the curate's command to leave.[28] Legal proceedings might have to be announced at the market cross rather than in the church. In January 1510 sir Thomas Auld, curate of Irvine, and a colleague publicly cited all interested parties to attend the trial of Humphrey Blair 'and other clerkis' before the archbishop of Glasgow for their part in the slaughter of young William Crawford of Baidland. Nobody came forward 'although several friends and relatives of the deceased were present', and the prosecution collapsed. It must have required a good deal of nerve to publicly denounce those on one side or the other in a feud. In more peaceable times curates like any other chaplains acted as notaries, as clerks to secular courts or as procurators in court for lay clients, as sir Richard Miller, curate of Ayr, continued to do after 1560.

Conditions of employment and remuneration varied. The contract of employment between sir William Hume, curate of Auchinleck, and Paisley abbey on 17 April 1523 is written into the abbey register:

> we ... grantis us to haif rentallit our servand sir William Hume curat of our kirk of Auchinlek in the haill kirkland of the samin payand yeirlie as it was wont to do and also we ordain and maks the said sir William our curat of our said kirk for all the tyme of his lyfe, and quhen the said sir William may nocht mak service in the parochin he sall caus ane othir to mak service for him that he the [deputy] sall be sufficient ....[29]

A lifetime contract like this supported by rents from the parish kirklands was a fairly secure appointment for sir William who had been active as a chaplain in the Cumnock and Ochiltree areas since at least 1514.[30] Curates were just as likely to be moved around. Sir William Bankhead is found at Loudoun (1527) and Riccarton (1533); sir Robert Leggat at Prestwick (1525–1558) and Ayr (1558–1560); sir David Neill at Largs (1549) and Monkton (1556); and sir John Mitchell at Irvine (1541) and Ardrossan (1552).

Salaries paid to Ayrshire curates were sometimes more and sometimes less than the minimum £13 6s 8d laid down by the provincial council.[31] However they fared, the working parish clergy received only a fraction of the parochial revenues. It could be argued that the middlemen tacksmen of teinds were probably making as much if not more out of this situation than the higher clergy who leased their benefices to them. One point can scarcely be argued, that in return for their modest incomes the parish priests carried most of the church's responsibility for the cure of souls. At their best these men are exemplified by sir James Mason, parish priest of Kilmarnock who died in 1537 but whose parishioners remembered him with affection twenty years later.[32] Their memories ranged from those of Lord Boyd to whom he had stood godfather, and William Hamilton, canon of Glasgow, who recalled how 'he had yeirlie drank at the kirk and manse oftymes', to that of John Adamson who remembered sir James tilling his glebe, whose father had been servant to the old priest who had gone blind towards the end of his life.

Perhaps there was more disillusionment among religious dissenters on the eve of the Reformation than outright hostility towards the church, more apathy than antagonism. If a reasonable service was conscientiously provided at parish level by the lower clergy, who were the laity's normal contact with the church, what then were the causes, if any, of complaint? It has been suggested that the local leaders of society may have been increasingly inclined to take their custom elsewhere, through their collegiate churches, private chapels and ability to pay for concessions such as that of being allowed to choose a confessor (perhaps a friar) or to have a portable altar so that facilities for worship might fit in with their lifestyle.[33] At the same time there is evidence of regular contact between the lairds, their families and their parish priests. The curate of Kilmarnock, as we saw, stood godfather to the heir to the lordship of Boyd, it was the curate who officiated at the marriages and burials of the gentry, it was the lady of Loudoun's curate, not her private chaplain, who testified that she was too ill to attend a court hearing,[34] and it was long familiarity surely which caused an Alloway farmer in 1569 to refer to the reader whom he asked to subscribe his will for him as 'curat of my paroch kirk'.[35] However much they might have absented themselves, the lairds regarded the parish kirk as theirs just as much as did humbler parishioners. If there was a target for their grievances, it was perhaps the normally absentee beneficed clergy who, they felt, had personally ceased to return spiritual value for money. The tone of much contemporary criticism is aimed at what was seen as the higher clergy's detachment from spiritual service, their apparent preoccupation with personal concerns:

> Our parson has na uthir pyne
> Bot tak his teind and spend it syne.

People were in no doubt what the teinds were for:

> The lawe is plaine,
> Our teindis suld furneish teachouris.

A more deep-seated criticism, however, was making itself felt two decades before the Reformation crisis of 1560:

> Sen layik men knew the veritie
> Pardoners gets no charitie
> Without that they debait it.[36]

Dissent, not simply dissatisfaction, was the ultimate cause of the demand for reform. While emphasising the continuity of personnel which often marked the formal religious changes of 1560 at parish level, we cannot forget that the Reformation was a schism. The serving pre-Reformation clergy who are found in office at parish kirks after 1560 were there because they were schismatics, of whatever degree of personal commitment to the new kirk.

It is also easy to mistake the occasions of the Reformation-rebellion and its outcome for the causes of support for reform. The international political setting of 1559–60 and the public actions and pronouncements of the lords of the Congregation are well documented and lend themselves to historical analysis, while the climate in which the movement for religious reform grew is elusive (although by no means unrecorded) and is in danger of being discounted as an explanation of what happened in these years. A purely confessional explanation of these events may no longer be acceptable, but it cannot simply be replaced by purely socio-economic or political explanations.

In the next four chapters we shall look at the emergence of religious dissent in Ayrshire which led to active support for church reform, at the involvement of Ayrshiremen in the growing confrontation with the establishment, religious and secular, and at their participation in the Reformation-rebellion which, by making skilful use of prevailing political circumstances, enabled proposals for reform to be carried through nationally and locally.

CHAPTER FOUR

The Lollards' Legacy

Reckoned in years, the trial at Glasgow of the so-called Lollards of Kyle in the spring of 1494 is remote from the Reformation-settlement of 1560. Yet it may not have seemed remote in the memories of the families involved. Indeed, the brief family history published in 1718 by Sergeant James Nisbet from Hardhill on the Ayrshire-Lanarkshire border highlights a perceived continuity of religious dissent (given the very different times) that linked his father John Nisbet the covenanter, executed in 1685, with his great-great-grandfather Murdoch Nisbet, whose 'Wycliffe's New Testament' the family still treasured, and who was believed to have joined Lollard circles at the end of the fifteenth century.[1] How much nearer must the trial of the Lollards have seemed to George Campbell, laird of Cessnock at the Reformation, whose father was old enough to have heard first-hand accounts of it from his father and uncle who had been among the accused?

Standing with the Ayrshire Lollards, as it were, and looking back into the fifteenth century it may be possible to provide them with an historical and geographical context. Our sole account of the event, left to us by John Knox who knew personally the descendants of some of the accused, has given their trial the character of an isolated incident.[2] This impression is reinforced by the fact that Knox named only a handful of them, although he speaks of some 30 persons, from King's Kyle, Kylestewart and Cunninghame, as having been charged. However, since lollardy was a recognised phenomenon in mid-fifteenth century Scotland, word of its existence there having reached even parts of Europe, not all of these people need have been recent or first-generation adherents.

Signs of the presence of heresy before 1500 are usually given a mention in accounts of the Scottish Reformation, if in rather incidental fashion. These include the burning of the Englishman James Reseby in 1407, the vigilance of the new St Andrews university for signs of lollardy among its staff and students, the appointment of Laurence of Lindores as inquisitor of heresy, and the burning of the Bohemian Hussite, Paul Kravar, in 1433. The early fifteenth century was a period of contact between Scotland and English lollard activists during which the points of contact may have lain along the communication routes between Roxburghshire, Lanarkshire and Ayrshire. The existence of these contacts is important in trying to account for the Lollards of Kyle at the end of the century.

Early Scottish contacts with lollardy may have been made through the

English presence at Roxburgh where Sir John Oldcastle was stationed in 1400. Some of the Scots lords made overtures to Oldcastle after negotiations with the English government for the release of King James I broke down in 1408. William Douglas of Drumlanrig, a leading border magnate, is said to have made contact with Oldcastle on the Welsh border in 1417, after the collapse of the latter's rebellion and shortly before his arrest.[3]

Also in these years the religious propositions of lollardy may have reached parts of southern Scotland. In 1401 some followers of Jerome of Prague, lately at Oxford, are said to have crossed the border into Scotland to escape prosecution. About 1402–03 three priests, one of whom was called Robert of Roxburgh (suggesting border origins) also crossed the border to avoid the heresy laws. It cannot now be determined whether their 'unsoundness of faith' was specifically lollard in character, but this is quite possible. The bishop of Durham's authorisation to his officials to arrest them is written into the register of Kelso abbey.[4] The scribe, possibly aware of the phenomenon of lollardy in the region, may have engrossed the document as a useful legal 'style' or model.

Personnel from Kelso would have routine connections with the abbey's dependant priory at Lesmahagow in Lanarkshire, which stood in what may have been the home parish of Scotland's first named lollard, Quintin Fockhart. It seems likely (from the combination of unusual names) that the Quintin Fockhart, a Scot who received safeconducts while travelling in England in 1407, is the Quintin Folkhyrd, or Folkhard, who sent four letters – 'News from Scotland' – to Prague in 1410 in which he described reaction to his demands for church reform.[5] Apparently an educated and landed man, it seems reasonable to believe that he belonged to the family of Fockhart who from the early thirteenth century held the lands of Fockhartoun, Poneil and Kype in Lesmahagow barony from Kelso abbey. The abbey register contains many documents relating to their holdings including a property dispute with the abbey which dragged on into the fifteenth century.[6] Fockhart was in England in 1407, the year of James Reseby's execution. While there is no documentary evidence that Fockhart came under the Englishman's influence, the characteristically lollard tone of 'News from Scotland' suggests some contact with English lollardy. Reseby had moved around in Scotland long enough for the main points of his teaching to be identified and brought against him, although so far there is no record of his activities. Fockhart was also evidently in touch with those who formed a link between English lollardy and the Hussites. One historian has suggested that his letters may have been taken to Prague in 1410 with two others, one from Wyche to Hus and one from Oldcastle to Waldenstein.[7]

Fockhart claimed to have travelled around advocating those propositions for reform set out in his letters. Although his professed aim had been to reform not to break away from the church, he asserted in his first letter that the clergy had tried to enlist the help of his fellow-laymen against him. In response he defended himself in writing to the bishop of Glasgow and the clergy. His criticisms were then denounced as heretical. In his second letter to Prague he continued to challenge his critics. In his third he explained that he had called for support from the secular lords and lay people, and in the fourth that he had appealed to the curates to implement reform, as though in an attempt to divide the higher and lower clergy over the issue in dispute.

Much of what Fockhart had to say about the clergy had lollard overtones, the basic criticism being that they had failed to deliver the service for which they were being paid. They ought, he said, to study and preach, to administer the sacraments 'without price'. They had spiritual responsibilities for which they were paid in tithes and offerings. Yet they did not work as they should, failing to teach the people in a way that they could understand, and they did not give away those goods that were surplus to their own needs.

He urged the curates to preach and read the gospels and epistles in the vernacular during divine service and to share their tithes and offerings, especially with the poor. He assured them that he spoke as their (the curates') friend. His tone, we might say, was constructively critical. There are built into his letters two pillars of lollardy as it came to be preached, which were to remain vitally important to later reformers – the availability of the vernacular scriptures, by reading or hearing, and the accountability of the clergy to those whom they served. Communications like Fockhart's letters probably helped to inform European sympathisers and opponents alike that the teachings of Wycliffe's followers had reached Scotland. In 1414, at the council of Constance, Dietrich von Nieme spoke of the spread of Wycliffe's doctrines in Bohemia, Moravia, England and Scotland, and the following year, when preaching before the pope, Jean d'Achery, envoy from Paris university, also included Scotland in those countries affected by heresy.[8]

In Scotland the authorities were well aware of the presence of lollardy. Walter Bower commends the vigilance of the regent Albany – 'All Lollard he hatet and heretik'. A blow was struck at the sect in 1425 with an act of parliament in the terms of which the secular power was envisaged as assisting in the conviction of 'heretiks and lollardis' who might be apprehended by episcopal inquisitions. John Knox claimed that in 1422, three years before the act was passed, a lollard was burnt at Glasgow. It is unlikely that Knox was confusing this heretic with either the earlier Reseby (1407) or later Kravar (1433) since he mentions both elsewhere. The Glasgow case could have involved someone from anywhere in the diocese. It was stated by Boece and Dempster that the conviction of Kravar was assisted by John Foggo who, they say, got the abbacy of Melrose as a reward. But since Foggo held the abbacy of Melrose from at least 1425, it may be that he helped to convict the unnamed heretic of 1422.[9] Vigilance and legislation did not prevent discussion of lollard ideas at St Andrews university with the Bohemian Paul Kravar when he came, which led to his accusation and death in 1433, or allay the suspicions of Prior Halderstone which fell on one of the St Andrews canons in 1436.[10] Although active inquisition appears to have died out by mid-century, the vehemence of Bower's attack on lollardy in the 1440s in the *Scotichronicon*, and the reminder to its students by St Andrews university in 1469 of the need to maintain a watchful orthodoxy suggests that the issue was not dead. The poet Walter Kennedy, an Ayrshireman, wrote, with some literary licence, of

> The Schip of Faith, tempestuous wind and rane
> Dryvis, in the see of Lollardy that blaws,

and used the word 'lollard' as a vituperative adjective in his 'Flyting' with Dunbar. This is no indication of the seriousness of the threat posed by lollardy but these writings evoke a climate in which people avoided the imputation because the term meant something at the time.

It is unlikely that the Lollards of Kyle who were accused in 1494 had suddenly attached themselves to a movement for which there is evidence from the early fifteenth century. It is more likely in the nature of things that their adherence suggests the survival since then of an interest in lollard propositions by families in the region. By his own testimony Quintin Fockhart rode about advocating his reforms. We can hardly credit him with having single-handedly spread the lollard message. Yet, if he is not to be seen as an isolated disciple, the suggestion is of a pocket of interest in the movement in south-west Scotland which could easily have spread from Lanarkshire into Kyle and Cunninghame.

Communication between the middle ward of Lanarkshire and Ayrshire was comparatively easy. The south-west corner of Lesmahagow parish, which may have been Fockhart's home territory, marched with a stretch of the huge parish of Mauchline which included Melrose abbey's barony of Kylesmure. Mauchline was bounded for about half the length of its northern limits by the parish of Galston. To the north of Galston parish lay that of Loudoun. These three parishes – Mauchline, Galston and Loudoun – were the home territory of some of Ayrshire's oldest protestant families, such as the Lockharts, Campbells and Nisbets, some of whose forebears had been active in what may be called the lollard phase of religious dissent in Ayrshire. Travel between Lanarkshire and Ayrshire was constant. In the early sixteenth century the teind grain from Mauchline parish bound for Melrose abbey in Roxburghshire was carted by way of Priesthill on the Mauchline/Lesmahagow parish border towards Lanark and on to Carnwath, where the carriagemen from Melrose met it and took it on the rest of its journey.[11] In the 1550s the feuars of Kylesmure travelled to Lesmahagow priory where the chamberlain of Kelso abbey and his officials sat to receive the rents and feus of Kylesmure on behalf of James Stewart, joint commendator of Kelso and Melrose.[12] The commendator's falconer of Lesmahagow barony, George Campbell, whose fee is noted in these accounts, was probably one of the Ayrshire Campbells.

Several of the Lollards of Kyle whom Knox actually names were related by blood or marriage to the Campbells of Cessnock from Galston parish who were among the most consistent supporters of religious reform in Ayrshire. George Campbell of Cessnock was himself accused in 1494 along with his second son, John Campbell of Newmilns. Two of the women who were tried, Helen and Marion Chalmers (married respectively to Mure of Polkellie and Dalrymple of Stair), were sisters of the laird of Cessnock's wife Margaret Chalmers. Their family, Chalmers of Gadgirth, who later strongly supported the public advancement of the Reformation, came from Coylton parish in King's Kyle south of the river Ayr. Also from King's Kyle came Adam Reid of Barskimming, another of the accused of 1494. Andrew Shaw, younger of Polkemmet in Linlithgowshire, the laird of Cessnock's nephew, had been drawn into the lollard circle. His father, William Shaw of Polkemmet, is found witnessing Ayrshire legal deeds in company with the lairds, Campbell of Cessnock and Lockhart of Bar, from at least 1491.[13]

The Lollards were tried in the presence of King James IV in the court of the Official of Glasgow, an example of the cooperation of secular and spiritual authorities envisaged in the anti-heresy statute of 1425. The impression from the surviving account of the trial is that the king took it in fairly relaxed fashion. It was claimed that some of the accused got off because they were his familiar servants; some of them held minor administrative and royal household posts and received grants of crown revenue at about this time. John Knox listed 34 articles brought against them which he claimed to have 'received ... forth of the Registers of Glasgow'. This suggests that details were passed on to him, possibly in the form of a legal extract from the register (now lost) of the diocesan Official, made at the time of the trial and preserved by descendants of one or other of the accused. Ayrshire contacts probably supplied Knox with information about other local events for inclusion in his *History*. In trying to assess the emphasis of the Lollards' assertions, we must allow for the fact that what survives, even if correctly extracted from the registers and faithfully transmitted to Knox, is the ecclesiastical authorities' summing up of the evidence gleaned and forwarded to them by informants. Given the authorities' condemnation of the potentially subversive element (spiritual and secular) in lollardy, we can expect the articles to be strongly worded.

Many of the accusations, 13 out of 34, challenged the ultimate spiritual authority of the church, especially in the person of the pope who was identified not as the successor of St Peter but as the antichrist, with no power to release from purgatory or to forgive sins, whose official communications such as bulls, pardons and indulgences were declared to be a deception. Excommunication, it was claimed, was not binding and therefore not to be feared. Four overtly anticlerical statements robbed the priesthood of their mediatory role, their spiritual authority and their distinctive clerical character which set them apart from the laity: that they had no power to consecrate, that every believing man and woman is a priest, that teinds should not be given to churchmen, and that priests should marry. The accountability of the higher clergy, who were accused of failing to deliver spiritual services in return for material support, was encapsulated in the cryptic accusation that 'they who are called principals are thieves and robbers'.

Theological prepositions included the denial of the efficacy of prayers for the dead, and transubstantiation, two major lollard objections: 'The mass profiteth not the souls in purgatory'; 'after consecration in the mass bread remains'; 'true Christians receive the body of Christ Jesus every day'. The lollard antipathy to the cult of images, relics and miracles was to leave Ayrshire reformers with a distinctively iconoclastic legacy: no worshipping of images, no worshipping of so-called relics of the saints; faith should not be placed in miracles; the veneration of the sacrament itself in church is idolatry. A secular attitude is not unexpected in followers of a movement which assumed a good deal of lay initiative in the Christian community. Kings were desanctified: since the coming of Christ they were no longer spiritual judges, and they should not be given a quasi-priestly character by anointing at coronation. The church had no authority to dissolve marriage. There was nothing specially sacred about church buildings that worship should take place only there. Two pacifist notes were struck: crusades and the indulgences that were sold to finance them were wrong, and the faith should not be defended by force of arms. The later reformers were to abandon the second of these positions. The accused denied the lawfulness of oath-taking.

The general overtones are of an historical perspective of the development of the church, the accountability of the priesthood in carrying out their functions, and the importance of the laity. As is generally the case with lollardy, there is no preoccupation with sinful man's predicament before a holy God, so central to later protestantism, but simply the advocacy of direct unmediated access to God by believing men and women at all times in circumstances shorn of all miraculous elements, perhaps not even in a consecrated building. Christian experience here is not simply anti-authority but extra-authority. This lay-orientated 'do-it-yourself' element must have been as disturbing to the ecclesiastical authorities as the outright denial of some of the church's central doctrines.

In the later tradition of south-west Scotland the advocates of religious reform in the 1520s and 1530s were seen as the spiritual heirs (some were the actual descendants) of the Lollards of Kyle, in the same way as English protestants were portrayed by such writers as John Foxe as the heirs of Wycliffe. If in England the 1530s saw fusion and adjustment of lollard and protestant ideas, we should not be surprised if Scottish chroniclers speak of lollards and the followers of lollardy in the reign of James V when the ideas of an earlier generation of religious dissenters came into contact with the influence of Luther's Germany and Tyndale's England. Interest in the vernacular scriptures, anti-clerical attitudes and iconoclastic activity, all of which characterised the lay reform movement in Ayrshire at an early stage, reflect its lollard origins.

The Lollards of Kyle had not been accused of possessing lollard literature or the vernacular scriptures, although a later source claims that John Campbell had the scriptures read to his household for which he, his wife and a priest, probably his household chaplain, were arrested.[14] Nevertheless, group-reading of the scriptures, a characteristic practice of English lollardy, took place among those who formed a personal link between the earlier lollards and later reformers in south-west Scotland. They included the circle of Alexander Gordon of Airds in Dumfriesshire, a region as accessible to Ayrshire as Ayrshire was to Lanarkshire. One of those in this circle was the son of Stewart of Garlies, who in 1558 invited the protestant preacher William Harlaw to Dumfries where he preached in the house of a burgess, Robert Cunningham.[15]

In Ayrshire a bible-reading group gathered around Murdoch Nisbet of Hardhill in Loudoun parish, whose identification with religious dissent spanned half a century.[16] Although not named by Knox in his account of the 1494 trial, Nisbet may have been among those accused who were said to have come from Cunninghame, of which Loudoun is the easternmost parish. If so, he would be well-known to near neighbours George Campbell of Cessnock and his son John Campbell of Newmilns. The chronology of Nisbet's early career is a little difficult to straighten out but it is said that as a young man he joined the lollard group about the turn of the century. He went 'abroad', to either England or Europe (perhaps both), to avoid prosecution, sometime after 1513. By the 1520s Lutheran literature was reaching Scotland, leading to the anti-heresy legislation of 1525, and in the later 1520s copies of Tyndale's new testament were entering the country, it was claimed, in considerable numbers. Nisbet appears to have been aware of these strands of bible translation. While in exile he prepared a rendering into Scots of the new testament. With his own connections with lollardy it is not surprising that he used as the basis of his work not Tyndale's English translation but the revision of a Lollard text, hitherto attributed to John Purvey, although his authorship has recently been questioned.[17] This was in all probability the vernacular text with which he was already familiar, of which he must either have had a copy of his own or borrowed one on long-term loan in order to complete his task. At the same time it has been noted that a large part of his prologue is a literal translation of Luther's preface to his German translation, and that here and there Nisbet also makes use of Tyndale's own use of Luther in the 1525 edition of the English new testament, as well as Tyndale's textual markings. It has been suggested that Nisbet's main text had been prepared before Luther's work appeared in print in 1522, because if Nisbet was able to translate Luther's preface he was doubtless able to translate the whole of Luther's text. He may, however, have had a personal preference for the familiar lollard text. Nisbet's work is not a painstaking scholarly translation, and it was probably not intended to be, only an intelligible working transcription in Scots for the use of himself and his friends; he did not trouble to render into Scots those English words that would be readily understood by his fellow-readers and hearers.

Nisbet returned to Scotland, probably at some time during the 1530s, in the company of others who 'had been elsewhere upon the same occasion'. Keeping a low profile, he held secret meetings with his friends and is said to have taught others who made contact with him. He lived on into the 1550s when he is said to have assisted with the more open advancement of the Reformation, helping those of his fellow-Ayrshiremen who 'went through many places of the land, demolishing idolatry wherever they went'. This iconoclasm would satisfy some of his earliest lollard convictions. He may or may not be the Murdoch Nisbet who practised as a notary in the 1520s and 1530s, who transacted business for the dissenting Campbells, Reids and Lockharts, as well as for other Nisbets, over an area stretching from Ayr itself to Loudoun parish. The burgess Nisbets of Ayr were friends of the heretic Glenluce monk John MacBrair in the 1550s.[18]

The acquittal of the Lollards in 1494, the first native Scots to be tried for heresy, left an enclave of dissenters more or less intact. A public abjuration, however, would in the interests of safety have the effect of sending their activities if any underground. This would not necesarily mean that they abandoned their opinions; one of the difficulties in trying to make lollard abjurations stick was the fact that they put no value on oath-taking and therefore recognised no personal perjury in adhering to opinions which they had publicly abjured at their trials.[19] The acquittal of the Ayrshire accused implies abjuration by at least some of them. Lack of official records, however, makes it difficult to tell what actually happened. Knox's account gives the impression that the case collapsed partly because the king's attitude took the wind out of the prosecution's sails. At the same time there was a tradition that John Campbell and his wife were only saved from the death penalty by the last-minute intervention of the king. The willingness of Archbishop Robert Blackadder in March 1504 to furnish the Campbells, father and son, with copies of the attestations produced at their trial echoes the English practice of documenting the process of abjuration by issuing copies of the charges laid against the accused. This process was seen by the heretics as a safeguard against being falsely accused at a later date. If the Campbells requested such documents, these may be some of the sources on which Knox later drew for his account of the trial.[20] The fact that the attestations were requested 10 years after the trial may suggest some unfinished business, may even hint at further accusations. Nevertheless, both men stood well with secular authority in the years following their trial. The laird of Cessnock himself was sheriff-depute of Ayr between 1500 and 1505, while his son John of Newmilns received regular crown gifts 'for his support' from the customs from 1507 to 1513.

The abjuration of another of the accused, Adam Reid of Barskimming, is described by Knox. The story of how Reid turned his recantation into an insolent riposte to the discomfiture of the archbishop would have lost nothing in the re-telling by the time Knox heard it. If there is any authenticity in the account, it suggests that Reid was confident of the king's sympathy. According to Knox's account, it was the king who asked Reid if he would burn his bill, to which Reid is said to have replied, 'Sir, the bishop and you will'. Later circumstances may suggest that Reid's lollardy was somewhat shallow, although some of these circumstances need to be considered in context.[21] The fact that he witnessed the grant of a chaplainry in Ayr parish kirk to sir William Reid by their kinsman Mr Martin Reid, chancellor of Glasgow cathedral, in 1507 need not imply a change of opinion, only an adjustment of conscience.[22] Whatever its spiritual significance, the chaplainry was a welcome piece of property for a family member drawn from an influential relative's fund of patronage. Since he had abjured his assertion that masses for the dead had no efficacy, it would have been asking for trouble to refuse to act as a witness now on grounds of conscience. More inconsistent is Reid's proposed pilgrimage in 1507, in company with another layman and a cleric, to the shrine of St Thomas of Canterbury and a French pilgrim shrine; inconsistent, that is, unless the pilgrimage was a penance handed out to him by the church authorities for his religious offence.[23] The crown granted him a respite (temporary immunity from legal prosecution) while on his journey. Of less significance is Reid's appointment of procurators to the papal court (as a court of appeal) as executor of his kinsman Mr Martin Reid in 1523.[24] This was a necessary legal step in regularising his late kinsman's affairs as the law then stood, whatever one might think privately of papal authority or the canon law. Whatever Reid's personal commitment, his branch of the family continued to support the movement for religious reform. His grandson and namesake with other Reids signed the Band of Ayr in 1562, and about the same time the leaders of the Catholic party, Archbishop Hamilton and Abbot Quintin Kennedy, tried unsuccessfully to foment trouble between the Reids and the Crawfords in a bid to crack the solidarity of the protestants of the west country.[25]

However the Lollards who were tried may have squared matters with the church authorities, the two decades that followed their trial saw a number of attacks on clerics and church property in Ayrshire. Although not all of these may have been deliberate acts of religious protest, they reveal a lack of respect for religious institutions and habitual lay intrusion into their affairs, a climate in which the more radical proponents of reform would find it easier to take steps towards their ends. The most serious incident, which took place in the winter of 1503–04, was the killing of the priest of Crosbie chapel, a quasi-parochial church in Dundonald parish.[26] The use of the term 'slaughter' in the record indicates that the priest was killed openly, perhaps during a fracas between rival groups. There were thefts of teinds from the lands of Kilwinning and Crossraguel abbeys;[27] the word 'theft' can simply denote that the teind crops were withheld or abstracted by tenants, great or small, in an era when resistance to the payment of teinds was endemic. There was the notorious occasion in 1512 when the earls of Angus and Glencairn with an armed company broke into the abbey church at Kilwinning and by physical force tried to make the last monastic superior, Abbot William Bunch, adhere to an earlier undertaking to resign in favour of crown nominee, John Forman.[28] Abbot Bunch stuck to his post but is believed to have been killed at Flodden the following year.

In 1511 George Campbell, son of the lollard laird of Cessnock, in company with a priest sir John Leitch and others broke into the royal chapel at Dundonald castle and carried off a chest containing the books, chalice and chapel ornaments.[29] When Leitch was summoned before the archbishop's commissary for his sacrilegious action, Campbell acted as his procurator – perhaps to make sure that the court heard his side of the story. Although the Campbells are known to have had objections to the purpose of the chapel – it was a non-parochial chapel endowed for the celebration of masses for the Stewarts – the fact that sir John Leitch had been the unsuccessful candidate for the chaplainry two years earlier may have had something to do with the attack; the loss of the liturgical property would make it difficult for the rival incumbent to prove his right. It also shows how dissenters like the Campbells were ready to become involved in ecclesiastical property disputes, if this was indeed the reason behind the incident.

It is difficult to avoid the impression that Ayrshire families such as the Cunninghams, Wallaces, Fullartons, Reids, Lockharts, Campbells, Stewarts and Chalmers, who were to be so prominent in the pro-reform ranks in the 1550s, had been nurtured in a tradition of dissent which went back to the turn of the century at least, a tradition which may have filtered through during even earlier decades from Lanarkshire, the borders and ultimately from England. Unlike the movement of people and goods that of ideas cannot be quantified but ideas can travel a fair distance in time and space. The Carmichaels of that Ilk, from the Lanarkshire parish of Carmichael which lay to the east of Lesmahagow parish (possibly the centre of Quintin Fockhart's activities), consistently supported the Reformation, one of its best known members being that 'stout gentleman' Peter Carmichael of Balmeddie, one of Cardinal Beaton's assassins. Peter's grandfather had married as his second wife in 1495 Elizabeth, joint-heiress of the Fockharts of Fockhartoun.[30] The family of the reformer Andrew Stewart, 2nd Lord Ochiltree, came from the Lanarkshire parish of Avondale to the west of Lesmahagow. Andrew Stewart 1st Lord Ochiltree exchanged the barony of Avondale for that of Ochiltree in Kyle in 1534. Adam Fullarton, expatriate Ayrshireman and prominent member of the protestant party in Edinburgh in the 1550s, was probably a son of a Fullarton of Dreghorn.[31] It is difficult to tell whether he was the brother or cousin of the laird of Dreghorn who supported the Reformation and signed the band of Ayr in 1562. If a brother, their mother was Helen Chalmers, said in family histories to be the daughter of Sir John Chalmers of Gadgirth and, presumably, the Helen Chalmers accused as a Lollard in 1494 and first married to Robert Mure of Polkellie. If a cousin, Adam's mother would have been Elizabeth Dalrymple of Stair, whose brother was the husband of Marion Chalmers, another of the accused Lollards. John Lockhart of Bar, the arch-iconoclast and enemy of priests in the 1540s, was a son of his father's first marriage to Margaret Stewart of the Garlies family whose nephew (John Lockhart's cousin) had in his youth been involved with lollard-style bible-reading groups. John's brother, Mr Robert Lockhart, negotiated with the English on behalf of the St Andrews castilians in 1547 and became a member with Adam Fullarton of the privy kirk in Edinburgh in the late 1550s. While children do not necessarily follow in the intellectual or spiritual footsteps of their parents, or students those of their teachers, it is a fact of life that ideas are spread through personal contact, through the spoken, written or printed word. It would be interesting to know more about the early life of William Aird who became a minister at St Cuthbert's outside Edinburgh in 1584, who was born at Burnmouth beside Newmilns in Loudoun parish and worked as a mason until the age of twenty. It is said that he was taught to read English by his wife -from a new testament? - and became proficient in the languages of the bible after being sent to university.[32] It is an interesting social vignette of the younger generation, male and female, in the home parish of the Lollards John Campbell of Newmilns and Murdoch Nisbet. The latter could still have been alive when William Aird was born.

It has been said that lollardy had no blueprint for a reformed church, that its followers held varied interpretations of certain parts of the scriptures and Christian doctrines, that its efforts lacked co-ordination. In other words it could not have brought about a Reformation. In those regions affected by it, however, it conditioned some people into asking searching questions about those aspects of the church which they had come to find unsatisfactory, to denounce those practices for which they claimed to find no biblical authority, and to take on board the idea of reform from outside the church establishment. Margaret Aston's observation that 'Lollards may not actually make Protestants but they could sow fertile seeds of doubt' would seem to fit the experience of those Ayrshire families among whom religious dissent was a marked feature in the first half of the sixteenth century.[33] Murdoch Nisbet's Scots new testament, with its links back to Wycliffe and his followers, is a legacy of that dissent on the eve of its contact with European protestantism.

CHAPTER FIVE

Towards Reform

Although religious dissent was by no means new to Ayrshire in the 1530s, its open activities were part of the spread of unorthodoxy across Scotland which gave both religious and secular authorities cause for concern in that decade, a concern which led to periodic anti-heresy legislation and prosecutions. The period saw the spread of Luther's influence outside Germany by means of printed literature, the appearance in Scotland of William Tyndale's two editions of the new testament in English, the continuing impact on the educated classes of the trial and death of Patrick Hamilton in 1528, the first Scot to be put to death for heresy, and at the close of the decade (1539) the succession to the archbishopric of St Andrews of the reactionary and pro-French Cardinal David Beaton.

In an act of parliament of 1525 the authorities took steps to curb 'ony opunyeounis contrare the Christin fayth', for which the penalties covered not only the importation of 'Lutheran' books but also the public discussion of Luther's teaching, unless in order to condemn it. In 1527 the scope of the act was extended to include native Scots, 'the kingis leigis assistaris to ony sic opunyeounis', and discussion such as was permitted was limited to 'clerkis in the sculis allanerlie', hinting at a widening extra-academic interest in Lutheran ideas. The legislation was ratified in 1535 and amplified in 1541.

Dissent in the 1530s although leaderless and unorganised was found among people of widely differing backgrounds: academics and students, some of the latter laymen; members of religious orders, notably friars and canons regular, who were genuinely concerned about internal reform of the church and interested in the written sources of Christianity in the original languages, to which Erasmus and others had recently drawn so much attention; laymen such as lawyers and crown officials who were increasingly keen to elbow the churchmen out of their chosen professions; lairds and other lay people, increasingly literate and self-determining even in religious matters, who resented the demands of the clerical establishment; merchants and shipmasters who had everyday contacts with European centres of protestantism.[1]

We can only guess at the effect of exposure to protestant literature, bible-reading or hearing, theological discussion of the new doctrines or neighbourly arguments around religious concerns on this wide range of people, from the convinced to the confused. Yet the varied grounds of the accusations against heretics in this decade, which are our only guide, comprise a body of recognisably protestant beliefs, however transmitted or partially understood. Apart from possession of the new testament in English and banned literature (rarely specified), these beliefs included objection to the sacrificial doctrine of the mass and to the doctrine of transubstantiation, to reliance on the intercession of the saints (even of the Virgin Mary) and their merits, and to the doctrine of purgatory and the associated sale of indulgences; a call for the dissolution of monastic property, the abolition of clerical privileges and for the marriage of the clergy to be permitted; revulsion towards the excess of temporal wealth and power in the hands of the higher clergy; and attempts to implement some of these beliefs by physically removing the visible and tangible props of traditional religious practice, such as images and what some saw as the superfluous symbolic decoration of church interiors.

Iconoclasm, because it takes the form of attacks on property, can easily be confused with ill-informed vandalism, which it could sometimes become. Its real significance, however, lies deeper then the expression of contempt for the objectionable or the last resort of the thwarted and frustrated reformer. Iconoclasm is the logical physical removal of things already abandoned in the mind, the outward result of having come to do without these things inwardly and of believing that their continued presence is wrong and misleading to others. The actual removal need not always have been accompanied by physical violence. The proceeding came to be called 'the work of reformation' by those who carried it out.

The earliest record of such an act in Scotland is the appearance before the archbishop's court in Glasgow in March 1533 of Walter Stewart, son of the 1st Lord Ochiltree, on a charge of 'casting doun ane image in the kirk of Ayr', as it is put in Calderwood's *History*, our only source of information.[2] As often happened in such cases, the specific charge against Walter Stewart led to a deeper investigation of the accused's beliefs and to a general charge of heresy. Stewart recanted only 'after long dealing with him', but was drowned in the Water of Calder on his way home, at the last moment bitterly regretting his recantation.

His trial actually took place some months before his father, Andrew Stewart, Lord Avondale, formally exchanged his Lanarkshire lordship for that of Ochiltree in Kyle and some years before he was officially recognised as Lord Ochiltree, although he was commonly known as such from at least 1537.[3] So it was probably to his Lanarkshire home near Strathaven that Walter and his party were travelling when the fateful crossing of the Calder Water was made. Interestingly, one of his companions, who had accompanied him to his trial, was George Good, a senior court of session clerk who was long retained as a legal factotum by the burgh of Ayr. His attack on the fabric of the Ayr church shows that Walter's family were involved in religious protest in Ayrshire before they settled in Kyle where his brother Andrew, 2nd Lord Ochiltree, became a prominent leader of the reform party. The parish of Avondale, marching as it did on the south and west with those of Mauchline, Loudoun and Galston, afforded the Stewarts easy contact with families in the old 'lollard' country of the Lanarkshire-Ayrshire border.

The incident involving Walter Stewart may or may not be the same as that recorded in the legal stylebook of Mr John Lauder who was employed in the Glasgow episcopal chancery in the 1530s.[4] Lauder's document refers to the decapitation of a statue of the Virgin Mary on the wall of the Franciscan monastery at Ayr, the defacement of an external feature suggesting some kind of public protest. The group who mutilated the Franciscans' statue were also accused of having expressed heretical opinions against the sacrament of the mass, of spreading Lutheran doctrines publicly and privately and of being in possession of the new testament in English and (unspecified) Lutheran works. There may have been some difficulty in bringing the law to bear fully on offenders, for in 1537 a search was being made for 'the heretiks in the westland' and a messenger-at-arms was dispatched to 'Summond the menne of Aire to compeir [appear in court] . . . anent the geir of thame quhilk wes convict of heresy'.[5] The prosecutors' difficulties may help to explain why so few south-west names turn up in the escheats (confiscations) for heresy recorded in the register of the privy seal, a circumstance which led one Reformation historian to conclude that heresy at this period was an east-coast phenomenon.[6]

This particular inquisition by the authorities may connect with the arrival at Carlisle in March 1537 of 'four Scotchmen of the toun of Ayr' who complained to Henry Clifford earl of Cumberland that 'they are cumbered [harassed] at home for the opinion that the Bishop of Rome ought not to be called Pope and for having the new testament in English'.[7] The fugitives asked to be allowed to remain in Carlisle until King James V returned from France, where he had recently married Princess Madeleine, saying that they hoped for better justice from him than from the churchmen in his absence. This and the attack on the Franciscans' kirk are the earliest references to open dissent in the burgh of Ayr itself, a state of affairs not unexpected considering how many relatives of the Lockharts, Campbells, Reids, Nisbets and other dissenting families from landward Ayrshire were prominent members of the burgh community.

The inquisition did not give up its efforts to bring west-country heretics to justice and in 1539 three young men were convicted, a friar and two laymen: Jerome Russell of the strict Observant Franciscans, a youth named Kennedy who was probably from Carrick, and Andrew Cunningham, a grandson of Cuthbert, earl of Glencairn.[8] John Knox describes Russell as being 'of good letters' and Kennedy, who was then under 18 years of age, as 'one of excellent engine [genius] in Scottish poesy'. Both are said to have been in the company of Murdoch Nisbet, himself a lettered man, while he took refuge outwith Scotland but were informed against after their return and arrested. Russell, who was apprehended in Dumfries and could have been from either the Ayr or Glasgow house of Observants, had apparently left his community. The cardinal sent two representatives, his secretary Mr John Lauder and Friar Maltman, to Glasgow to influence Archbishop Gavin Dunbar into taking a firm line with Russell and Kennedy, who were tried together. Dunbar acquiesced and they were condemned and burnt. Their deaths were among the clutch of executions in 1539 that heralded the new primate's determined, if short-lived, drive against heresy.

Andrew Cunningham, the third accused, was found guilty but was later granted his own escheat, presumably following a formal recantation. No details of the accusations against him survive but his beliefs were evidently such as to condemn him in the eyes of the judges. His opinions were shared by other members of his family, including his father and older brother who were never prosecuted. If the authorities' treatment of Andrew was meant to be a warning to them, it failed to take effect. The 1530s saw three generations of the Cunningham family active together in public affairs after weathering earlier political storms. Alexander 1st earl of Glencairn was killed at the battle of Sauchieburn in 1488 fighting for King James III. In retribution his son Robert was deprived of the title by the new regime but it was restored to Andrew Cunningham's grandfather, Cuthbert 2nd earl of Glencairn, at James IV's marriage to Margaret Tudor in 1503. Cuthbert was wounded at but survived the battle at Linlithgow in 1526 when he supported the earl of Lennox against the Douglases and lived on until between May 1540 and May 1541, a patriarchal and somewhat turbulent figure at the centre of a huge family network and following in the south-west. The Cunningham chiefs enjoyed a remarkably strong line of succession in the sixteenth century; no head of the family or heir fell at Flodden, Pinkie or other national engagement or even in the continual private wars and vendettas that dogged their relations with other Ayrshire families, notably the Montgomeries of Eglinton. Andrew Cunningham the heretic's father, William Master of Kilmaurs, was by the late 1530s an active man in middle age whose sons were already taking part in public affairs. The Master's oldest son Alexander, who was later to become the lay leader of the Reformation in the south-west, had himself an heir of marriageable age when his grandfather Cuthbert died and his father William became the 3rd earl of Glencairn about 1541.[9]

Earl William and his sons soon came to the forefront of the anglophile-reforming party whose activities found a focus in their association with Henry VIII's Scottish policy which they believed to be in their own interest in advancing reform of the church, at least in as far as reform measures might clip the wings of the ecclesiastical aristocracy. Like many of their contemporaries, the attitude of the Cunninghams to the religious establishment was both paternalist and opportunist. At home they used their patronage of Kilmaurs collegiate church, the family's foundation, to benefit various dependants and were themselves tacksmen of the teinds of several parishes. Two of the heretic Andrew Cunningham's brothers, Robert and William, exploited the dual character of the ecclesiastical establishment by living on church revenues without undertaking the religious responsibilities attached to them. Robert Cunningham was head – or Minister – of the house of Trinitarian friars at Fail in Barnweil parish, a community whose internal standards had been the subject of investigations since the mid-fifteenth century and which rarely had more than six or seven friars besides the superior.[10] By 1546 Robert Cunningham was married, when he and his wife had a charter of the lands of Montgreenan, although he continued to be known as Minister of Fail and to act as provincial of the Trinitarian order in Scotland. Without doubt his sole concern was with the temporal possessions of the monastery as a piece of property. The youngest Cunningham son, William, was provided to the bishopric of Argyll in 1539 but remained technically bishop-elect and unconsecrated (a not unknown situation) for about 14 years. Although his see was described by his royal sponsor James V at the time of William's nomination as a mountainous and barren country yielding a meagre revenue, it no doubt provided some income as it undoubtedly brought social prestige and political patronage to William Cunningham, while locally-born Gaelic-speaking deputies administered the bishopric lands and held its courts on his behalf. In 1553 William exchanged the bishopric of Argyll with James Hamilton, a natural brother of Chatelherault, for the deanery of Brechin. While he acted as vicar-general of Brechin in 1557 during a vacancy in that see, the bailiary of the bishopric lands was held successively by family allies in the protestant Congregation, John Erskine of Dun and the earl of Argyll.[11] Families on both sides of the increasingly apparent religious divide were able to take advantage of inherent weaknesses in the ecclesiastical structure.

The decade after the death of Patrick Hamilton was an intellectual phase in the early movement towards reform in Scotland as the debate between dissent and orthodoxy, banned in public, worked its way through educated circles. It was also a decade of defection when the need to evade prosecution drove many of the dissenters into England or across to Europe, some of them to an academic career or foreign pulpit. A few were arrested, condemned and put to death for heresy in the occasional prosecutions of the mid-1530s and in 1539.[12]

Those who defected included a number of Augustinian canons who not only discussed the new doctrines with colleagues but through their practice of serving parishes in some cases influenced the laity. They included Alexander Allan, Augustinian canon of St Andrews, who left to escape prosecution and taught successively at Malmo, Cologne, Wittenberg, Frankfurt-on-Oder and

Leipzig; John Gaw, also of St Andrews, who fled to Sweden where in 1533 he published *The Richt Way to the Kingdom of Hevine*, a translation of a treatise by Christiern Pedersen; Thomas Forret, canon of Inchcolm and vicar of Dollar (where the memory of his pastoral work is commemorated in the 'vicar's bridge'), who was among those burnt for heresy in 1539 having been accused of catechising his parishioners from the English new testament; Thomas Cocklaw, canon of Cambuskenneth and vicar of Tullibody, who was condemned after his secret marriage but managed to escape to England with the help of friends; and Robert Richardson, also of Cambuskenneth, who is said to have gone over to protestantism shortly after writing his Commentary on the rule of St Augustine and was one of a number of Scottish exiles who came within the patronage of Henry VIII's minister Thomas Cromwell.

The dissenters in this period also included Gavin Logie, the principal of St Leonard's college, St Andrews, where Lutheran ideas were so alive (if underground) that those suspected of unorthodox views were said to have 'drunk of St Leonard's well'. St Leonard's college came under the particular influence of the priory of St Andrews where the sub-prior John Winram long led a double life of participant in heresy trials and crypto-reformer.

The Scottish houses of friars, Dominican, Franciscan and others, were also in ferment in the 1530s.[13] At least 19 friars left their communities in these years, including three priors and two subpriors. Clearly, the debate over the means of internal reform had in a number of cases crystallised into adherence to protestant doctrine, as the later careers of many of those friars who left their houses demonstrate. By 1534 the trend had become sufficiently pronounced for a meeting to be held between representatives of the orders of friars and the lords of council to consider what to do about those friars 'quha are thollit [allowed] to pas furthe of the realme in apostacy'.[14] With their preaching role and ability (unlike monks) to move around the country, the influence of unorthodox friars among the laity was particularly worrying for the establishment. Friar William Arth (who remained a seriously reform-minded catholic) and Friar Alexander Seton (mentioned again below) were both arrested after publicly preaching against ecclesiastical abuses of various kinds.[15]

King James V through the chancellor, Archbishop Gavin Dunbar of Glasgow – probably in the latter's words – warned the provincials of the friars to

> tak gud tent [care] and diligence that na sermones be maid be thair brethir quhair throu ony new opinionis mai ryis in the comone peple and to advertise all thair Wardanis and brethir thairof quhilk thai promitit to do to the weill of all our soverane leigis.[16]

Among the apostate friars were Alexander Seton, prior of the St Andrews Dominicans, the king's confessor, accused of heresy after preaching in St Andrews and Dundee, who fled to England in 1537 where he became a chaplain to the duke of Suffolk and died in 1542; Thomas Gillem from East Lothian, a Franciscan who is said to have had some influence on the ideas of the young John Knox; John McDowall, subprior of the Glasgow Dominicans in 1531 and later head of the Whithorn community, who left for England in 1534 and subsequently went to Germany; John MacAlpine, Perth Dominican, who was suspected of Lutheranism in 1534 but fled to England, later to Wittenberg and Copenhagen; John Lyne, a Franciscan described by Knox as having 'left his hypocritical habit' about 1539–40, who also went to Wittenberg; and John Craig, a Dominican who was imprisoned for heresy in both Scotland and Italy but eventually returned to Scotland in 1559.

That the trouble had affected Ayr is suggested by the departure from the Dominican friary there about 1535 of John Willock, from a local burgess family, who went to England where he followed the career of public preacher and private chaplain, later going to Emden before returning to Scotland in 1555.[17] It has been suggested that a personal scandal as well as religious misgivings may have driven Willock from Ayr. Questions about marital and moral principles put in a letter to the Swiss reformer Henry Bullinger by Willock in 1552 may, it is thought, refer to an attempt to sort out a tangle in his own life. If so, he would not be the only kirkman of his times to combine scholarly abilities and an active career in the religious establishment with a less than perfect private life, although this was less common among friars than among the secular clergy. At least in Willock's case, if the surmise is correct, his conscience appears to have troubled him.[18]

Of Willock's interest in protestant doctrine and practice there can be little doubt. Holding English benefices (at times as an absentee), he preached for some time in London where about 1540 he was imprisoned for preaching against confession, the use of holy water, praying to the saints and for the dead, and for advocating that priests should marry. During Edward VI's reign he became a chaplain in the household of the marquis of Dorset, father of Lady Jane Grey, in whose circle he became acquainted with John ab Ulmis. Bullinger dedicated one of his works, the fifth book of his *Decades*, jointly to Dorset and Willock.

Exchange of reforming ideas and discussion of Luther's doctrines in the 1530s took place in Scotland among those whose Christian humanism, linguistic scholarship and habits of debate motivated them to try to find some means of reform within the church which would equip it to make a better job of leading and teaching the laity. Even the eminent traditional theologian John Mair said that Luther had done a good thing in recalling theologians to the study of the original scriptures. By the 1530s, however, the idea of reform outside orthodoxy was beginning to take hold of a number of these would-be reformers, and the idea became acceptable that a parting of the ways could come between those who sought to renew and strengthen the sources of traditional belief and piety and those who wished to remove (and when this became impossible within the establishment, to remove themselves) from all doctrine and religious practice which they claimed were not explicitly taught in scripture.

The educated laity had their own interest in and even agenda for reform. These laymen included professionals and landed men, like the advocates Mr David Borthwick and Mr William Johnston who had been fellow-students at St Leonard's college, and their colleague Mr Henry Balnaves, who studied at St Andrews university when Patrick Hamilton was there, who expressed his protestant beliefs in a treatise on justification by faith; royal servants such as the king's physician Dr Michael Durham and his apothecary Francis Aikman; Sir James Kirkcaldy of Grange, treasurer (1537–1542), who was reputed to carry a forbidden new testament in his pouch; and the king's 'familiar servant' Sir John Borthwick whose Cromwellian programme for the dissolution of ecclesiastical authority as it was then constituted provoked the cardinal into staging Borthwick's showpiece heresy trial (*in absentia*, due to a tip-off by his friends) in 1540.[19]

Ayrshire had its share of literate laymen whose interest in the reform movement was both pragmatic and ideological. They ranged from the iconoclast John Lockhart of Bar whose recipe for reform was to get rid of 'the bishops and priests for they have brought much sorrow to the country',[20] to Alexander 4th earl of Glencairn who could lead an armed contingent of the Congregation when the time came and also write satirical verses exposing what he saw as the fraudulent cult of miracles.[21] Gilbert 3rd earl of Cassillis, who was a constant envoy on behalf of the anglophile party in the early 1540s, had been a student at St Andrews university when Patrick Hamilton was condemned in 1528 and was tutored at Paris by the heretic Mr George Buchanan.[22] Cassillis was one of a growing number of university-educated men from landed families who were not destined for a career in the church. Some were from other Ayrshire families, such as Mr Robert Chalmers of Gadgirth (d.1529) whose sisters were among those accused of lollardy in 1494 and whose nephew Sir James Chalmers of Gadgirth was one of the leaders of reform in Ayrshire in the 1550s; Mr John Fullarton of Dreghorn, head of a branch of a strongly protestant family; and Mr Michael Wallace of Wausford, brother of the prominent reforming laird John Wallace of Craigie whose commitment he shared, who was an influential member of Ayr town council in the critical 1550s. The survival of Murdoch Nisbet's Scots rendering of the new testament reveals a facility for study and writing which might be acquired without a university education, which he may have shared with other countrymen from smaller landed families like his own.

Levels of literacy which would facilitate access to heretical literature are notoriously difficult to assess. One of the few basic indications in this period, the ability to sign one's name, may indicate little more than a skill acquired to protect the possessors of property from fraudulent documents being issued in their names, as did the possession of a seal. The writing skills of individuals may be tentatively judged from the quality of their signatures. A number of Ayrshire lairds are found able to sign before 1520, including Sir Mungo Lockhart of Lee (1487), John Logan of Grougar (1490), Sir George Campbell of Loudoun (c.1494), William Wallace of Sorn (1504), George Campbell of Cessnock (1505), Alan Cathcart of Carlton (1506), Robert Wallace of Shewalton (1509) and John Lockhart of Bar (1518).[23] However, in the context of early religious dissent through the dissemination of bible knowledge and the circulation of heretical books and tracts, we have to remember that people could sometimes read without having acquired the ability to write, and that most people who became familiar with the message of such literature probably did so through hearing and discussion of the contents rather than by reading it for themselves. Technical illiteracy need not have been a bar to becoming familiar with the purpose and argument of such literature in days when much knowledge was commmitted to memory and transmitted orally.

England had long been a source of ideological contact and when need be a place of refuge for Scottish religious dissenters, including those from the south-west. In the 1530s Henry VIII's ecclesiastical policy (for whatever personal purposes he employed it) appealed to reform-minded Scottish laymen. On one occasion the leading lawyers Sir Thomas Bellenden of Auchnoule and Mr Henry Balnaves had a meeting with the English commissioner Sir Ralph Eure who was impressed with their desire for 'reformation of the misdemeanors of the clergy'. They asked Eure for copies of the English acts of parliament on ecclesiastical affairs.[24] Sir John Borthwick, whose anticlerical attitude was shared by fellow-laymen, was accused in 1540 of having stated that the pope's authority was no higher than that of any other bishop, that the pope was a simoniac, indulgences had no force, priests should marry, churchmen (not only the religious orders) should have no temporal possessions, King James should follow King Henry's example and get back what his forebears had granted away to the church, the canon law was not binding, and that the religious orders should be dissolved as in England. It was the possibility of a Henrician-style assault on ecclesiastical authority and property that caused the embattled first estate to capitulate in the early 1530s to James V's demands for a grant and ongoing subsidy towards the endowment of a professional civil court – the college of justice as it became known. The learned lawyer Bellenden and the resentful laird Lockhart of Bar may have expressed their opinions differently but both wanted some kind of 'stay of the spirituality', and both saw an example in what had been happening in the 1530s south of the border. 'The whole pollution and plague of Anglican impiety' was how Cardinal Beaton forcefully described their disaffection in a letter to the pope.[25]

The death of James V in early December 1542 soon after the rout of Solway Moss was a watershed in the fortunes of the party who favoured religious reform, as circumstances raised the possibility of implementing reform by political means. A struggle for the regency in January 1543 resulted in the sole appointment as governor of the earl of Arran, chief of the Hamiltons and heir presumptive to the throne, and a few weeks later in the forcible removal and detention of the cardinal.[26] The anglophile-reformists near the centre of power quickly took advantage of these circumstances to put certain measures for religious reform through parliament in March 1543, and to negotiate for peace and a marriage alliance with England in the spring and early summer of that year. Under the influence of the reform party the governor appointed known protestants as preachers at court.

An important article of the existing heresy laws was removed in a bill introduced by Lord Maxwell,

> That it salbe lefull to all our sovirane ladyis leigis to have the haly write baith the new testament and the auld in the vulgar toung in Inglis or Scottis . . .

although a qualification was retained:

> provyding alwayis that na man despute or haid [i.e. openly] oppunyeonis under the panis contenit in the actis of parliament.[27]

The bill was formally accepted by the lords of the articles (who customarily presented legislation to parliament), some of them no doubt with misgivings, and was enacted in spite of a divided assembly, to the satisfaction of the reformists but the outrage of the prelates on whose behalf Archbishop Gavin Dunbar protested that the matter should be postponed until a provincial council should have time to consider the advisability of the measure.

At the afternoon session on 3 March instructions were approved for the ambassadors who were to negotiate a perpetual peace with England and the terms for a marriage between the Scottish queen Mary and the English prince Edward. The nature of the terms offered by the Scottish parliament as a basis for the dynastic union absolutely protected Scottish sovereignty: no removal of the queen to England before her marriage; the queen dowager to be her daughter's chief guardian, with four lords to be chosen; no men or castles to be given as pledges for the eventual delivery of the queen when she came of age; after conclusion of the treaty Scotland to 'stand in the awin libertie and fredomes as it is now and hes bene in all tymes bygane'; Arran to remain governor during Mary's minority; and the realm to continue to be called Scotland, keeping her own distinct laws and institutions, with no legal appeals to English courts and no calling of Scots to an English parliament.

Relaxation of the law against possession of the vernacular bible and positive steps towards Anglo-Scottish dynastic union must have encouraged most of the Ayrshire representatives: the reformist earls of Cassillis and Glencairn, Andrew Stewart Lord Ochiltree and Sir William Hamilton of Sanquhar, provost of Ayr, who saw the burgh's seal attached to the act permitting the use of the scriptures in English.[28] The attitude of Irvine's representative Thomas Auld is not known. Abbot Quintin Kennedy of Crossraguel was no doubt far from happy.

Glencairn and Cassillis were among those leading Scots who became 'assured' to the English king after their capture at Solway Moss, having been released on promising to set forward the Anglo-Scottish marriage alliance and to give Henry their practical support in bringing it about. Both earls were soon to take part in the diplomatic activity surrounding the negotiation of the peace and royal marriage and both, with others whom Henry found useful, were in receipt of English pensions. Henry particularly valued the services of the powerful William earl of Glencairn and was prepared, so he said through his privy council, to forget that the earl was his prisoner on parole should the governor Arran make him chancellor in place of the ousted cardinal.[29]

The nature and extent of the assured (or as some might say, traitor) earls' support for Henry VIII's Scottish plans have to be looked at realistically. First, their action in becoming assured was not unique. Collaboration with England had long been a device for putting pressure on the Scottish government, particularly used by magnates on the western seaboard. During the English military occupation of south-east Scotland which was to fall on the country in less than a year after the March 1543 parliament, large numbers of lairds, gentlemen and lesser people assured with the English in the conviction that their own government could not protect them from the enemy.[30] Second, as prisoners of war, Glencairn, Cassillis and the others would expect to pay some price for their release and it may have seemed to them cheap at the price to promise support for a dynastic union which they and many others already believed in and for a peace that would make their southern homelands safer. Their initial detention had caused dislocations in their territories. In December 1542 it was reported that 'the Keterickes in the North parts were angry with the taking of their lord the earl of Glencairn and would come to fetch him home'.[31] Having promised to be Henry's friends, the earls were among those released in return for hostages, in Glencairn's case his sons Alexander and Robert, for Cassillis his two brothers and his uncle Kennedy of Coif. The absence of their relatives, in a society where an armed following underwrote political power, was on the debit side of being a collaborator, to be weighed against the value of an English pension. In March 1543 Sadler the English ambassador wrote to Henry VIII that Glencairn badly wanted his eldest son at home, drawing a pen-portrait of Alexander Cunningham the future 4th earl on the eve of his assumption of lay leadership of the reform movement in the south-west:

> if he [Alexander] were at home he should stand him [his father] in great stead. I assure your Majesty I think he feigneth not: for such a man as his son is may not be spared out of so wild a country. I have talked with the man . . . the Master of Glencairn; and in my poor opinion there be few such Scottish in Scotland, both for his wisdom and learning, and well dedicate to the truth of Christ's word and doctrine. So that I think if he were at home he would . . . do much good here in the country where now the gospel is set forth in English and open proclamations made . . .[32]

The third point to be made about collaboration is that once on parole the extent of the earls' military co-operation with England depended on circumstances not always within their own control. A weather-eye had to be kept on the changing Scottish political scene where the cardinal's detention was something of a fiction and the possibility of his regaining control was far from remote. Collaborators with England and advocates of church reforms that had been pushed through parliament in the face of ecclesiastical opposition would get short shrift if Beaton achieved his summer's goal of wearing down the governor. In spite of their promises to facilitate the progress of an English army into the Scottish heartland and to hand over the young queen to her future father-in-law, the 'loyalty' of the assured lords sometimes fell short of Henry's demands in 1543–44. English agents on the border and around the Scottish court kept Henry and his council posted with a kind of weather report on the political loyalty of his Scottish friends – as indeed they did with regard to the alliances of all prominent Scots, whose real motives continually seem to have baffled the English establishment.[33] While leading anglophiles were telling Sadler that they had 'given hands to go together in Henry's service against France', Henry was remarking sourly to his ambassador that he found 'a great difference between words and deeds', and that he suspected that they were only concerned with their own profit. It is difficult not to conclude that all along the assured were playing a dangerous game for their own ends.

Apart from their useful English pensions, the assured earls Glencairn and Cassillis, in common with many lay leaders from their Ayrshire homeland and beyond, had a strong ideological reason for wanting union with England, a country that had thrown off allegiance to a foreign religious head, with state control over the wealth and ambitions of prelates and an open (English) bible and preachers to disseminate its message. The present head of the church in England was himself far from being a protestant but Scottish religious dissidents, clerical and lay, had by now made many contacts south of the border whose help would be welcome in setting forward a programme of religious reform which would radically change the character and message of the church. There seems no reason to doubt that laymen like Cassillis and Glencairn and families such as the Lockharts, Campbells and Fullartons, reared in a late-medieval world in which religious belief and experience were part of the substructure of everyday life, having changed the ground of their belief, should now hold their protestantism as strongly as they had formerly held the catholicism in which they had been nurtured. It seemed to them natural that they should closely ally and even politically unite with a neighbouring country where (so their personal contacts convinced them at least) similar religious change was taking place.

Some of the anglophile-reformists were attracted to the idea of Scotland's absorption into an imperial protestant Britain on the western edge of Europe, the nearest portions of which were catholic.[34] This vision was delineated for them in English propaganda of the 1540s, notably in Hertford's tract 'An Epistle Exhortatorie' which was meant to blunt the impact of and lessen Scottish resistance to Henry VIII's aggressive methods of bringing about the dynastic union. It was also put over in the writings of the dissident James Henderson who identified the proposed royal marriage as the 'blessed meane and remedy' which would make this vision a reality. Were men like Glencairn and Cassillis visionaries, pragmatists or just plain gullible about Scotland's place in the new protestant Britain? Would they have sold Scotland for it or did they hope to bargain for acceptable terms of accommodation? The tough negotiating terms set out for Henry VIII by the Scottish parliament in March 1543 suggest that bargaining rather than submission to an English imperial crown was in their minds at this time.

The fact was that the assured lords, far from being an organised party or a single-minded band of secret agents, were held together by intention rather than adherence to a programme. Their efforts on Henry's behalf were liable to be pulled apart by the reaction of individuals to changing political situations. Indeed much of their time and many of their written communications were taken up with the repair and maintenance of personal relations among them. While making a public gesture of solidarity by refusing to attend the queen's coronation on 9 September 1543 unless the marriage and peace treaties were honoured, they assembled at Angus's home of Douglas castle in Lanarkshire where they 'signed a bond to abide together' and tried to work out their strategy in the face of coming retribution at home while appearing to keep their promises to the English king.

Parliament which met in December 1543 under the domination of the cardinal, supported by the governor whom he had publicly absolved from his flirtation with heresy, threw out the English marriage treaty (which Beaton told the English ambassador had been agreed to only by a 'private party'), reaffirmed the Franco-Scottish alliance and re-enacted the heresy laws including the ban on possession of the English bible.[35] Many people had dared to raise their heads above the parapet of religious orthodoxy in

Towards Reform

the months following the pro-reform legislation of March 1543. John Knox later recalled (with some cynicism) how some had flaunted their copies of the English new testament hitherto read only in secret.

In the burgh of Ayr where dissent had simmered on since the iconoclastic protests of the 1530s, trouble broke out in 1543 during a visit of one of Arran's preachers, the Dominican John Rough. An unnamed Grey Friar who publicly opposed him was warded in the burgh tolbooth, an extraordinary step by the secular authorities suggesting fear of a public disturbance. Rough, from what is known of him, was a confrontational character who joined the Dominicans, so he maintained, to spite his family after an inconclusive spell at St Leonard's college, St Andrews. He also claimed to have spent four years in Ayr at one stage, making the burgh an obvious refuge when trying to avoid the cardinal's net in 1543. At one point during his preaching visit there was a stand-off between a group gathered by the Master of Montgomerie with a view to rescuing the Grey Friar from the tolbooth and 'the town's friends', probably gentlemen from Kyle, who presumably defended Rough. The battle of wills – there does not seem to have been any actual fighting – was won by the latter who were afterwards treated to a celebration drink at the town's expense. After the episode Rough, his expenses paid by the burgh, was seen off to make his explanations to the governor who under the cardinal's influence had now abandoned his recently-appointed preachers. Cryptic entries in Ayr burgh accounts hint at explanations also having to be made to Archbishop Dunbar, and at a reprimand delivered in his name by the rural dean whose diocesan authority the burgh appears to have been reluctant to acknowledge.[36] His censure was presumably for having allowed unlicensed preaching to take place in the burgh, since Rough had already been inhibited from preaching, after sermons by him and Friar Gillem in Dundee had provoked attacks on the local friaries. The Glasgow diocesan authorities were obviously determined to head off the same thing happening in Ayr.

Ever since the trial of Russell and Kennedy in his first year of office the cardinal had sent forewarnings of trouble and instructions on how to handle it to his colleague the archbishop of Glasgow with whom he was on uneasy terms in matters of precedence. Having failed to catch Rough at Dundee, he also failed to prevent his arrival in sympathetic Kyle, 'that receptacle of God's servants of old', as Knox called it. Yet public preaching by invitation came to be a characteristic of the pro-reform movement in the 1540s and 1550s when, in spite of reversals in the political field, the anglophile-reformists pressed on with their attempts, however sporadically successful, to raise the profile of religious reform. Ayrshire shared fully in these attempts through the successive visits of John Rough, George Wishart, John Knox and John Willock until the eve of the Reformation-settlement in 1560. The iconoclastic activity which tended to follow in the wake of the preachers demonstrated the determination of the more energetic reformers to bring about open religious change.

Throughout the autumn and winter of 1543–44 the south-west, especially Lanarkshire, Renfrewshire, Ayrshire and the Firth of Clyde, witnessed the comings and goings of the leaders of the broadly-based party which now supported the anglophile earl of Angus and the governor's dynastic rival the earl of Lennox against the reactionary central government. At Christmas 1543 the western leadership, Angus, Glencairn, Cassillis, Hugh Campbell of Loudoun, usually known as the Sheriff of Ayr, Douglas of Drumlanrig and Lords Maxwell and Somerville, met at Ayr, one of their grievances being what they saw as the unconstitutional arrest of the earl of Rothes and Lord Gray, two of the cardinal's most powerful opponents.[37] In spite of an elaborately-staged but hollow public reconciliation and agreement between the two parties at Edinburgh in January 1544 open confrontation grew increasingly likely.

By March Lennox, supported by Glencairn, was occupying Glasgow including the archbishop's castle to which the governor laid siege. The archbishop had his own confrontation with the cardinal over the question of ecclesiastical pre-eminence, the cardinal promising in writing not to elevate his cross in the archdiocese of Glasgow: prelude to the undignified fracas about precedence which took place in the cathedral in June 1544. The power struggle between the two prelates took place against a background of street fighting in which the cardinal's brother Walter, a canon of Glasgow, was attacked and a skirmish on Glasgow moor in which Andrew Cunningham, the pardoned heretic son of Glencairn, was killed.[38] Prolonged civil war was avoided when Angus, Cassillis and Lord Maxwell were arrested, temporarily as it fell out. Lennox, with his own interests in mind, departed soon afterwards for England leaving the strategic castle of Dumbarton in the hands of Glencairn.

The English invasions which followed in the spring of 1544 and the winter of 1544–45 had the effect of drawing all parties together in self-defence and of encouraging instinctive Scottish antipathy to the 'auld enemy'. Cassillis at one point urged Henry to hold his hand because the need to defend themselves was likely to dampen his collaborators' loyalty. During the summer of 1544 Mary of Guise tried to form a party of her own in opposition to Arran and for some time she was successful in attracting to herself some influential supporters who included even Glencairn, Lord Maxwell, Angus's brother Sir George Douglas and a few of the cardinal's natural allies such as the four bishops of Moray, Orkney, Dunblane and Glasgow. However, this emergency coalition, who may simply have been drawn together by a desire for peace as an alternative to the cardinal's belligerent anglophobia, fell apart.[39] At the November parliament the Douglases were pardoned and began a period of co-operation with the government which gave them an opportunity to wreak revenge on the English for the devastation of their ancestors' tombs in Melrose abbey, and allowed Angus to lead the Scots to their only victory in the entire period of hostilities, at Ancrum Moor on 27 February 1545. In the previous December parliament had pardoned Glencairn, Cassillis and the Sheriff of

Towards Reform

Ayr 'for all crimes of treason bygone' and in return for 'the true and thankful service to be done to the Queen's Grace'.

Cassillis still carried on underground diplomacy with his fellow anglophiles on Henry's behalf. At a reconciliatory mass at Holyrood attended by Mary of Guise, Glencairn managed to whisper to a spy that he had every intention of keeping his promises to Henry about the peace and royal marriage.[40] Henry, however, already suspected his Scottish allies' behaviour, his agents referring to the 'treason and falsehood' of Glencairn and his son Alexander. The Cunninghams continued to walk their political tightrope into the spring of 1545 when Henry sent Lennox to Carlisle to 'practice' with Angus, Glencairn and their associates. Early in April Cassillis, on yet another diplomatic mission, found Angus and Glencairn with the Scottish army on the border waiting to defend themselves against the expected English invasion. He felt it necessary to urge Henry to spell out to them the nature of the rewards for their continued co-operation. Henry's response, through his agent Foster, was to demand from them how they intended to serve him.

However blurred their political alignments had become, the anglophiles demonstrated their ongoing commitment to religious reform by their support of the preacher Mr George Wishart who arrived in Scotland in 1544, a support which in the end forced the cardinal's hand against heresy after a two-year gap in prosecutions.

CHAPTER SIX

A Receptacle of God's Servants

It has been said that from the time of George Wishart's preaching in 1544–45 initiative in the movement for religious reform passed to the laity who were eventually to spearhead the confrontation with authority in the late 1550s. Their public support for protestant preachers and determination to implement changes in religious practice was by the 1540s making the protestant lords an element, if scarcely yet a force, to be reckoned with. In April 1545 Lord Methven, whose son was at one point accused of holding heretical ideas, advised Mary of Guise of the futility of prosecutions, recommending instead 'your graice and all my lordis to recounsall in tendir maner all greit gentilmen that be innorance is of ill mynd towartis haly kirk, because it is now dowtsum to pursue be the law as the samyn requiris'.[1] Lay support for Wishart's preaching in churches in the east of Scotland, such as the earl Marischal's outspoken expression of support in Dundee, illustrates the kind of open attitude which now faced the authorities.

In Ayrshire the laity had long had a prominent role in the movement for reform. All the known Lollards in the 1494 case were lay men and women, and from then onwards those accused of heresy or who caused trouble for the authorities in that connection were mainly lay. Nor was it necessary to be a fully committed anglophile to be in favour of reformation. Although Lord Methven, again writing to the queen dowager, in 1548, listed 'new aponzionis [opinions] of the scriptour' as the chief reason 'that Inglis men is fauvorit and the authorite nocht obeyit nor servit',[2] Mr Robert Lockhart, whose brother John Lockhart of Bar was an anglophile reformer of the most radical sort, gave it as his opinion that only a small number of Scots 'loif the said English mariage and unione and wald spend thar lyves and all that thai have'.[3] As has recently been remarked, 'It was one thing to ask for a supply of English bibles and testaments . . . but quite another to render oneself open to a charge of treason'.[4]

Reform-minded laymen in Ayrshire as elsewhere were interested in religious reform long before they combined to defend the Reformation by force of arms against the secular authority. A desire for access to the vernacular scriptures had been an element in their commitment from the time of Murdoch Nisbet's reading group onwards. Central lollard antipathies such as those towards images, the sacrificial doctrine of the mass and the church's possession of property remained prominent among those opinions of which Ayrshire heretics were accused, as did discussion of the new doctrines 'in public and private'. The welcome given to preachers by the Ayrshire dissenting community from 1543 onwards was part and parcel of their attempts to bring about religious transformation.

George Wishart's preaching tour of mid-Ayrshire in the summer of 1545, like the earlier visit of John Rough, is evidence of the links forged between the reform-minded of east and west Scotland.[5] Glencairn, Cassillis, Ochiltree, Lockhart of Bar and others already had associations with activists from Fife, Angus and the Mearns, including the earl of Rothes, John Erskine of Dun, the earl Marischal and James Wishart of Pittarrow, the preacher's brother. The earl Marischal, the earl of Errol and the laird of Pittarrow had supported the forces led by Lennox and Glencairn at Glasgow in the spring of 1544 in opposition to the governor after he capitulated to the cardinal.

Wishart, like Rough, was a volatile personality whose preaching aroused both euphoria and antagonism in his hearers. His journey towards his doctrinal position in 1545–6 had been a stormy one. Imputations of alleged anabaptist heresies still clung to him at the time of his trial, which he denied. The partisanship engendered by his preaching caused riots in the English city of Bristol where the reformer was made to go through three separate recantations, during one of which he tossed the ceremonial faggot (to be burned instead of himself) back at the summoner. At Cambridge university where he next went, the severity of his approach aroused extreme antagonism in some students although others remembered his piety and generosity. Nevertheless, there can be little doubt of his bravery both in facing the consequences of ecclesiastical censure and in preaching to the plague-stricken inhabitants of Dundee, or of the extent to which he impressed his hearers with his personal conviction and commitment to the evangelical message. He must have appealed enormously to John Lockhart of Bar.

Under his influence the emphasis of Scottish protestantism moved from the evangelical Lutheranism of the 1530s, with its central concern with justification before God, through reading or hearing the scriptures, to the more practical reform of belief and practice associated with such European centres of reform as Strasbourg and Zürich, with its iconoclastic clearing of the way for change and concentration on the corporate experiences of the Christian community, such as an understanding of the Lord's Supper, the parting of the ways from the mass which lay at the heart of traditional worship. Wishart's charismatic presence was the catalyst needed to bring 'the work of Reformation' in Ayrshire out of discussion groups and into the open.

John Knox's account of Wishart's movements implies that he had spent some time in the west before going to Ayr itself. Relying on information on the preacher's movements, the cardinal sent word to Archbishop Gavin Dunbar to prevent the heretic's taking possession of the pulpit in St John's kirk. Hearing what was afoot, Glencairn and some of his friends made for the burgh in support of the preacher where they were joined by some gentlemen of Kyle, no doubt with the confrontations during the Rough episode in their minds. Their first impulse was to forcibly enter the church and defy the archbishop, but Wishart himself opted to avoid confrontation and chose instead the larger audience at the market cross. Ayr had two market crosses, each with its tolbooth, one where the High Street widened near the end of the bridge over the river Ayr and the other at the convergence of the High Street and the Sandgate. Either would provide the preacher with a busy vantage point, where people would be less likely to incur ecclesiastical censure for listening to him than if they had deliberately entered the parish kirk.

Knox has left a dismissive account of how the archbishop tried in a short sermon to defuse a potential public disturbance.[7] It is a fact that, having complied with the cardinal's specific request, Dunbar did nothing thereafter to curb Wishart's movements in Ayrshire. No episcopal inhibition for unlicensed preaching was issued, as had been issued at Dundee. Having made an impression on the burgh audience and avoided trouble, Wishart accompanied by his friends made his way north-eastwards towards the Irvine valley where he 'commonly' preached in Galston kirk under the protection of the young laird from a veteran dissenting family, George Campbell of Cessnock. This was a congenial neighbourhood for the preacher. There was very little ecclesiastical presence in Galston parish where the kirk was served by a curate. The parochial revenues were annexed to the monastery of Fail which was at that time undergoing secularisation in the hands of its superior Robert Cunningham, Glencairn's son, by then a married man. The lands of Galston were divided among the Lennox interest, including the Stewarts of Galston, a Lennox cadet, and the Campbells of Cessnock.

The parish was also home to John Lockhart of Bar, an older kinsman of the laird of Cessnock, who extended hospitality to Wishart at the tower of Bar which stood in the clachan of Galston itself. None of John Lockhart's forebears is named in the surviving account of the Lollards' trial but his anti-papal, anticlerical, iconoclastic brand of reform suggests that he grew up in a family circle and neighbourhood permeated with the attitudes of that earlier generation, probably reinforced by those of his cousins on his mother's side, the Stewarts of Garlies, who had a similar background. Lockhart's anglophile tendency was also confirmed by personal and family experience. In 1535 he had travelled through England in the entourage of his kinsman, William Stewart, bishop of Aberdeen, at that time ambassador to France in the early stages of negotiating James V's first French marriage.[8] The bishop's patronage was extended to John's brother Mr Robert Lockhart, canon of Aberdeen cathedral, who may have become compromised in religion in the 1540s through his association with the circle of Meldrum of Fyvie, Fraser of Philorth, Wishart of Pitarrow, Sir James Menzies, the provost of Aberdeen, and the earl Marischal who were charged in 1544 with failing to join the army against the English invasion and with reading prohibited heretical books.[9] Mr Robert Lockhart, who was later drawn into the communication channel between the St Andrews castilians and the English government, may have been one of the links between the gentlemen of Kyle and Wishart's friends in the Lothians whose company Lockhart frequented, including Cockburn of Ormiston and Crichton of Brunston. John Lockhart of Bar saw not only the pro-French cardinal but the whole reactionary hierarchy as a hindrance to Anglo-Scottish friendship and the cessation of hostilities between the two countries. The Ayrshire valley of Wishart's sojourn was anything but remote from those national events that were working to change Scotland's traditional alignments in mid-sixteenth century.

While Wishart's access to Galston church was free of tensions, matters were more difficult when he accepted an invitation to preach in the church of Mauchline in Kylesmure. Knox describes how Campbell of Loudoun, supported by four others, barred the entrance to the church 'for preservation of a tabernacle that was there, beautiful to the eye'. Sir Hugh Campbell of Loudoun was not himself a parishioner of Mauchline (although the other four were) but he did have a double responsibility for public order, as sheriff of Ayr for the crown and as bailie of the barony of Kylesmure for Melrose abbey.[10] As at Galston, there was little ecclesiastical presence in the huge parish of Mauchline which, apart from two chapels of ease, was served by successive curates from local families, sir James and sir Andrew Mitchell. The abbey's administrative headquarters, the tower of Mauchline, which stood in the clachan itself near the church, had been in Sir Hugh Campbell's possession for over 20 years.

It is quite likely that the tabernacle mentioned by Knox, the shrine in which the reserved sacrament was held, had been presented to the church by Melrose abbey to which the parish revenues were annexed. The sheriff may have feared that the tabernacle, being so closely associated with the doctrine of the mass, might be the first victim in an iconoclastic attack, when it would fall to him to explain to the abbot and monks what had happened to their property. His attitude to the reformers' religious programme remained ambivalent, although his son Matthew joined them during his father's lifetime. Two of those who guarded the church at Mauchline with Sir Hugh were Campbells, dependants of his house, and a third, George Reid of Daldilling, was also in his patronage.

Hugh Campbell of Kinzeancleuch, whose son Robert, then in his teens, was to become an influential leader of the Reformation a decade later, was keen to force entry to the church. He and 'some zealous of the parish' took exception to being shut out of their own parish church by the sheriff. As at Ayr, however, Wishart chose an open-air congregation. His hearers' lasting memory of this proto-conventicle, with the preacher standing on the turf dyke on the edge of the moor in the hot sunshine, may have been the dramatic conversion of a well-known sinner, Laurence Rankin of Shiel from Ochiltree parish, whose presence suggests that people came from further afield to hear Wishart at Mauchline.[11]

The aftermath of Wishart's visit to Ayrshire was much as the sheriff may have feared, as the more radical spirits among the reformers embarked on an iconoclastic campaign to remove the apparatus of traditional worship, especially that associated with the mass and the veneration of images of the saints, from a number of churches and chapels. There seems to have been some activity in Ayr itself, about which there is a little information in a few suggestive entries in the burgh accounts.[12] The dean of guild's account for 1544–45 includes the payment of 5 shillings to James Nicol 'for taking down the broken images' in St John's kirk; not for repairing them but taking them down. No further references to images occur in the accounts. At the same time substantial work was done on the church windows for which a glazier was brought from his work at Kilwinning and Paisley abbeys. Although there is no corroborative evidence of such an attack on St John's, other churches in Ayrshire, as well as Paisley and Kilwinning abbeys, are known to have been attacked about this time. Images and glass windows depicting biblical scenes and the lives of the saints were targets in 'reforming' church interiors. It is quite feasible that Ayr town council sympathised with this kind of public cleansing while maintaining other features of traditional worship. So, about the same time the dean of guild paid for strings for the censers, oil for the bells, candles for the organ loft, and cord for the Easter candle and even the making of a 'god's house' or shrine for the sacrament.

There is firmer record of iconoclastic activity in the countryside in the wake of Wishart's preaching and the death of the cardinal in May 1546 when church property of all kinds was felt to be under threat of attack, causing the privy council in turn to threaten with punishment all 'evill disposit personis' who it was feared would 'invaid, distroy, cast doun, and withhald abbays, abbay places, kirkis, alswele paroche kirkis as utheris religious places, freiris ... nunreis, chapellis and other spirituale mennis houssis, aganis the lawis of God and man'.[13] In the south-west between 1545 and 1548 John Lockhart of Bar and Charles Campbell of Bargour from Mauchline parish, with presumably a number of helpers, carried out a widespread campaign of removing 'eucharistic chalices, altars, breaking up choir stalls and breaking church windows in Cunninghame, Kyle and Carrick as well as in Renfrewshire and Lanarkshire'.[14] Lockhart and his helpers seem to have carried on for some time with impunity from the law courts, for it was not until 1550 that he and Campbell, with their surety the earl of Argyll, were fined for non-compearance in the criminal court. The case papers have not survived which might have told us more about the success or failure of their campaign to cleanse the churches and would have named their collaborators and the churches concerned. It would be simplistic to see these activities as

A Receptacle of God's Servants

private enterprise on the part of Lockhart; he and Campbell may have been directing a campaign with the co-operation of others in at least some areas, but there is nothing to inform us one way or the other.

About the time he was summoned for these offences, Lockhart and some friends, including Charles Campbell of Skerrington from Cumnock parish, defied the authority of Archbishop Hamilton over the latter's imprisonment of John MacBrair, a former monk of Glenluce who was charged with heresy.[15] Heresy already had a longish history in Galloway whence the prior of the Wigtown Dominicans, John MacDowall, had fled in 1534 to England and then to Germany; and another Glenluce monk, Donald MacCartnay, was accused of heresy but abjured in 1539. MacBrair, a graduate of St Andrews, who may have been a student when Patrick Hamilton was there, was a product of the Lutheran phase of Scottish dissent. In the 1540s he found friends in Ayrshire who included the Ayr relatives of the Nisbet family. In 1550 he was accused among other things of alleging that Archbishop Dunbar neglected his diocese, was arrested on Archbishop Hamilton's orders in the house of Lord Ochiltree and was imprisoned in Hamilton castle. From there he was rescued by John Lockhart and his friends and given shelter at the Bar and elsewhere until he was able to slip over the border into England, where he stayed until the accession of Mary Tudor drove him to Europe. Campbell of Cessnock and Dalrymple of Stair stood caution that Lockhart would compear in court for assisting MacBrair, but like Argyll they failed to produce him and all were outlawed for their defiance in July 1550. In the general friction caused by bringing off this coup Lockhart found himself pursuing an old family feud against his fellow-reformer Lord Ochiltree.

Any hope Ayrshire dissidents may have had of continuing to openly defy ecclesiastical authority received a jolt in the summer of 1550 with the arrest, trial and execution of one of their countrymen, Adam Wallace.[16] His trial was Archbishop Hamilton's first major demonstration of authority against heresy since taking office. Wallace's exact identity has never been established but, coming from the parish of Barnweil in Kyle, where he claimed to have been born within two miles of Fail monastery, he is likely to have belonged to one of the many offshoots of the Wallaces of Craigie in neighbouring Craigie parish who were active on the side of reform. The fact that he was commonly known by an alternative surname – Feane – may suggest that he was an illegitimate son.

Adam Wallace was the kind of self-taught layman who turns up from time to time in the annals of early protestantism in Ayrshire. Knox's description of him as a 'simple servant of God' probably underrates his intellectual capacity. After all he became tutor to the children of Cockburn of Ormiston, the friend of Wishart, after their father's arrest, which may have led to Wallace's own arrest in that suspect East Lothian circle. He may have become associated with Wishart's Lothian friends after the preacher's Ayrshire visit; Wallace's wife Beatrice Levington, from an East Lothian family, married Mr Robert Lockhart, another Ayrshireman in Lothian reforming circles, after his death. Wallace admitted that he had not much Latin but he could read the bible, a copy of which he took from his pocket during his trial, in French, German and English.

When accused of having preached without a licence he disclaimed the ability to do so but admitted that

> sometimes at table and sometimes in other privy places he would read, ... the scriptures, and had given such exhortation as God pleaseth to give him to such as pleased to hear him.

When asked why he meddled with scripture at all, he replied,

> I think it is the duty of every Christian to seek the will of God, and the assurance of his salvation where it is to be found, and that is within the old and new testaments.

He reckoned that he and others like him had still left the bishops with plenty of preaching to do,

> ... although we search out our own salvation where it is to be found, considering they are but dumb dogs and unsavoury salt that has altogether lost the season.

His preliminary defence thus focused attention on the social world in which the new doctrines might spread — 'at table and sometimes in other privy places' — and on the invitation to help themselves to the means of salvation, which seems to have so appealed to laymen like himself.

The chief accusations against him were that he had baptised his own child; that he denied purgatory; that he called prayer to the saints and for the dead idolatry and superstition; that he asserted that the bread and wine in the mass remained bread and wine even after the words of consecration, thus denying the doctrine of transubstantiation. He refused to be drawn into answering 'yea' or 'nay' to the question, whether or not he had taught these things, but continually insisted that he had taught nothing except what he found in scripture. His judges just as determinedly avoided slipping into a debate as to what the relevant passages of scripture signified. The question hanging over the trial proceedings was whether or not the accused had denied the teaching of the church, not whether his assertions, argued from scripture, were valid or not.

Some of Wallace's arguments concerning the central accusations were arguments that went all the way back to the Lollards in his home country, others showed the influence of those Zwinglian emphases which appealed to many Scots dissidents, clerical and lay, in this middle period of the movement for reform. When asked to admit to or deny what he was alleged to have said about the nature of the bread and wine in the eucharist, he focused his reply on the historic circumstances of the Last Supper and on the commemorative purpose of the institution of the communion:

> I said that after our Lord Jesus Christ had eaten the Paschal lamb in his last supper with his apostles and fulfilled the ceremonies of the old law, he instituted a new sacrament in remembrance of his death then to come . . . 'Take eat; this is my body'. And he then took the cup . . . saying, 'Drink ye all of it; for this is my blood of the new testament, which is shed for many for the remission of sins . . .'

> I know not what that word consecrate means . . . but I believe that the Son of God . . . has a natural body . . .; and in the same body he walked up and down in the world . . . he suffered death . . .; and that by his godly power he raised that same body again the third day; . . . and ascended into heavin . . . and that this body is a natural body . . . and cannot be in two places at once.

He based his denial of purgatory and of the efficacy of prayers to the saints and for the dead on his inability to find authority for them in scripture, claiming that they were 'mere inventions of men, devised for covetousness only'. To the accusation that he had baptised his own child he replied that he had done so 'for lack of a true minister', not because of any danger that the child might die without baptism, which was the one circumstance in which lay persons were permitted to do so. His action hints at private religious practice independent of orthodox provision; 'for lack of a true minister' does not sound the same as 'for lack of a priest'. This is probably the kind of unorthodox practice which the provincial council referred to in 1559, when it decreed that for 'better assuring of salvation of infants, that all infants shall be baptised by priests conform to the method instituted by Christ and accepted by the church'.[17]

When Wallace asked for an impartial judge he was told that he would get no other than those present. He replied that in that case he expected no other verdict than condemnation; 'I know that I shall die, but be ye assured that my blood shall be required at your hands'. At which Alexander Cunningham the new earl of Glencairn immediately disassociated himself from the impending judgement. Turning to Robert Reid, bishop of Orkney, and other clergy near him he said, 'Take you yon [the responsibility] my lords of the clergy; for here I protest, for my part, that I consent not to his death'.

Although Glencairn had long since come to a parting of the ways with orthodoxy, he was one of those who took advantage of the apparently conciliatory mood of the establishment, secular and religious, in the early 1550s. He and others likeminded may have hoped that this state of affairs might hold out the possibility of some kind of *modus vivendi* between the parties. In material terms, French pensions were as useful as English.

The first signs of a change in the attitude of the religious establishment were the deliberations of the provincial council of the church which met in the autumn of 1549. The council, having adjourned from an inaugural meeting at Linlithgow, met in the Dominican monastery in Edinburgh in the wake of the first session of the general council of Trent which later launched the Counter-Reformation.[18] The printed decrees of that first session of Trent, probably forwarded by Robert Wauchope, the blind Scottish theologian who played a prominent part in Trent's affairs, were used in the provincial council.[19] The church might be in dire straits but the times were auspicious and the intention to get down to the roots of the problems besetting the church must have cheered the genuinely reform-minded clerics present.

In deploring 'how many heresies cruelly assail the Lord's flocks committed to their pastoral care, and wishing utterly to extirpate these same . . . from the very roots', the council decided that reform should begin at home. The 'roots of evil' were identified as 'the corruption of morals and profane lewdness of life of ecclesiastics of almost every rank, together with the crass ignorance of literature and all the liberal arts'. Even allowing for the customary rhetoric of public assemblies, this is a fearful indictment which cannot be explained away. If we are not to regard it with complete cynicism, it can only be seen as a desperate attempt by the genuinely spiritual men present to bring the kirk to its senses. The picture conveyed is of a serious collapse of those moral standards of personal life which were meant to distinguish the pastors from the flock who needed their ministrations; a lack of teaching of the faith itself to those who were supposed to teach and show an example to the faithful people; a preoccupation with material wealth and property to the detriment of spiritual values; and a vitiation of the appointments system which prevented the appointment of committed pastors with ability and spiritual priorities. The picture drawn did not portray all, or even a majority, of kirkmen but it was felt to be representative enough to have deprived the church in recent times of her authority and impact. It was certainly true of all too many of those prelates who were expected to lead the church and give it its moral tone.

The proposed remedies were positive enough. The question of clerical immorality – more realistically, perhaps, the tendency of many of them to live like the laity with 'wife' and children, material pursuits, property interests, and dynastic ambitions – was tackled by simply endorsing the decrees of the general council of Basle against clerical concubinage: a procedure which spared those offenders on the episcopal bench (who included the primate) the embarrassment of having to frame a self-denying ordinance on the subject. There followed provision for the regular visitation of monasteries and the return of apostate monks and nuns to their houses, regular visitation of the secular clergy, responsible management of church lands, the provision of qualified preachers – 'heretofore neglected' – in every church, cathedral and monastery, with detailed guidance for such preachers, an injunction to bishops to preach at least four times a year (episcopal deficiencies being remedied by taking 'men learned in Scripture' into episcopal households), and a call to all those with the cure of souls to preach on Sundays and holy days. The suitability and educational standards of parish priests were to be ascertained by examining curates before appointment, while vicars-pensioner were to be resident in their parishes. The decrees against heresy listed punishable opinions, including the growing phenomenon of the 'sacramentaris' who denied the sacrificial doctrine of the mass and transubstantiation.

As Lord Eustace Percy put it, 'If the passing of resolutions could bring about reform, the Church would have forestalled the coming revolution'. If carried out with conviction and expedition, the programme for internal reform and the confirmation of orthodox belief might have rescued the church from criticism, giving a well-informed and committed clergy the opportunity to arm the faithful against the onslaught of heresy, and restoring a sense of self-esteem to those who genuinely cared about the church's wellbeing. Unfortunately, not all present were in earnest about the business in hand. Commenting on the attitude of lay rulers and nobles who practised conventional piety while undermining the church's resources for their own ends, one historian of the Scottish provincial councils has said:

> For this attitude of mind the bishops must shoulder much of the responsibility, for they had become so secular in their ministry that abuses were allowed to spread unchallenged and suffered to become almost accepted behaviour ... and if the Auld Kirk was to survive, she had to save herself, for there were too many vested interests at stake for her to rely on monarch or noble.[20]

On the whole the occupants of the episcopal bench in 1549 could hardly have inspired the confidence of genuine reformers. Patrick Hepburn, bishop of Moray (from 1538) and commendator of Scone abbey, and Andrew Durie, bishop of Galloway (from 1541) and abbot of Melrose until he was bought out by James V in favour of an illegitimate royal son, were dissolute by any standards and quite unfit for the episcopal office. William Cunningham, bishop of Argyll (from 1539), son of the 3rd earl of Glencairn, remained unconsecrated throughout his tenure of office, administering his episcopal lands as part of his anglophile protestant family's territorial possessions on the Highland border. William Gordon, bishop of Aberdeen (from 1545), has left behind an impressive library, but was nevertheless a career cleric whose appointment was a reward for his father the 3rd earl of Huntly's support of the governor Arran. Gordon's own cathedral chapter remonstrated with him about the open nature of his relationship with Janet Knowis, daughter of an Aberdeen merchant, while the magistrates once wrote to him asking him to pay the town a visit, 'so that there may be some remembrance of your

Lordship as of your reverend predecessoris'. William Chisholm, bishop of Dunblane (from 1526), who gave his daughter Jane a tocher of £1000 when she married Stirling of Keir, was the second of three successive Chisholm bishops of Dunblane. He had succeeded his brother in 1526, and passed on the see (under the technicality of a coadjutorship) to his nephew in 1561, by which time it merely represented income. The eminent role of Archbishop John Hamilton, his association with proposals for internal church reform and the so-called 'Hamilton's Catechism', and his miserable fate in 1573 on a somewhat tenuous charge of complicity in the plot to murder Darnley, have endowed him with an aura of moderation and wisdom which it is difficult to substantiate from his actions, which were sometimes petty and vindictive. Whatever his personal commitment to reform (drastically contradicted by his private life), he was a partner with his half-brother the governor in the latter's attempts to take as much land as possible into the territorial hegemony of the Hamiltons. Although he is seen at the side of the queen dowager at certain important moments in the Reformation drama, it is known that Mary of Guise disliked him, partly because she was competing with the Hamiltons for control of church appointments. Knox's shrewd comment that the archbishop when in possession of a piece of information could not keep it to himself, hints at a basically weak personality.

The remaining occupant of the episcopal bench in 1549, and its only ornament, was Robert Reid, bishop of Orkney (from 1541) and commendator of Kinloss abbey. As a humanist scholar and conscientious administrator of his ecclesiastical office and possessions, he must have hoped for much from the council's work, not least in improving the educational standards of the clergy. His famous library at Kinloss and the abbey's education programme directed by the Italian scholar Ferreri, set a high standard to follow.[21] The sees of Glasgow and Dunkeld were vacant in 1549, the former represented at the council by Gavin Hamilton, dean of Glasgow, Caithness meant little more than a title to the royal incumbent Robert Stewart, while those of Ross and the Isles were at that time being contested by several applicants. The impression is inescapable that the bishops were not interested in reform which would undercut their secular priorities. In their own way they exploited the system they were appointed to nurture.

The council that opened in Edinburgh in January 1552 regretted that 'owing to troublous times and their manifold embarrassments' certain statutes of 1549 had not been fulfilled, but all were agreed about the need to move forward swiftly with their implementation.[22] The most significant move by this council was to give its approval to a Catechism, a simple exposition of the commandments, the creed and the Lord's prayer, to be distributed in the archbishop's and council's names to the bishops and in turn by them to their clergy to read (without commentary) to their parishioners. In facing the increasingly doctrinal assault on her defences, the church chose this positive means of response rather than a mere denunciation of heretical propositions which might have gone little further than the council itself.

The Catechism of 1552 was to be followed in 1559 by A Godly Exhortation, or 'The Twopenny Faith' as it came to be known, a cheap two-page leaflet which focused on the mass itself, the point of departure for protestants and from the mid-1540s onwards the chief target of their doctrinal objections to traditional teaching. It is eloquent of the council's intention to contain rather than confront the threat that the tone of the Catechism and the Godly Exhortation is moderate and middle-of-the-way in its explanations, to the point of modifying some of the definitions of Trent itself. Many curious but puzzled people on hearing them read might conclude that there was little difference of interpretation between orthodox teaching and the 'new opinions' to which they might have been exposed. Moderate reformers, more concerned about externals (such as the secularisation of church property) rather than doctrine might have been satisfied. For example,

On the eucharist (the Catechism);

> First it is callit the eucharist, that is to say, because it contenis him really and essentially . . . Christin men and wemen are joynit al togidder amang thame self as spiritual memberis of ane body . . . It is callit the sacrifice of the altar because it is ane quick and special remembrance of the passioun of Christ . . .'

On the mass (The Twopenny Faith):

> Devote Christiane men and wemen . . . wytt ye perfitlie and beleve ye fermlie that under the forme of bread quhilk I am now presentlie to minister to yow, is contenit trewlie, and realie, our Salveour Jesus Christ, . . . quha in his mortale lyve offerit hym self upon the Croce to the father of hevin, ane acceptable sacrifyce for our redemptioun . . . And wit ye that ressave this blyssit sacrament worthelie, ye ressave the blyssit bodie and blude of our Salveour Chryst for the fude of your saulis . . . to cause yow have quick remembrance of the blyssit passioun of our Salveour . . .[23]

If a threat is a small one it can often be knocked out of the way. If it is a substantial one and one that seems likely to persist, tactics must become more sophisticated. The compromising tone of the documents issued by the reforming councils of 1552 and 1559 suggest that the sentiments conveyed in Lord Methven's advice to the establishment to 'recounsall in tender manner' – meaning 'reconcile those who really belong but have gone astray' – may have been taken to heart by those genuinely-concerned religious leaders who were behind the intentions of the councils. Inspiration for the internal reform-programme, with its emphasis on improved clerical standards and theological education, came largely from those who were in touch with similar programmes of Catholic reform in Germany and France, and Archbishop Hamilton may well have seen himself as patron of such a programme in the manner of European episcopal colleagues who were committed to reform.[24]

The explanations of the faith in the Catechism and Godly Exhortation are not orthodox. Twenty years previously Patrick Hamilton had been put to death for saying something very like them, showing how far the new doctrines had penetrated in that length of time. These were either desperate measures for desperate times or they were the words, not of Archbishop Hamilton but of those still in the establishment who were nevertheless privately moving beyond orthodoxy.[25] If, however, there was any truth in the rumour that the archbishop had toyed with Lutheranism earlier in his career, it may have been easy for the promoters of the Catechism to persuade him that its chosen words were the best way now of maintaining the church's credibility in the eyes of those exposed to heresy.

It was too late for reform from within by the time the 'Twopenny Faith' made its appearance in 1559. It was too late, not just because by that time the protestant reformers had got the bit between their teeth but because the prelates in 1549 and 1552 had not taken it firmly enough between theirs. Even the brave attempt in 1559 to goad them into action with a petition to the regent calling for wide-ranging reforms, which purported to come from the leaders of the orthodox laity but judging by its content was probably compiled by the reform-minded clergy, failed to have the desired effect. The text of that petition (which will be considered again shortly) reads like a description of what-might-have-been, and the failure of the bishops to implement it must have been a source of disappointment and frustration to the genuine reformers in the council, who were among the real ecclesiastical casualties of the Reformation battle, betrayed by their leaders. We must salute them for trying so hard.

Conciliation was also in the air in the councils of state in the early 1550s as Mary of Guise became the agent of French interests in Scotland, while at the same time working towards her goal of ousting Chatelherault from the regency. In the spring of 1550 Scotland was comprehended in the Anglo-French treaty of Boulogne by the terms of which English garrisons in Scotland were abandoned. There was a price to pay, however, for the departure of the auld enemy as Frenchmen filtered into administrative posts and even offices of state to the resentment of the Scottish office-holding class. The dowager's task was to appease both the power-hungry house of Hamilton who might react to her increasing authority by seeking allies among other malcontents (such as the protestants whose channels of communication with England were blocked off with the accession of Mary Tudor in 1553), and the Scottish nobility who saw the French, as the earl of Argyll put it, 'come and sitten doun in this realme to occupy it and put out the inhabitants thereof'.[26]

In the early years of the decade, therefore, the dowager used her influence with the French king through her powerful family the Guises to reward and pardon recent wrongdoers and potential troublemakers. She obtained the release of the St Andrews castilians from their French prisons. The earls of Arran, Argyll, Angus and Huntly received the French Order of St Michael. Huntly was restored to the chancellorship and the earl of Cassillis was made treasurer. In September 1550 the queen dowager sailed for France to visit her daughter and discuss her plans with Henry II and the Guises, taking with her on an expenses-paid trip a number of Scots who might create trouble if left behind, including the anglophile protestants, Glencairn, Cassillis, Marischal, Lord Maxwell and Sir George Douglas. It was the opinion of some observers that the French king had 'bought Scotland completely'. In April 1554 parliament formally transferred the regency from Chatelherault to Mary of Guise. From then on her policy became more openly francophile, and as opposition to it built up in the second half of the decade it was backed by an increasing French military presence. Friction between the Scots and the French had become so marked by 1555 that parliament passed an act against those 'speiking aganis the Quenis grace and sawing evill brute [rumour] anent the maist Christin king of Frances subjectis send to this realme for the commoun weill and suppressing of the auld inimeis furth of the samin . . .'[27] Scotland increasingly became an element in French foreign policy as the decade advanced.

The cessation of prosecutions for heresy in the first half of the decade, the apparent accommodation of the leading religious dissidents with the political establishment and the church's own attempt to take the initiative in reform by tackling clerical standards and papering over the doctrinal cracks in the religious fabric may suggest that the movement for reform had lost pace at this time. Given that open dissidence in any way associated with England now attracted a clear-cut charge of treason (with the shadow of forfeiture in its wake), this may be so. However, perhaps not too much weight should be attached to the spectacle of protestant trips to France, or the acceptance of French pensions by men like the earl of Glencairn. He and others were ready to accept pensions from either France or England, but in neither instance did they do much in return, as Henry VIII constantly complained.

Rather, there is reason to believe that in the early to mid-1550s the problem of heresy was still a real one. This is suggested by the wording of the legislation of 1551, doubtless influenced by the grievances of the first estate, which was aimed at curbing criticism and debate, and the circulation of the kind of literature that encouraged it.[28] The legislation singled out those who in irreverent manner interrupted divine service and 'the preaching of the Word of God, stopping the same to be heard'; perhaps the critics included both conservatives who objected to the current attempts to water down traditional teaching and dissidents who disagreed with orthodoxy or were demanding that the scripture readings be in the vernacular. In either case it indicates that criticism and disrespect were quite open. We have to remember that the instructions to the clergy who were supplied with the Catechism of 1552 reveal that people did not always feel intimidated in church and did not always behave in a seemly manner even at mass, creating an atmosphere in which it might be easy to stage a protest. Just as serious in the eyes of authority was the circulation of subversive literature said to be produced by Scottish printers who 'daily continually print . . . concerning the faith, ballads, songs, blasphemies, rhymes as well of churchmen as temporall men'. This sounds like the kind of material which was to be gathered together in *The Gude and Godly Ballatis*, but it may also have referred to verses like those by the earl of Glencairn on the wonder-working shrine at Loretto. In 1554 letters of protection had to be issued in favour of the Dominican friary and Charterhouse of Perth in a resurgence of attacks on church property. Attacks on the friaries were perhaps a protest against those religious institutions which radical reformers regarded as dispensible, as distinct from the 'cleansing' of parish kirks and chapels which was a positive attempt to transform worship in accordance with the doctrinal stance of committed protestants.

The picture that comes across at this juncture is of those who were committed to reform meeting in private, where the bible was read and expounded, psalms and ballads sung, protest literature distributed and even religious practice observed in the absence of the clergy, publicly criticising orthodoxy, removing the apparatus of traditional worship, expressing antipathy towards religious institutions such as friaries, and even on occasion ostentatiously flouting orthodox rules, like the 'insolent and evill personis' who publicly ate meat in Lent. The extent of protest, the quantity of available literature and the numbers of people involved cannot be determined for lack of evidence, so there is no point in our insisting that they were either many or few. Nevertheless, the reaction, both accommodating and punitive, of the religious establishment through the mediums of provincial councils and civil legislation suggests that the protest was sufficiently visible and audible to cause concern and that, led as it was by persons of influence, it was now beyond eradication. The above are group activities, suggesting the existence of like-minded groups based on households, coming together occasionally and spontaneously rather than continually in being, but nevertheless foreshadowing the privy kirks which in the later 1550s met in such areas as Edinburgh and parts of the Lothians, Fife, Angus and the Mearns, and Ayrshire.

It was for the encouragement and instruction of such people that John Knox was invited into influential households while he was in Scotland in 1555–56. John Knox's uneventful early career as a notary and private tutor was dramatically interrupted when he met George Wishart, the friend of his employer Douglas of Longniddry and other East Lothian lairds who were drawn to the new doctrines. He found his own talents in a crisis, in preaching to the murderers of the cardinal in St Andrews castle; there is something dramatic about the way he appeared from the wings the moment the cardinal's body was dragged off the stage of Scottish history. Of all the notable Scottish reformers, Knox made the quickest and cleanest break with the religion in which he had been nurtured. Even by 1546 he could dismiss 'pilgrimage, pardons and other such baggage', while those who heard him preach from the pulpit of St Andrews parish kirk in 1547 exclaimed that 'Others sned [chopped] the branches of papistry, but he strikes at the root to destroy the whole'.[29] Not for Knox the personal sadness of broken friendships as a result of his religious alignment. For him it was 'us' and 'them' right from the start. His concern during his 1555–56 visit to Scotland was to encourage others to make that clean break.[30] The focus of his teaching was the need to recognise the mass as the supreme identifying mark of the pope's kirk and the height of her 'idolatry', upon which those who wished to establish a reformed kirk must turn their backs. It is an indication of the growing cohesion of attitude among the dissident groups that Knox could urge the 'zealous' to have the courage of their convictions and stay away from the celebration of mass, at the same time encouraging them to hold their own alternative communion. At the same time, coming back to Scotland after a ministry in England and with English-speaking congregations in Europe who had already become used to protestant practice, he was perhaps somewhat impatient with the members of what was still an underground if increasingly confident movement.

In the winter of 1555 he expounded the need for this essential break to a group of friends assembled at supper in John Erskine of Dun's Edinburgh lodging, who included David Forrest, an old friend from East Lothian, the worldy-wise William Maitland, younger of Lethington and two Ayrshiremen, Mr Robert Lockhart and John Willock, the latter like Knox himself recently returned from Europe.[31] To his lay friends who 'had a zeal to godliness' but 'made scruple to go to the mass or to communicate with the abused sacraments in the papisticall manner', Knox insisted that there was no excuse for continuing to give their presence to 'the idol'. After the preacher had dealt with all their misgivings Lethington remarked ruefully, 'I see that our shifts will serve nothing before God, seeing that they stand us in so small stead before man'. That winter similar teaching took place at John Erskine's home at Dun near Montrose, attended by 'the principal men of that country', and at Calder at the house of Sir James Sandilands who ten years before had befriended Wishart, where the gatherings drew the earl of Argyll's heir, Lord Lorne, and Lord James Stewart, prior of St Andrews. Then 'after Yule', following in George Wishart's footsteps, Knox left for Ayrshire.

He may have had earlier if brief contacts with Ayrshire reformers. William 3rd earl of Glencairn had visited the castilians at St Andrews in 1547.[32] It was John Rough at the instigation of the castilians who had bullied Knox into preaching publicly for the first time, at St Andrews. In January 1556 John Lockhart of Bar, his two sons and his brother were in Edinburgh and may have attended some of Knox's preaching.[33] Contact must have been made at some point, possibly through Mr Robert Lockhart, for it was the laird of Bar and Robert Campbell of Kinzeancleuch, whose father had supported Wishart at Mauchline, who accompanied Knox on his wintry journey down into Ayrshire.

It was in private households rather than in churches that Knox taught during his Ayrshire visit, in some of which he ministered the Lord's Supper. Such private gatherings were in keeping with the purpose of his instruction on this journey, which was concerned not so much with making public proclamation in public places — as Wishart had done — as with encouraging withdrawal from traditional worship by those who over the decade since Wishart's visit had become increasingly attached to protestantism. His visits may have encouraged the formation of privy kirks in Ayrshire, which although unrecorded must surely have existed around households where there had been commitment to reform for several generations, fortified by visits from preachers from time to time. Knox's first stopping place on entering Ayrshire by the old route from Edinburgh through the middle ward of Lanarkshire was Galston where he stayed with John Lockhart at the tower of Bar.[34] The laird's reputation as a sweeper away of the old things must have provided the preacher and him with much common ground. Galston parish had been a seedbed of reform for half a century by the time Knox arrived. He next moved westwards to Carnell in Riccarton parish on the border of Cunninghame, whose laird Hugh Wallace, then a young man still in his twenties, was soon to take a prominent part in events.

His next host was one of his guides into Ayrshire, another young man, Robert Campbell of Kinzeancleuch near Mauchline. The private occasion, which would attract only friends and sympathisers, pre-empted the kind of public difference of opinion which had marked Wishart's visit. The activities of Robert Campbell of Kinzeancleuch illustrate the stage the reform movement had reached in Ayrshire by the 1550s, with increasingly open attempts to implement a local transformation in religious practice.[35] He is said to have lent his hand to the removal of the apparatus of catholic worship from Ayrshire churches. He also arranged preachings out of doors, in kirkyards and other places where people tended to gather; the preachers may have had to compete with the attractions of Sunday shopping from chapmen's packs in the kirkyards of 'upland' Ayrshire kirks about which the burgh merchants had complained as early as the 1520s. The laird of Kinzeancleuch was one of those who by the 1550s felt that it was time for the leaders of reform to take advantage of the queen regent's conciliatory mood by requesting freedom to set up their alternative forms of worship where there was a local consensus in favour, reminding her at the same time of their local authority to order things as they wished. In one sense this would have been a revolutionary move, in another it would simply have been a radical extension of the local gentry's longstanding ability to arrange for the ministrations of the church to suit their needs and wishes. It is not surprising to find Robert Campbell in the company of the older laird of Bar whose iconoclastic campaigns in the region had possibly made an impression on him while he was still in his teens. It is said that it was the particular friendship of Kinzeancleuch with the young Matthew Campbell of Loudoun that drew the latter more firmly into protestant circles than his father Sir Hugh had been. Robert's wife, Elizabeth Campbell from the house of Cessnock, who shared his commitment to protestantism, is one of a number of women whose names are associated with the history of the Reformation in Ayrshire.

Like Wishart, Knox preached in the burgh of Ayr, which was probably the next place on his itinerary.[36] In the early spring of 1556 when John Knox arrived in the burgh, the influence of a group of office-bearers and their families who were inclined to protestantism may have provided him with the pulpit in St John's kirk as well as opportunities for household gatherings.[37] The bailies were John Lockhart, a kinsman of the laird of Bar who also had two merchant brothers in the town, and Mr Michael Wallace, brother of the laird of Craigie, a prominent reformer. The dean of guild, the merchant John Kirkpatrick, had a brother William, a monk at Kilwinning abbey, who was to become the first minister of that parish. Of the clergy of St John's whose services would be suspended if Knox did preach there, the curate sir Richard Miller was doubtless disapproving since two years later he was to be replaced by a cleric who was more amenable to the town council's religious changes. His future replacement, sir Robert Leggat, curate of Prestwick where he was to become reader, was also vicar of Ayr in which capacity he may have been present. George Cochrane, the organist and master of the song school, and the chorister James Dalrymple, both of whom later took office in the reformed church, may have been among those who listened with interest whether or not they were already committed to protestantism at that point. The town of Ayr continued to be a meeting place for those who were behind the increasing momentum of events leading to the revolution of 1559–60.

There followed visits to two households in south Kyle, those of Andrew Stewart Lord Ochiltree, in Ochiltree parish, and Sir James Chalmers of Gadgirth in the parish of Coylton. Andrew Stewart 2nd Lord Ochiltree, whose older brother Walter had been tried for heresy in 1533, was probably then still in his thirties, with a young family one of whom, Margaret, was to become Knox's second wife in 1564. Lord Ochiltree was one of the most consistent supporters of the Reformation. Sir James Chalmers, who was probably in the same age-group as Lord Ochiltree, came from a family with a reformist tradition. His aunts, Marion and Helen Chalmers, when young married women had been accused with the Lollards of Kyle. Since their own father Sir John Chalmers remained faithful to his religious traditions – he founded an obit in the Ayr Dominican church in 1501 – perhaps it was their husbands' families that were the source of their heretical beliefs. Marion's son, Sir James Dalrymple of Stair, was an ardent reformer. Sir James Chalmers, Knox's host, was a man of blunt manner who two years later strode into the regent's presence and threw down the gauntlet on behalf of his party.

Knox's last recorded stop on his tour of the west was Finlayston castle on the shores of the Clyde estuary, the Renfrewshire home of Alexander Cunningham, 4th earl of Glencairn. The earl, who had succeeded his father in 1548, was probably at this time in his early fifties. In the year in which he succeeded to the earldom he had watched the turning of the political tide which carried the young queen off to France from Dumbarton castle, the very stronghold which his father had once held for the anglophile party.[38] The need to come to a working accommodation with the government in the 1550s left his commitment to the realisation of reform intact. It was in time for the Easter festival, at which parishioners were particularly enjoined to take mass, that Glencairn sent his invitation to John Knox to Finlayston where 'after doctrine' he ministered the protestant communion to the earl and his household. These included, besides himself, his second wife Jane Cunningham (a daughter of John Cunningham of Caprington), two of his sons of whom the eldest (by his first marriage), William, had been married for nine years, and certain friends. It would be illuminating to know who these friends were. One cleric who may well have been present was sir James Walker, parson of Inchcailoch, a parish on Loch Lomondside in Glencairn's patronage, a personal friend and in all likelihood household chaplain, who had regularly witnessed the business and legal transactions of the earls of Glencairn and their sons since at least 1537. Sir James was sufficiently versed in protestant doctrine to be appointed the first minister of Stevenston in Ayrshire, a parish where Glencairn held land.

After returning to Sir James Sandiland's house at Calder where his teaching and the celebration of the reformed communion attracted hearers from Edinburgh as well as from the neighbourhood, Knox travelled north to Dun a second time where even larger gatherings attended comparatively open meetings and the administration of the sacrament.[39] Political conciliation did not guarantee ecclesiastical toleration, however, and Knox found a summons to appear before the bishops waiting for him when he returned to Edinburgh. The situation edged towards confrontation when Erskine of Dun and others arrived in the town prepared to defend the preacher at his interrogation. Their unforeseen action caused the summons to be withdrawn, possibly on the regent's instructions, as she was unwilling at this time to damage the semblance of rapprochement with prominent dissidents. Knox's friends then arranged meetings for him to which Glencairn, who had followed him eastwards, brought along the earl Marischal. In a positive mood the two earls decided to call the regent's bluff by urging Knox to write to her inviting her

A Receptacle of God's Servants

to hear the preaching and offering her the role of patron of reform which had been adopted by some European rulers.

Mary of Guise declined the challenge. She did not reply to the letter, handed to her by Glencairn on Knox's behalf, later passing it on with a quip to Archbishop James Beaton of Glasgow: 'Please you, my lord, to read a pasquil?'[40] Apart from her reaction to Knox's blunt way of pointing out her duty – 'the negligence of bishops shall no less be required at the hand of the magistrates than the oppression of false judges' – a protestant reformation did not come within the scope of her policy of appeasement. 'I am forced to keep up many pretences until I come to the proper time', she wrote to her brother the Cardinal of Lorraine. When the proper time arrived two years later, and appeasement had given way to opposition, and reformation to revolution, Knox's Ayrshire friends were in the forefront of the battle.

CHAPTER SEVEN

The Work of Reformation

The significance of what happened to the reform movement in the two and a half years between John Knox's sudden departure in the autumn of 1556 and his return in the spring of 1559 has been obscured by the dramatic nature of the events that took place following his re-appearance, giving the impression that nothing of note in the reformers' progress happened unless he was around. The murmur of voices in negotiation (even although they did occasionally rise to a shout) has been drowned in the later sounds of conflict when, as Knox himself put it in a letter to Mrs Locke in September 1559, 'we do nothing but goe about Jericho blowing with trumpets as God giveth strength, hoping victorie by his power alone'.[1]

Nevertheless, it was during these two and a half years that the leaders of the reform party made their clearest peaceful demands for recognition and for liberty to openly practice alternative forms of worship, and in their relations with the secular government passed from negotiation to confrontation. During this time they protected the activities of an increasing number of protestant preachers, in the spring of 1557 cancelling an invitation to Knox to return, at a point when their prospects of success seemed to diminish.[2] At the end of 1557, conscious of representing groups of protestants in their own homelands, the earls of Argyll, Glencairn and Morton, with Argyll's heir Lord Lorne and John Erskine of Dun, made a resolution in the characteristic Scottish form of a Band (or Bond) to

> apply our whole power, substance and our very lives, to maintain, set forward and establish the most blessed word of God and his Congregation; and shall labour at our possibility to have faithful Ministers purely and truly to minister Christ's Evangel and Sacraments to his people . . . and also does forsake and renounce the congregation of Sathan, with all superstitions, abomination and idolatry thereof . . .[3]

Since it led to little public action, the First Band of the Congregation tends to be regarded as premature and ineffective. On the contrary it did what it set out to do, which was to commit the signatories to protecting the scattered 'privy kirks', their withdrawal at local level from the religious establishment and alternative religious practice where it took hold in amenable localities. The lords of the Congregation drew up a handful of practical resolutions, enough to strengthen the spiritual cohesion of these groups without provoking a clampdown on their activities: reading of the common prayers in the vulgar tongue on Sundays and feast days, with similar reading from the old and new testaments; and 'doctrine, preaching and interpretation of the Scriptures . . . privately in quiet houses, without great conventions of people thereto, while afterward that God move the Prince to grant public preaching by faithful and true ministers'. In this way the minimum of change could be introduced into actual church services, the more controversial protestant teaching (and the reformed sacraments) taking place in the private familiar surroundings of the household. With regard to public reading in the vernacular of the prayers and scriptures, if the incumbents in the parish churches could not or would not do so, 'the most qualified in the parish use and read the same';[4] a situation which may have helped to clarify the alignments of local clergy and prepare the way for greater change. It was hoped that this low-key but persistent programme of practical reform would enable dialogue to continue with the secular authority, who might be encouraged to implement a programme of reform in spite of opposition from the hierarchy. It was a bid for a peaceful, possibly piecemeal, Reformation of the kind that had the backing of Robert Campbell of Kinzencleuch and his friends. At the same time the First Band marked the formation of an active public body, pledged (we might say, covenanted) to use every means in their power, including political and if need be military means, to advance the cause of religious reform. In this they were prepared to act in the role of the godly 'lesser' magistrates already delineated for them in Knox's letter to them of the previous October.

Among the first confrontations with the establishment was that early in 1558 between the archbishop of St Andrews and the aged earl of Argyll when the earl implemented his promise made in the 1557 Band by employing the ex-Carmelite friar John Douglas to preach in his household. The powerful chief of Clan Campbell fended off all the archbishop's objections, refusing to dismiss the preacher:

> I praise God that of his goodness now in my latter days he has of his infinite mercy opened his bosom of grace to me, to acknowledge him the Eternal Wisdom, his son Jesus Christ my omnisufficient satisfaction, to refuse all manner of idolatry, superstition, and ignorance, wherewith I have been blinded in tymes bygone, and now believe that God will be merciful to me, for now he has declared his blessed will clearly to me, before my departing of this transitory life.[5]

Meantime the privy kirks continued to meet, with the appointment of elders in some places and, in the absence of sufficient numbers of clerical preachers, exhortation by a mixture of clergy and laymen, who included the laird of Dun, David Forrest, Mr Robert Hamilton, Mr Robert Lockhart, William Harlaw, John Willock and others. Changes at Dundee are said to have amounted to the emergence of 'the face of a public church reformed, in the which the Word was openly preached and Christ's sacrament truly administered'.[6]

Into this evolutionary situation, in the summer of 1558, came a summons to the protestant preachers to answer a charge of preaching without licence. Their lay supporters determined to accompany them to their interrogation. In an attempt, so it was alleged, to detach the preachers' bodyguards an order was issued to all lords and gentlemen then in Edinburgh without the regent's specific request to muster on the border. This tactic was attributed to the bishops by those whom it was intended to inconvenience, a suspicion that got around just as the 'west land' contingent arrived back in Edinburgh from a somewhat abortive border raid during which the nobles told the French commander to his face that 'in no wise would they invade England'. Feeling distinctly messed about, the gentlemen of the west tramped through the palace corridors and into the room where the regent, Archbishop Hamilton and others were in consultation. There, without ceremony, Sir James Chalmers of Gadgirth stepped forward and confronted Mary of Guise:

> Madam, we know that this is the malice and device of those jeswells [rascals] and of that bastard [the archbishop] that stand beside you: We avow to God we shall make a day of it. They oppress us and our tenants for feeding of their bellies: they trouble our preachers, and would murder them and us. Shall we suffer this any longer? No, Madam. It shall not be.[7]

At which outburst the laird's companions, by way of emphasis, reached for their weapons and clapped on their steel bonnets. It is eloquent of the finely balanced nature of the contest of wills that this insubordinate gesture was not reprimanded. Instead, the regent tried to mollify the protesters, assuring them that if their suspicions were correct she would protect them from the bishops. As with the earlier summons to Knox, this one was withdrawn. The protestant protagonists regarded this as another loss of face for the bishops who a few months earlier, having failed to prosecute Knox, pounced on the aged schismatic priest Walter Mill, whose death at the stake at St Andrews provoked a popular local backlash.[8]

According to Knox, it was partly the influence of John Willock that caused the protestant lords to press their advantage towards the end of 1558 by presenting a petition to the regent and parliament requesting 'a public reformation, as well in religion as in temporal government . . . lest that the adversaries hereafter shall object to us, that place was granted to Reformation, and yet no man suited for the same'.[9] The job of handing the petition to the regent was given to 'that ancient and honorable father Sir James Sandilands of Calder', whom it was felt she was bound to respect. The petition, which Willock probably had a hand in framing, asked for public recognition of those steps already taken in private towards reformation: public use of the old and new testaments and common prayers, to be read in the vernacular; qualified persons to be permitted to publicly expound the scriptures; the baptismal service to be conducted in the vernacular so that those taking part might understand its significance; the celebration of the Lord's Supper to be in both kinds, according to reformed practice; that there be reformation of the private lives of the prelates, calling on them either to 'desist from ecclesiastical administration, or ... discharge their duties as becometh true ministers ... so that the grave and godly face of the primitive church [be] reduced [recovered]'

This petition and another calling for the repeal of the heresy laws and recognition of confessional dissent, as in parts of Europe, was followed by a protest to parliament against the decision not to engross the petitions in the parliamentary register. There ensued a brief and somewhat hollow attempt at a negotiated compromise between the protesters and the hierarchy, in which the former tried to manoeuvre the regent into the role of their champion against the bishops. The bishops held out an offer of a disputation which the protestant lords declined to accept unless 'the plain and written scriptures of God should decide all controversy'; this was refused. The bishops then drew up a list of 'Articles of Reconciliation' which offered to exchange liberty to pray and baptise using the vernacular, in private, for acceptance by the reformers of the mass, purgatory, prayers to the saints and for the dead, and recognition of the church's right to possess property: two small concessions in return for recognition of the religious status quo.[10] No mention was made of the public use of the vernacular scriptures or of the protestant communion. There was no reflection in the Articles of the tone of the recent Catechism sanctioned by the archbishop, or of the spirit of compromise shortly to be reflected in the Twopenny Faith. If the reformists in the church councils were prepared to compromise, the bishops were not. The opportunity for conciliation, such as it was, passed.

Nor, as it was soon made clear, was the regent sympathetic to protestant reform. John Knox, in order to emphasise the regent's alleged duplicity, dwells on the trusting nature of the reformers in these negotiations, but it is difficult to believe that by the end of 1558 they really expected 'a public reformation' on their terms at her hands, especially in the light of political developments.

In December 1557, the month in which the lords of the Congregation subscribed the First Band, Scottish commissioners were summoned to negotiate the details of Queen Mary's marriage to the dauphin Francis. The marriage took place in April 1558, and the Scots looked forward to having an absentee monarch in years to come. French control of certain public offices and military command had already indicated what the balance of power was likely to be between the united kingdoms. The Scots commissioners saw Mary, her husband and father-in-law sign documents which promised to preserve Scotland's sovereignty and the autonomy of her institutions. They did not see those secret papers which Mary signed just before her marriage, which conveyed her kingdom to the French crown should she die without heirs, thus reducing Scotland to a part of the French dominions.[11] Throughout 1558 all politically active Scots knew that it was the French intention through the regent's agency to gain the crown matrimonial for the dauphin, making him king of Scotland, not simply the queen's consort.

This concession was actually made in the same parliament as the protestant lords laid their demands on the table. They must have been aware of how political and constitutional developments were strengthening the queen regent's hand against subversive subjects, and how the forces of orthodoxy would naturally add their support to her French-backed administration. They may have gained some hope from the accession of Elizabeth in November 1558, but it was to be some time before they could count on help from that quarter. The tone of their protest in parliament shows that they had already made contingency plans (in principle at least if not in practice) for a time when the regent might be in a position to throw off any semblance of conciliation and protection:

> we protest that seeing we cannot obtain a just reformation, according to God's word, that it be lawful to us to use ourselves in matters of religion and conscience, as we must answer to God, unto such time as our adversaries be able to prove themselves the true ministers of Christ's church . . .
>
> . . . that if any tumult or uproar shall arise amongst the members of this realm for diversity of religion and it shall chance that abuses be violently reformed, that the crime thereof be not imputed to us, who most humbly do now seek all things to be reformed by an order. But rather whatsoever inconveniences shall happen to follow for lack of order taken, that may be imputed to those that do refuse the same . . .
>
> . . . that our requests, proceeding from conscience, do tend to no other end but to the reformation of abuses in religion only . . . beseeching the sacred authority [i.e. the civil power] to take us, faithful and obedient subjects, in protection against our adversaries . . . as it becometh God's Lieutenants to do . . .[12]

This protest was at one and the same time a unilateral declaration of reformation, a disclaimer in advance of responsibility for any ensuing trouble, an affirmation that the protesters' motive was only religious (having dropped the original request for reformation in religion and secular government) and a desire to appear as loyal subjects under the cloak of the regent's protection. The message was, 'We did ask; we shall not hold ourselves responsible if, due to the recalcitrance of the hierarchy and the regent's failure to do her duty as God's agent in advancing reform, trouble ensues from our determination to go it alone'. As a public manifesto of the protestant lords it could not have had more, or more representative, witnesses than the assembled estates.

After the bishops' limited response to this challenge already mentioned the initiative in the contest of wills was taken by the queen regent on her own terms. With the crown matrimonial of Scotland now safely in French hands and the peace negotiations between France and Spain going forward that winter, the conclusion of which was likely to leave the French king with more time and resources for Scottish affairs, Mary of Guise took a firm line with both sides in the religious dispute. Taking on her role of patron of reform, but on the side of orthodoxy, she asked Archbishop Hamilton to call a provincial council of the church, partly so that the clergy might respond to a petition which had been handed to her in the name of the orthodox laity, entitled 'Articles proponit to the Quene Regent of Scotland be sum temporall Lordis and Barronis . . .'[13] Recalling the initiative of King James V who had called upon the first estate to reform their lives, and the efforts of recent provincial councils in tackling internal reform, these Articles were an attempt to work out an acceptable compromise which might undercut the protestants' programme, revitalise the familiar beliefs and practices of traditional religion and goad the prelates into more positive reform than that offered to the lords of the Congregation in the 'Articles of Reconciliation'.

The proposals, some of which were later to be transformed into the statutes of the church's last provincial council, included regular preaching by qualified priests or their substitutes, and the regular reading of the Catechism. There was also a call for a clear explanation in print of the sacraments, which came to fruition in the Twopenny Faith, although its use was in the event limited. The common prayers should be said in the vulgar tongue, the payment of kirk dues and Easter offerings should be voluntary and the use of cursing against non-payers should be abolished. Steps ought to be taken to speed up the procedures of the church courts and there should be no need to obtain confirmation of feu charters from Rome, a lengthy and expensive process. The privileges of the Scottish crown in church appointments should be safeguarded. At the same time, there must be stricter prosecution of those who spoke irreverently against the mass; baptism must be administered in accordance with the church's practice only; and there must be punishment of those found defacing the fabric and ornaments of churches and of 'deforming or innovating the lovable ceremonies and rites therof usit in Haly kirk'. It is believed that although these Articles ran in the name of the faithful laity and undoubtedly had their support, they were probably drawn up by the clergy most committed to reform, who thus provided an advance agenda for the provincial council.[14] They even managed to formulate much more stringent rules for the private lives of the clergy and bravely attempted to put the bishops on the mat in this respect.

Having provided the ecclesiastical establishment with an opportunity to upstage the dissidents, and now that the political tide was turning in her favour, the regent's attitude towards the protestants hardened. At Easter

1559 a proclamation was issued against preaching without licence, and when it was ignored another summons, this time to appear at Stirling, went out. In a final attempt to reach an accommodation, two Ayrshiremen, the earl of Glencairn and the elderly sheriff of Ayr, Sir Hugh Campbell, had a meeting with Mary of Guise to protest at the summons, at which she told them that their preachers would be banished the country 'albeit they preached as truly as ever did Saint Paul', and reminded them that 'it became not subjects to burden their Princes with promises further than it pleaseth them to keep the same'.[15] Upon which, Knox claimed, they 'plainly forewarned her of the inconvenients that were to follow'.

It was between the summer of 1558 and the early months of 1559, while the representatives of the establishment and the dissidents grew nearer to confrontation, that the first public religious changes took place in the burgh of Ayr. The curate sir Richard Miller, who also held a chaplainry in St John's kirk, was paid his chaplain's fees until 1558. When in 1564 he sued the town for arrears of his chaplain's annuals, the magistrates accused him of having forfeited them by deserting his chaplainry 'lang before ony mutation of religion', having instead taken on 'a cuir to landward'.[16] Although his desertion (which also deprived the town of a curate) comes to light because of the dispute about his chaplainry, it may be that he found new duties laid upon him as curate uncongenial. It was during 1558 that the public practice of reading the common prayers and scripture lessons in the vernacular was gradually implemented in those localities where there was support for reform, with the provision for a qualified replacement for unwilling incumbents. Miller appears to have left while masses for the dead were still being said at the altars of St John's kirk (otherwise he would not have been charged with deserting his post) but perhaps while less controversial innovations in worship were being introduced. Sir Richard, not liking these innovations, may have jumped before he was pushed and found a chaplainry in the country with a more conservative employer. He was still around the area in 1559 but no longer employed at the burgh kirk.

His replacement as curate of Ayr was sir Robert Leggat, then also curate of Prestwick, clerk to Prestwick burgh court and since 1548 vicar of Ayr.[17] Sir Robert, who became reader at Prestwick at the Reformation and had begun his career before 1520 in the circle of the Wallaces of Newton, is likely to have been more amenable to possible changes in 1558. He is on record as 'vicar and curate' of Ayr as early as midsummer that year when he conducted the burial service of a parishioner.[18] On 5 November he formally put himself under the jurisdiction of the magistrates, agreeing to appear before them in the burgh court if anyone raised an action against him, renouncing his clerical privilege and right to be repledged to the church courts.[19]

In the spring of 1559 the town council discharged the chaplains of the burgh kirk and banned the saying of masses at its altars. In an action for

The Work of Reformation

arrears of choristers' annuals brought to court in 1564 it was answered on behalf of those burgesses who were being sued for payment that 'so long as the choristers had place they received payment of annuals ... and as for 1559 and 1560 there is no order taken to whom the same should be paid'.[20] The designations 'chaplain' and 'chorister' are used interchangeably in the burgh records, as the chaplains formed the choir of the parish kirk. Chaplainries, however small their remuneration, were pieces of property, some of them granted for life. Sir John Sinclair, who had been inducted as a chaplain in St John's for life in 1551, tried to hold the magistrates to the payment of his fees notwithstanding the ban on altar services.[21] On his first complaint, on 11 May 1559, the bailies conceded that he should have the arrears of his annuals for Martinmas 1558 and Witsunday 1559; this covered the burgh's accounting year which ran from Michaelmas (29 September) to Michaelmas. Having received his fees to date, sir John then tried to extract further payments by stating in court that he was personally prepared to carry out the duties laid down in his letters of appointment, by saying mass at his altar. The only reason he had not done so, he explained, was the refusal of the curate sir Robert Leggat to lend him the necessary vestments, 'alleging the bailies and dene of gild haid forbiddin him becaus thai haid dischargit the chaplandis of the said kirk thair service and feis, for sic caus as ar contenit in the actis maid thereupon'. Since he was willing to fulfil his duties, he argued, their discharge should not affect his liferent of his chaplainry.

Later the magistrates were able to prove that sir John had been the first to break the terms of his appointment, because he had 'divers tymes without leif or licence of the provost, bailies, dein of gild and communitie of the said burgh absentit him self furthe of the said kirk and service usit be the remanent chaiplanis ... to the number of 15 or 20 dayis togiddir, passing be the said space quhair it plesit him, nocht regarding his promeis ... and laitlie hes made thaim na service be the space of ane yeir and ane half'. They therefore felt no longer under obligation to pay him. Sir John failed in his bid to turn his desertion into a lock-out. His brief verbal exchange with the curate who was himself taking part in these changes is a rare vignette of the dislocations that must have occurred in Ayrshire and elsewhere at this time in the religious habits of a lifetime. Also in May the organist and master of the song school George Cochrane had been asked to leave his post, which suggests that use of the organ ceased about the same time as commemorative masses were abandoned.[22] When handing the bailies the keys of the organ loft, Cochrane protested that it be noted that he left only because they had discharged him and not 'for ony opinionis'. This made clear that he had not deserted his post, as the curate may have done, out of disagreement with current changes in the church. Cochrane's opinions were in any case with the reformers: he was soon to become reader in the nearby parish of St Quivox. It is to be regretted that the town council's acts which introduced these changes have not survived, but the reference to them during the Sinclair case at least records, even if it does not describe or precisely date, the emergence of reformed worship in the burgh kirk almost a year and a half before the ratification of the Reformation in August 1560.

No-one, however much they believed in their respective causes, could have foreseen the outcome of the events of that next year and a half. The provincial council which closed on 10 April 1559 set 11 February 1560 as the date of its next meeting.[23] It had issued the most constructive set of statutes to date for ecclesiastical reform and religious renewal within the bounds of orthodoxy, the strongest attempt yet by those who had diagnosed the church's ills to prescribe an effective remedy. Besides, this had not simply been a churchman's council, for its agenda had largely been set by the Articles presented to the regent in name of the faithful laity, indicating the kind of church they wanted and were prepared to defend. It was still the people's church, if no longer the church of all the people.

Yet, although there are indications that the church authorities in both provinces of St Andrews and Glasgow quickly set about implementing the council's edicts, it was too late to save the church as it was. By now, those who had withdrawn wanted not a better but a different church. Having failed to gain official sponsorship and episcopal toleration for their progrmme for reform outside orthodoxy, they had already proclaimed their intention to honour their conscience, as they put it, by proceeding with their own kind of reformation whatever the consequences. If they failed, Scotland might yet have a catholic Reformation, but because the civil authority relying on France stood by orthodoxy, church and state stood together in the heretics' line of fire.

The provincial council had met under the shadow of an accomplished piece of protestant propaganda, 'The Beggars' Summons', which had appeared on the doors of friaries on 1 January 1559, giving the friars a statutory 40 days' warning to quit at Whitsunday, which fell on 14 May.[24] The wording echoes that of a legal notice served on those who occupy property without right, ordering them to remove so that the rightful owners might enter and enjoy it as their own proper possession. The friars' alleged falsity consisted of their claims to be poor, simple and holy, entitling them to the alms of Christian people, whereas, the Summons claimed, on the authority of God's word all alms belong to the real poor, the blind, lame, bedridden, widows, orphans and other poor who, unlike the friars, are unable to work. The power behind the poor is revealed as God's 'sanctis on erthe, of quhais reddie support we dout not'. The bill is cast in the mould of Simon Fish the London anticlerical pamphleteer's 'Supplication of Beggars' which appeared in England in the late 1520s and is said to have been known in Scotland by 1540. Unlike the poor in Fish's pamphlet, however, who appealed to the king for redress against the greedy clergy, the Scottish poor of 1559 appealed to the 'lesser magistrates', the Lords of the Congregation here called the saints in the protestant sense of living believers, in place of the civil authority who had (in their eyes) failed the cause of reform. Little is known about how this propaganda event was organised or how widely the notices appeared, but it is eloquent of the effectiveness of the protestant network by the winter of 1558-59. Since 'tickets' with a similar warning had appeared on the friars' premises the previous autumn without any consequences (like a kind of first notice), those who were now threatened may have hoped that this warning might pass off without incident. Until 'flitting Friday' (12 May) had passed they could not be sure.[25]

Also ominous was the reaction in some localities to the regent's proclamation that Easter should be celebrated with all traditional ceremonies; the need for such a reminder is itself eloquent of the extent of secession in some places. The injunction was sufficiently ignored to indicate a mood of defiance, which was underlined by the activities of the preachers who, three days before Easter, had again been forbidden to preach without licence. Just before Easter John Willock travelled west and publicly preached in St John's in Ayr during the festival. According to the outraged abbot of Crossraguel, Quintin Kennedy, he did so

> with intolerabill exclamations, cryand out on the Messe, persuadand the haill people, that he exponit certane Scripturis allegit be him, truellie conforme to the jugement of the doctoris, and allegit thame to be expreslie aganis the Mess, and the ydolatrie usit be it.[26]

What nettled the abbot particularly was Willock's use of the writings of the early fathers in support of his exposition, which seemed to pay some lip-service to the traditions of the church, whereas the protestants normally proclaimed their reliance on scripture alone. He was thus teaching heresy from the church's own ground, as it were, and the abbot prepared to confound him from his own extensive library of the early fathers. However, when negotiations for debate between them got going, Willock demanded that the scriptures should decide all controversy, to which Kennedy refused to agree:

> For quhy? Yee will say that the Scripture is for you, and I in likewise will say it is for me; and appearandlie we are not able to have a competent juge presentlie to decerne quhilk of us allegeis the Scripture maist truelie ... Quhairfor the maist competent jugeis quhilkis we can haif presentlie ... are the anceant fatheris and doctouris ...

And so the argument about the ground of debate went round in circles and the debate itself never took place. The circumstances surrounding the exchanges, however, give a useful picture of the town of Ayr and St John's kirk as the arena of this controversy which in itself is a microcosm of the argument between orthodoxy and the protestants.

On Easter Sunday (26 March) Kennedy sent a note to Willock offering to meet him in a private house, each with 12 'hearers', when the abbot offered to prove that anyone stating that the mass was idolatry was a heretic. Willock replied the following day that, while anyone who said he could prove the pope's mass to be the Lord's Supper by the word of God 'affirmis that thing quhilk he sall not be hable to preif thereby', he also was prepared to meet with 12 hearers whom he would choose from the 'gentlemen of the schyr quha ... will be in this town schortly'. Two days later (29 March) he was able to name his chosen (15) witnesses: Glencairn, Boyd, Ochiltree, Campbell of Loudoun, the lairds of Craigie, Cessnock, Bar, Carnell, Kerse, Rowallan, Dreghorn, Kinzeancleuch, Carlton, Sornbeg and Kelwood, a considerable roster of the leaders of the Congregation of Kyle and Cunninghame. The venue was switched, probably at the gentlemen's suggestion, from the private house to 'ten houris of the clok afoir noon in Sanct Johnis kirk of Ayr oppinlye', because, Willock explained, 'I do teache my doctryne oppinlye befoir the pepill thair'.

In a letter to Archbishop James Beaton of Glasgow relating these events the abbot claimed that

> quhen the day of our ressoning come [Sunday 2 April] ... thair convened above four or five hundred to fortifie him: Truellie my Lord and I had pleissit I culd haif beyn twyse als mony; for my broder sone [Cassillis], my Lord Eglinton and all thair freindis and servandis, wes in reddines as I wald pleisse to charge, bot alwyse I wold nolder suffer thameselfis nor yit thair servandis to cum, for gif I had done utherwyse, it had not failzied cummyr [trouble].

It is difficult to believe that the Kennedy and Montgomerie chiefs were so easily persuaded to avoid 'cummyr', given their usual readiness to prove a point by force. It is just as likely that since Willock preached to the parishioners at Easter without the open support of the lords of the Congregation, Kennedy expected him to continue to do so and, being unprepared for a convocation of Willock's friends, had come himself accompanied 'alluterly ... with religious men' and a few gentlemen from Carrick as witnesses. His personal wish to avoid trouble, however, was doubtless genuine.

Willock's letter about the change of venue was delivered to the abbot by David Crawford of Kerse at the Grey Friars' monastery where Kennedy was lodging. The abbot stuck to his preference for a private venue before a maximum of 24 witnesses as originally agreed, with no packing of stairs, lofts and back doors, 'for I desyr nolder tumultatioun, cummyr nor stryf bot only the just tryal of Goddis worde, in sic manner as may be to the glore of God and quietness of the Congregation'. Thursday 30 March was a day of shuttle diplomacy. Willock agreed to a private meeting in the lodging of his supporter Hugh Wallace of Carnell. It was in his reply to this note that Kennedy declined to make scripture the sole judge. Willock in turn replied that he stood by 'the jugement of Goddis worde onlie, be which all manner of heresies must be confoundit', upon which the abbot accused Willock of himself standing in judgement on the early fathers of the church. If Willock could produce one 'anceant doctour' who agreed with him about the alleged idolatrous nature of the mass, he promised to abandon the rest of the proposed disputation.

In reply Willock spelled out the protestant confession about reliance on scripture. Far from his judging the fathers, he insisted, the latter had themselves expected believers to judge their writings for themselves and to submit them to the test of scripture.

In his final communication Kennedy expressed the revulsion of orthodoxy to what he saw as private interpretation:

> Quhat say ye in that pairt bot as . . . the maist deplorit heretykis quhilk evir wes sayd, ay allegeand Scripture for thame, standand at thair awin interpretation for the samyn?

The exchanges illuminate the doctrinal gulf, over which no provincial council however well-intentioned could now throw a bridge, be it constructed of spiritual renewal or concessionary terminology. The protestant reformers had taken another route altogether to a reformed church. Much attention has rightly been given to Quintin Kennedy's 1562 theological debate with John Knox, yet his exchanges with John Willock at Easter 1559, abortive though they were, are also significant in demonstrating the respective positions of the orthodox and apostate protagonists. On Sunday 2 April, while Willock was preaching in the church of Ayr, Quintin Kennedy took a notarial instrument at the market cross and kirk door recording that Willock had failed to keep his appointment, although he himself was willing to debate. Among those with him was the prior of the Ayr Dominicans who was refused entry to the church when he tried in the archbishop's name to inhibit Willock's unlicensed preaching. Those who watched the taking of legal instruments at the market cross may have reflected on how times had changed since George Wishart had preached at the cross and the archbishop of Glasgow in the church 14 years before.

The turn-round in the fortunes of dissent in Ayr could scarcely have happened without a measure of consensus in favour of reform. Religious change in the burgh seems to have taken place gradually but perceptibly, in a way that perhaps gave people time to get used to it. Walter Stewart's iconoclastic action (1533) had been a protest; John Rough's presence (1543) provoked the makings of a disturbance but established the phenomenon of public protestant preaching; George Wishart's visit (1545) initiated an iconoclastic campaign of four years' duration, during which the burgh kirk may have experienced the first stages of the removal of the apparatus of traditional worship, in the taking down of the images; John Knox's visit (1556) helped to consolidate commitment to reform outside orthodoxy; the months between the summer of 1558 and Willock's preaching at Easter 1559 saw the replacement of a probably conservative with a progressive curate and the introduction of vernacular into the services, followed by the abandonment of the use of the organ and the greatest outward change so far, the cessation of masses at the altars of the burgh kirk.

This last change must have required some accommodation between the burgh authorities and the patrons of obits and chaplainries. Perhaps enthusiasm for these particular religious services was waning in any case. At Ayr, as in some other towns, such endowments dwindled markedly from mid-century onwards. The obit book of St John's, Ayr, contains 11 such endowments from the 1520s, two in the 1530s, one in 1542, by the scholarly dean of Glasgow, Mr George Lockhart, and after that only the record of a few obits founded earlier by people who died well after 1560.[27] Charitable bequests to Ayr Dominicans, in so far as these can be judged from their surviving charters, were few after 1540.[28] Of 104 testaments recorded in Glasgow commissary court between 1547 and 1555, only four include the foundation of an obit or commemorative mass in perpetuity.[29] In three other cases small sums were left to priests to say special prayers for the soul of the testator. Of these seven individuals, three were from Ayrshire: Thomas Kennedy of Knockdaw left money for 24 masses to be said for him in Colmonell parish kirk (1549); Margaret Fullarton of Irvine left money to the Ayr Franciscans for masses (1550); and William Cunningham of Glengarnock left 20 merks to the Ayr and Glasgow Franciscans and £20 to the chaplains of Kilbirnie parish church to pray for him (1547). Of just over £26 left in donations to the Ayr Franciscans between 1545 and 1552, the archbishop of Glasgow and the earl of Eglinton left £10 each.[30] When it came to 'flitting Friday', 12 May 1559, and the Ayr friars were told to quit, although the churches were purged the friars themselves are said to have suffered no violence, in contrast to their experience in some other burghs. Two younger representatives of the Congregation, Robert Campbell of Kinzeancleuch and Hugh Wallace of Carnell, went along, to whom the friars handed over their keys before filing out, taking their personal belongings with them.[31] Perhaps this is how they preferred to do things in Ayr, where gradual acclimatisation to the idea of radical religious change may have soaked up local aggression over the years.

There is no doubt, of course, that the presence of the 'gentlemen of the shire' and their followings who arrived in the burgh to support the various preachers over the years would cause potential protestors to change their tactics. Nevertheless, John Willock had preached publicly on Easter Sunday 1559 without their supporting presence, which makes it look as if he had done so by invitation from his home town. A reference in the burgh accounts ending Michaelmas 1559 to the expenses incurred in 'bringing hame ane preacher'

The Work of Reformation

may refer to Willock.[32] Probably more influential over the years was the long tradition of religious dissent which the families of the Kyle hinterland had shared with their burgess relatives in Ayr, which may have acted as a leaven of change in the lump of traditional religion in the burgh. Lists of magistrates and other office bearers, burgh court juries and burgesses in general are peppered with the surnames Wallace, Lockhart, Nisbet, Cunningham, Campbell, Crawford, Reid, Chalmers and others whose landward kinsmen were active leaders of reform. At the same time, there was scarcely a substantial laird who did not have a permanent family lodging in the burgh.

Before the end of 1559 an appointment had been made to the reformed ministry at Ayr.[33] The minister was the Englishman Mr Christopher Goodman who had been a colleague of John Knox at Geneva. The burgh accounts record the arrangements made for his reception towards the end of the year, including the furnishing of his chamber, the expenses of his journey from Edinburgh in the company of Knox's servant Richard Bannatyne, the gift of money and a 'gowning'. The construction of a new pulpit and the purchase of wine and white bread for the communion mark the final emergence of the full protestant service in the parish church.

About the time the protestant minister arrived the bailies heard the 'lamentabill bill of support and complaint' of sir Alexander Kerr, the elderly sacrist of the church, the last of the chaplains to have his future decided. He represents some of the real casualties of the Reformation, the redundant labour force of chantry priests. The bailies agreed to give sir Alexander £10 yearly from the common purse, less than he had received as sacrist and chaplain,

> he keipand the paroche kirk of the said burght honest and clein, ringand the bellis yeirlie and on ilk day neidfull to the commoun prayeris and preiching, and cumand the morne to the said kirk and thair opinlie in presence of the haill congregatioun sal confess his offences done to his God and neighbouris and sal sourlie promit nocht to comit sic error nor offence in tyme comying; and willinglie to amend, sal witht his hail hart renunce the devill, the paip and all thair workis, otherwayis he is to haif na fie of the toun.[34]

And so, the only recorded public recantation in Ayr kirk was a Catholic one. Perhaps sir Alexander had been surreptitiously saying mass for some recusant family. If so, we shall never know whether they represented a silent minority or majority of the townspeople. All that can be said is that among the scattered and localised instances of Catholic recusancy reported from the south-west later in the century, only one was from Ayr.[35]

Ayr's new minister was a busy man with far-flung connections and responsibilities who found it necessary to spend some time away from his charge in the early days. Mindful of the old evil of non-residence, the town council made provision for this contingency. On 20 November 1559 they appointed a new schoolmaster John Orr, who was also charged to 'say and reid the commoun prayaris and minister the sacrament' in Christopher Goodman's absence, 'quhilk salbe bot 8 or 9 dayis at the maist at aneis'.[36] A concern for the maintenance of the new parish service once established took precedence over narrowly defined functions and job-descriptions in the early days of the Reformation. Readers were often called 'ministers' in the general sense of ministering to the people. The records that survive have preserved an illuminating glimpse of the transitional year at Ayr, which began with the service of the vicar-curate sir Robert Leggat and ended with that of the minister Mr Christopher Goodman, whose appointment illustrates Ayr's outside contacts, and his assistant the schoolmaster-reader John Orr.

Public events as well as local reformation occupied the Congregation of Kyle and Cunninghame between the summer of 1559 and the meeting of the Reformation parliament in August 1560. John Knox arrived back in Scotland on 2 May 1559 and soon afterwards the protestant preachers were summoned to Stirling. They included John Willock who on 10 May was denounced rebel for failure to answer for his unlicensed preaching at Ayr. His surety Robert Campbell of Kinzeancleuch was fined for failing to produce him in court.[37] It was in protest at this latest summons that Glencairn and Campbell of Loudoun warned the regent of further resistance. Perth became the scene of confrontation and disorder. Knox preached there on 11 May, the day before 'flitting Friday', following which several friaries in the east of Scotland and the friaries and Charterhouse at Perth were sacked, and the abbey of Scone looted. The leading burgesses of Dundee and the Congregation of Angus and the Mearns prepared to go to Perth in a gesture of solidarity with the preachers. Sir James Croft, writing to the English privy council on 19 May, reported the 'great dissension in Scotland', with the resort of many noblemen to the defence of Knox and the preachers. He had noted the earl of Argyll's brother, Donald Campbell abbot of Coupar Angus, 'in secular weed' and even the presence of Huntly, an experienced 'trimmer', among the Congregation.

Towards the end of May the Congregation of Kyle and Cunninghame held their own muster at Craigie kirk to decide whether to support their colleagues at Perth, having received copies of a letter to the nobility from the beleaguered preachers and their supporters, urging those who were against actively supporting them to think again, and those in favour of showing solidarity but doubtful of the best means of resisting the civil authority to do their duty, obey their conscience and come to the support of their brethren.[38] Of the gathering at Craigie, Glencairn being the senior nobleman present and because of his record was the acknowledged leader. One of his younger clansmen there, William Cunningham of Cunninghamhead, was soon to play an important part in negotiations with the regent. With them from

Cunninghame was Lord Boyd who although he was to be a staunch friend of Queen Mary was also a lifelong committed protestant. Also at the muster was Knox's friend Andrew Stewart, Lord Ochiltree, and Matthew Campbell, 'young sheriff of Ayr' and a clutch of younger lairds of his own generation who included Hugh Wallace of Carnell, John Wallace of Craigie, Glencairn's son-in-law on whose home-territory the Congregation had gathered, and George Campbell, the great-grandson of the Lollard laird of Cessnock. No muster of the Ayrshire Congregation would have been complete without the presence of the veteran John Lockhart of Bar, who had with him his brother Alexander, burgess of Ayr, who was to lose his life at the siege of Leith. The company also included Sir James Chalmers of Gadgirth, the story of whose defiance of the regent almost a year before was probably common property by then in Kyle and Cunninghame.

There was some debate about the course of action, for armed defiance of the civil authority, with its possible consequences, was not something to be undertaken lightly. There may have been some leaders who felt that in the light of recent advances in the reform programme in the south-west and given a little more time they could deliver the Reformation to the people of their own region and find their own preachers. But Glencairn spoke out impulsively, as he had done at Adam Wallace's trial, announcing his own decision:

> Let every man serve his conscience. I will by God's grace see my brethren at St Johnston; yea, albeit never man should accompany me, I will go, and if it were but with a pike upon my shoulder; for I had rather die with that company than live after them.

His initiative decided the rest, who rode off after him and the laird of Craigie: about 2,500 men, it is said, of whom about 1200 were horsemen. It was a decision in favour of solidarity with national issues rather than preoccupation with local concerns.

The burgh of Ayr appears to have sent a contingent: a carriage man was hired by the town council to take gear to Perth, and on 3 July the meeting of the burgh court was suspended 'because there is few nychtbouris present for the tyme'. With the armed company went the outlawed preacher John Willock. Defying Lyon Herald's command at Glasgow to turn back, and avoiding obstruction laid in their path by the regent's men beyond Stirling, they reached the outskirts of Perth and made contact with the rest of the Congregation's forces.

Meantime on 22 May the lords of the Congregation had confronted the regent with the possibility of armed revolt 'from our accustomed obedience' in defence of what they saw as their religious liberties. Secession might become civil as well as religious. The regent had accused them of withdrawing their obedience; now they admitted the possibility but vowed that it would take place only in defence of the religious freedom of themselves and their fellow seceders which it was their duty under God to defend:

> ... except this cruelty be stayed by your wisdom we will be compelled to take the sword of just defence against all that shall pursue us for the matter of religion, and for our conscience sake; which ought not, nor may not be subject to mortal creatures, further than by God's word man be able to prove that he hath power to command us ... .[39]

Agreement was finally reached about the evacuation of Perth. The Congregation should be free to leave the town; no townspeople should be prosecuted over the religious changes in the burgh, with all grievances on the subject of such changes to be remitted to a meeting of parliament; the town should be open to the regent but she should not bring in the French; should the regent break this promise, the Congregation would take appropriate steps to defend those whom she threatened.

About the time they left Perth the Congregation drew up a bond of mutual amity and defence in the light of their agreement with Mary of Guise:

> in case that any trouble be intended against the said Congregation or any part or member thereof they promised themselves ready to act against whatever power that shall intend the said trouble, for the cause of religion, or any other cause dependant thereon, or lay to their charge under pretence thereof, although it happen to be coloured with any other outward cause.[40]

Thus they justified in advance any military action they might take in the light of their agreement with the regent, were it to defend the Perth burgesses from a charge of disobeying her orders in matters of religion, or to resist any attempt by the French to take over the town. In the event the Congregation left Perth unmolested, but hard on their heels came the regent and the Frenchmen in apparent contravention of the agreement, for whom mass was set up again, according to Knox on altars improvised from tavern tables. The Congregation claimed a moral victory when, the regent in their eyes having broken her promise, her former negotiators Argyll and the Lord James joined them at Stirling. When accused by his sovereign of sedition on this account Lord James replied that his and the Congregation's actions were 'for the advancement of God's glory (as it does indeed) without any manner derogation to your Majesty's obedience ... being grounded upon the commandment of the eternal God, we dare not leave the same unaccomplished'. Others followed suit. The French ambassador remarked that 'You cannot tell friend from enemy, and he who is with us in the morning is on the other side after dinner'.[41]

A battle for the control of Perth ensued and after the town's relief various attempts at negotiation between the two sides took place, without agreement.

The Work of Reformation

The Congregation made periodic resolutions for their own defence; word of a proposed meeting of the Congregation of the west on Govan Muir for 12 August reached Mary of Guise. The insurgents continued to protest that they did not intend civil disobedience, except in so far as the civil power demanded them to obey in things 'repugnant to God's word', which obliged them to protect the advancement of the Reformation by military means if necessary. Qualified civil obedience was now justified and could be expected. In the autumn large numbers of professional soldiers arrived from France, at whose hands the Congregation's untrained forces suffered serious reversals. Many of their troops, their minds on the approaching harvest season, deserted. The Congregation's overtly political tactic of deposing the regent (the ultimate gesture of resistance) and transferring power to a great council of the realm was followed by an unsuccessful assault on French-held Leith and an ignominious evacuation of Edinburgh pursued by the French and numbers of the inhabitants, the latter doubtless motivated as much by self-interest as religious conservatism in evicting the 'rebels'.[42] Money sent by Queen Elizabeth was hijacked by the earl of Bothwell after a tip-off had reached the regent. The French dug themselves in at Leith and harried the nearby coastal regions. In the early winter of 1559 the fortunes of the Congregation, militarily and materially, were at a seriously low ebb. 'All concord is gone', Sadler and Croft reported to Cecil.

In November the Congregation sent William Maitland, younger of Lethington, to London to negotiate for military help. Until his return, Henry Balnaves explained to Cecil, Chatelherault, Argyll and Glencairn would be based in Glasgow, with Arran, Rothes, Lord James, Ruthven, Erskine of Dun and Pittarrow in St Andrews, the two groups keeping in touch. On 23 January an English fleet appeared in the Firth of Forth, effectively cutting the French off from seaborne reinforcements from home. In February 1560 English help was promised in the treaty of Berwick.[43] Since it was against English interest that the French 'intend to conquer the realm of Scotland, suppresse the liberties therof and unyte the same to the crown of France perpetuallie' (in contravention of the public agreements made at the time of Queen Mary's marriage to the dauphin), Queen Elizabeth agreed to take Scotland under her protection for the duration of the marriage of Mary and Francis and one year thereafter, and to send 'a convenient ayd of men of warre . . . alsweall by sea as by land', in order to help remove the French threat. In return the Scots lords made the centuries-old promise, formerly made to France, to assist their new ally against her enemy France if need be. They vowed that all of this was in defence of the rights of the Scottish crown only and did not imply disobedience to their native queen or resistance to her husband the king of France.

The English army arrived in Scotland on 2 April 1560, when the commanders were met by the lords of the Congregation, including the

Ayrshire leaders Glencairn, Boyd and Ochiltree. Yet another conference between the two sides, at Leith on 25 April, was mostly concerned with 'the assurance of our obedience', according to Maitland. On 27 April the Congregation drew up their last Band of this period of conflict, mutually promising to 'set forward the Reformation of Religion' and with Queen Elizabeth's help to expel the French 'oppressors of our liberty, forth of the realm' and recover 'our ancient freedoms and liberties'.[44]

On 6 June the treaty of Edinburgh was concluded between representatives of the real political protagonists. England and France.[45] All foreign forces were to leave Scotland. Francis and Mary were to abandon their recent use of the royal arms and style of England. The French commissioners in name of the absent rulers who still regarded the Congregation as rebels refused to negotiate with the insurgents but on petition from them granted certain Concessions, the most important of which was that a parliament might meet 'according to use and custom'. This parliament was not empowered to deal with the religious question – a prohibition which pinpoints the root cause of the recent 'uproar' – but must submit the question to the king and queen. With the death of the regent Mary of Guise in Edinburgh castle on the night of 10–11 June the Scots were under the direct rule of their sovereigns, Mary and Francis.

Whatever the vested interests of the different parties, France, England, and the Congregation, in the outcome of the conflict, the international situation in the run-up to the treaty of Cateau-Cambrésis in April 1560 and afterwards was bound to have a decisive effect on Scottish affairs. Peace with Spain meant that France would have more time to give to consolidating its hold on Scotland. The regent had seen this as strengthening her arm against the insurgents. For Elizabeth and her ministers, faced with Mary Stewart's claim to the throne of England, this would mean a permanent French presence on England's northern frontier where trouble was notoriously easy to hatch. To the Congregation, whatever dreams of Anglo-Scottish union some of them may have had, the pressing question was the immediate military crisis in which they found themselves, in which there was little hope of victory without English help. The English solution, however, gave them two associated problems. They must not look like rebels to Queen Elizabeth, and they must be able to calm the instinctive anglophobia of their fellow-Scots and reassure them about their real reason for inviting the auld enemy within the gates.

Their initial claim to be obedient subjects (with a serious grievance), which had been a necessary element in the Congregation's public statements in the early vulnerable days of their resistance, was a time-honoured safeguard of rebels. Their eventual arguments were that the regent had failed in her role of 'God's Lieutenant' (a role rather thrust upon her), that she had broken her promises to them leaving them free to take the matter of reformation into their own hands, and that they were under promise to God's higher authority

The Work of Reformation

to do so despite her call on their civil obedience in lesser matters. Their line with Queen Elizabeth was that they were asking her to help them expel the French who threatened their country's sovereignty and their native liberties. If they used anti-French propaganda to reassure Queen Elizabeth that they were not rebels, it was also used to reassure their fellow-Scots that they were not traitors. Here, there was little need to exaggerate the French threat if contemporary resentment is anything to go by, from that of the earl of Argyll and his fellow-nobles who saw French officials taking over their hereditary role in the nation's affairs, to that of the Scottish townsfolk who roughed-up the unpopular French soldiers. Quite apart from its real propaganda uses, however, the removal of the French threat, real as it was seen to be by all parties affected, had become a politico-religious necessity. The reformation of religion outwith orthodoxy, which was the Congregation's ultimate aim (stated or assumed) in all its professions of intent, required the ending of the auld alliance and the forging of the new. It was a necessity, nationally and internationally. It is easy to see Scotland as the vulnerable point in this international triangle, with England as the real winner in terms of the treaty of Edinburgh, and this is largely true. The crisis can also be seen, however, as the last bid by the Scots – or at least by an influential party of Scots – to benefit from their country's role as a small but vital piece in the diplomatic machinery that kept the balance of power in Europe, in the religiously-divided Europe as it had now become. In doing so, the Congregation used the device earlier used by Cardinal Beaton to keep his country within the arena of European politics, but to terminate not maintain the auld alliance, and for a purpose that must have had him turning in his unmarked grave.

Probably only a minority of protestants were enthusiastic about the idea of Scotland as part of a protestant Britain. To most, the new amity with England was a pragmatic necessity and one not easily accepted. The avowal of the anglophile-reformer earl of Cassillis that 'we would die, every mother's son of us, rather than be subject to England' probably accounted for a good many of them. One stalwart soldier in the ranks of the reformed kirk militant, William Douglas of Lochleven, recalled how difficult it had been to accept co-operation with the English, only the prospect of victory for the Congregation having made it possible for him to do so:

> Quhilk wes a begyning of the reconciliatioun amang us and that the hairtis of thaim quhilkis wer in malice aganis thaim [the English] throw want of thair predecessouris in battaill wes begun to be slokinit [assuaged], as I knaw be experience in my selff for the want of my fader at the feild of Pinky, quhilk wes the first occasioun that I did remit the sam with my hairt.[46]

In the end the cause of reform probably decided many who may otherwise have felt that unpatriotic collaboration with England was an unpalatable corollary to the Congregation's seemingly patriotic call to eject the French. It is also likely that distrust of the English – even anglophobia – outlived the need to co-operate with them in the crisis of the Reformation rebellion. Even the dream of those who saw Scotland's future as part of a protestant Britain began to fall apart as the two countries increasingly went their separate ways, culturally and politically, and plans for actual union came to nothing in the early seventeenth century.[47]

The Congregation's anti-French propaganda and English diplomacy was not a bid for support for a religious Reformation; such support was given or withheld for quite different reasons. Their political strategy was aimed at creating a situation in which the reform programme which they championed might be implemented. By 1559, on the strength of various public statements, they had abandoned the role of defenders of reform and had not only declared unilateral Reformation but exonerated their consciences from the consequences of having done so. The fact that, having been handed the necessary military victory, they were able to proceed as a provisional government to implement their programme in defiance of the wishes of their absent rulers suggests that they could count on the necessary support for reform itself. The ability to make the religious settlement stick, however threatened it might be by its unconstitutionality at the time or the effects of rival interests in the future, could not have been possessed by a mere faction or pressure group, but only by a body of representatives whose programme could draw on the necessary support, however variously motivated – even though, as William Douglas grudgingly put it later, they must have been grateful for the help of the 'few ships of England' who came to their rescue in the crisis. The next step was to sit down and work out the details of Reformation for all, not just for those who had supported it publicly and had taken up arms in its defence.

CHAPTER EIGHT

Faithful Workmen

In the autumn of 1560 there would be many in Ayrshire who waited for parliament to ratify a situation which in varying degrees already existed across the sheriffdom. Twenty-two Ayrshiremen of various ranks and stations, according to the official record, were present at the Reformation parliament which met in Edinburgh on 1, 17 and 24 August, having been prorogued from a meeting on 10 July.[1]

All the Ayrshire nobles and lords of parliament were present: four of them in favour of protestant reform – Glencairn, Boyd, Ochiltree and Cathcart – and two against it – Cassillis and Eglinton. William Master of Glencairn was also there. There were 11 lairds: seven from Cunninghame – Cunninghamhead, Glengarnock, Caprington, Rowallan, Lainshaw, Giffen and Hessilhead – and four from Kyle – Craigie, Lefnorris, Carnell and Sir William Hamilton of Sanquhar who had large holdings in Ayrshire and was provost of Ayr. The Cunninghams of Cunninghamhead, Glengarnock and Caprington supported Glencairn's stance, but the Montgomeries of Lainshaw, Giffen and Hessilhead parted company in matters of religion from their chief the earl of Eglinton.

Attendance at parliament did not in itself imply total commitment to reform, any more than absence denoted hesitation or opposition – the zealous lairds of Bar, Cessnock, Kinzeancleuch and Gadgirth, for example, did not attend. Nevertheless, the presence of the Ayrshire lairds contributed to the message of support conveyed by the attendance of over 100 lairds at the parliament, in contravention of the royal Concessions which had stipulated that only those 'in use to be present' should attend: government was clearly aware of the support of the lairds for radical reform. The lairds openly defended their attendance on the grounds that the matters to be discussed were of vital importance to them, although consideration of these very (religious) matters had also been forbidden in the Concessions. The whole aspect and purpose of the parliamentary sessions were a demonstration of the confidence of the lords of the Congregation that they had sufficient support to carry their programme through.

The only Ayrshire ecclesiastical magnates present were Mr Gavin Hamilton, commendator of Kilwinning abbey, soon to transform himself into a layman but as yet hedging his bets about the extent of his support for radical reform, and Robert Cunningham, Glencairn's brother, Minister of Fail, whose lifestyle had long been secular. Abbot Quintin Kennedy of Crossraguel was absent. The names of the burgh commissioners are not given in the parliamentary record but both Irvine and Ayr were represented. Four men are mentioned in Ayr burgh accounts as having gone to the parliament, although the expense of sealing only one commission is recorded: £8 4s. was paid to bailie Paul Reid and James Bannatyne 'quhen they raid to parliament' and £20 5s. was spent by Mr Michael Wallace and bailie Charles Campbell who left Ayr on 1 August (the day of the first parliamentary session) and 'raid to Edinburgh to the parliament at the town's command', where they remained 24 days.[2] It was not unknown for different burgh commissioners to attend different sesssions of parliament. Judging by the comparative amounts of their expenditure, either Reid or Bannatyne may have attended the first session and either Wallace or Campbell the other two, staying 24 days in the capital. It may be, however, that observers were sent in addition to the burgh's official commissioners.

It was against the background of recent military operations, political change and diplomatic dialogue with the new English ally that parliament got down to the business of ratifying the official victory of the lords of the Congregation and of defining the faith of the new church. The treaty of Edinburgh was ratified, the Confession of Faith (recently compiled by the religious leaders of reform) was adopted, the papal authority in Scotland abolished and the saying of or attendance at mass made a punishable offence. We know something of what actually took place during the parliamentary sessions from the reports of the English ambassador Thomas Randolph and the correspondence of William Maitland of Lethington.[3] Business struck a personal note on 17 August when those present were asked to vote for or against the adoption of the Confession of Faith, which was read out in its entirety. Maitland of Lethington gave Cecil the impression that support for the Confession was virtually unanimous among the laity: 'It was no small wonder to see what victory the truth obtained by so uniform consent'. In fact, there are conflicting reports of the extent and nature of the opposition, with some giving as many as seven, others as few as two nobles who either abstained or voted against adoption. Clearly, these reports were meant to impress different sections of the interested public.

One source of opposition, the clergy, was anticipated. Archbishop Hamilton spoke for himself and his colleagues when he said that the Confession

> was a matter he had not been accustomed with and had had no sufficient time to examine it or confer with his friends. Howbeit he would not utterly condemn it, so was he loth to give his consent thereto.

When called upon to answer 'Yea' or 'Nay' to the adoption some, according to Randolph,

> with protestation of the conscience and faythe desyred rather presently to end ther lyves, than ever to thynke contrarie unto that thaye

allowed ther. Many also offered to sheede ther blude in defence of the same.

Commenting on the response of the clergy, Lord James Stewart, himself prior of St Andrews, said 'he must sooner believe it true as some others in cumpany did not', adding that 'he knewe Goddes trothe wolde never be without his adversaries'. The earl Marischal, champion of Wishart 15 years earlier, declared that

> thoughe he were otherwyse assured that it was trewe, yet might he be the bolder to pronunce it, that he sawe ther present the pyllars of the pope's church and not one of them wold speake agaynste it.

There was an emotional moment when the aged Lord Lindsay got to his feet to give his vote, 'as grave and goodly a man as ever I saw', commented Randolph:

> I have lived manie yeris, I am the eldest in this cumpanie of my sorte, nowe that it hath pleased God to lett me see thys daye when so manie nobles and otheris have allowed so worthie a work, I will say with Simeon, 'Nunc dimitis'.

He was followed by the old laird of Lundie who, according to Randolph, made a profession of his faith and 'confessed how long he had lived in blindness, repented therof and embraced the same as his true belief'. Many others, the ambassador reported, did likewise, including Lord Erskine, Mark Kerr, commendator of Newbattle abbey and John Winram, subprior of St Andrews, having at last removed his mask of orthodoxy.

As it turned out, there were those who were happy to give their consent to the ratification of the confessional Reformation in the charged, even euphoric atmosphere of this parliament who were more hesitant about (even hostile to) the Book of Discipline, the blueprint for the endowment of the new church in the light of its functions, which threatened to make unwelcome demands on their purses.[4] However, while allowing for the time-serving and self-seeking instincts of some who had long supported the cause of reform-from-without, instincts present in public affairs in any age, it seems fair to credit many of those present at the 1560 parliament with a sense of achievement and relief, and of hope for the future of the Christian commonwealth. The Anglo-Scottish union lobby had their own particular hopes raised, although not for long. 'I wish to God,' William Maitland wrote to Cecil before leaving on embassy to England, 'I may rather die in the voyage than that it turn not to the union of the two realmes.'[5]

As parliament rose, the thoughts of many would turn to matters much nearer home, especially as to how the newly commissioned but as yet unendowed church was to be established locally. In this the laity were to play an even larger part than previously in the church's affairs, through the kirk sessions and general assembly. However long laymen had been theoretically included in the judicial affairs of the church, in recent times their role had mainly been a passive one. However, as we saw earlier, they had long had an important influence on its staffing, maintenance and social involvement as an institution. For the protestant laity, however, emphasis on the doctrine of the priesthood of all believers gave them a *de jure* role not only in reforming but in sustaining the church in which they were active agents, a role which was both a right and a responsibility. In this sense, it has been said, 'Protestantism was not a reform; it was a revolution. Even in its mildest shape ... It was a shifting of the seat of authority'.[6]

This role was particularly evident in localities like Ayrshire where the lay leaders of society had taken the initiative in the reform movement, and was to be especially operative in those parts of Ayrshire where pressure for reform had been most vociferous. In this connection some apparent unevenness has to be set in context. Firstly, although reference has been made most frequently to Kyle, support for reform was also strong in Cunninghame, led by the earl of Glencairn and Lord Boyd and attracting the support of even some of the conservative earl of Eglinton's Montgomerie kinsmen. The difference was that Kyle was full of lairds and gentlemen who were free to act on their own initiative and to co-operate without a lead from a superior magnate, whereas in Cunninghame such men appear in the followings of the nobles and are therefore less often named individually, William Cunningham of Cunninghamhead who appears to have had some diplomatic ability being a notable exception. English agents could quote the opinions of John Lockhart of Bar directly, but Glencairn spoke to them on behalf of 'my people'. Sir James Chalmers of Gadgirth could personally accost Mary of Guise, but it was less likely that a Cunningham laird would have done so had his chief been around. These circumstances make mere head-counts of relatively minor value in the long run when trying to assess the extent of support for reform. This applies to the evaluation of lists of signatories to public statements such as the various protestant bonds. These were not plebiscites, but public statements of intent guaranteed by representative signatories.

Even within Kyle itself the gentlemen of the Irvine and Ayr valleys were most frequently in the news, and indeed religious dissent in Ayrshire had first made its appearance among them. Yet the bailiary of Kyle was a large area with a variety of social networks among protestant families, from those of the Fullartons of Fullarton and Dreghorn in the north on the edge of Cunninghame to those of the Dalrymples of Stair in the south on the Carrick border. In the bailiary of Carrick itself the reform movement lost a prominent leader with the death in 1558 of the 3rd earl of Cassillis, who was succeeded by his son the conservative 4th earl who had been brought up under the influence of his uncle Abbot Quintin Kennedy. The 3rd earl's place in the protestant ranks was taken by Thomas Kennedy of Bargany, younger, described as 'wise and courteous . . . stout and passing kind', an influential magnate who rivalled his chief in substance, who long before his succession in 1564 made his alignment clear in agreeing to the implementation of the Book of Discipline.

Another apparent imbalance has been the seemingly minor role of the Ayrshire clergy compared to the positive action of the laity in moving forward the cause of reform. However, in the absence of the appropriate records of the pre-Reformation church we shall never know how many clerics were suspected of, or even charged with, unorthodoxy. Occasional references to the activities of chaplains in dissenting households suggest the existence of a reform-minded clerical circle echoing that among the laity, especially after 1557 when the lords of the Congregation first encouraged private reformed religious observance. However, the driving force of the laity and the dearth — with the notable exception of John Willock — of indigenous clerical intellectual leadership, meant that the Reformation in Ayrshire was a supremely practical affair, symbolised in its long-established iconoclastic programme of practical change. It is significant that in the 1560s and '70s, again with the exception of Willock as superintendent of the west, the planting and supervision of the Ayrshire churches was devolved by the general assembly to native laymen and clerics from outwith the shire.

The problem of staffing the new church in the 1560s was an enormous one; the wonder is not that so few but that so many pastors were found. For even the most committed reformers, to find over 1000 men nationwide with the authority and knowledge to act as full-time ministers, to dispense the sacraments, expound the scriptures several times a week and ensure congregational discipline, would have taken a miracle. The late-medieval church at local level had been a church of working subordinates, the curates, habitually taking their orders from above while running a fairly routine essential service for the parishioners. With this kind of background, and personal reaction to protestantism aside, it was unlikely that such subordinates, or their superiors who were notoriously detached from the parishes, would throw themselves into the demanding renewal of the parish service. There must have been many who, although they accepted protestantism, felt themselves or were judged unfit for these new duties, a qualifying factor that must be taken into account when putting emphasis (positive or negative) on the likely number of 'conformists' among the clergy. The fact that so many of those who did take office did so at the lowest grade of responsibility, that of reader, reflects the fact that the old system had not turned out the kind of men at local level who could take on teaching responsibilities even although they were willing to serve. When all this has been said, however, of those in the early reformed ministry in Ayrshire's 44 parishes, at least 28 had been in orders before 1560.

The staffing of Ayrshire's churches in the 1560s suggests a determined effort to fill the charges, an intention conveyed by the nine nominations for readers and an exhorter put forward by the lairds of Kyle at the general assembly of December 1560,[7] and the willingness of four Ayrshire magnates, Glencairn, Boyd, Ochiltree and Kennedy of Bargany, younger, to subscribe the Book of Discipline a month or so later, providing that the prelates, on being allowed their revenues for life, should become responsible for the ministers' stipends in those parishes annexed to their prelacies.[8] Could this arrangement be implemented, the superiors of Paisley, Kilwinning, Fail, Melrose and Crossraguel among them could provide for 30 Ayrshire parishes.

In spite of failure to gain an immediate and nationwide provision for the new ministry, which was to survive on piecemeal allocation of the old church's revenues for much of the century, 38 out of Ayrshire's 44 parishes (counting Crosbie) are recorded as having a minister, exhorter or reader in the 1560s, at least 16 of them being first mentioned before 1567. The following survey takes the parishes in the order in which they appear in Chapter 3, beginning in the northern bailiary of Cunninghame where conforming clergy were appointed to 11 out of the bailiary's 15 parishes. The date in brackets is that of the earliest known reference to an appointment.[9]

Sir David Neill, who became exhorter at Largs (1563), had been a chaplain acting as curate at Paisley abbey's kirks of Largs and Monkton. He belonged to an Ayr burgess family, with relatives in the barony of Monkton, and practised as a notary in the Largs area both before and after the Reformation. In 1590 when he must have been quite old he was described as 'sometime reader at Largs and now indweller in Ayr'. Sir John Maxwell, probably the former curate of West Kilbride, became 'minister' there (1565) and remained until 1580. In 1567 he was designated exhorter and in 1574 reader, by which time the office of exhorter was being phased out. Alexander Henderson, one of two Kilwinning monks to take office in the new church, became exhorter at Ardrossan (1567). The appointee at Stevenston was Glencairn's chaplain and friend, sir James Walker, who became the parish's first minister (1561) and sat in the general assembly of June 1562. In neighbouring Kilwinning parish William Kirkpatrick, who had been a monk at the abbey since at least 1545 and who belonged to an Ayr burgess family, became the first minister (1563). Sir George Boyd, a chaplain and notary in the circle of Lord Boyd in the 1550s, became exhorter at Dalry (1567) and a kinsman, sir Thomas Boyd, perhaps from the local family of Boyd of Baddinhaith, became reader at Beith (1574), after spells at Riccarton and Ardrossan.

The first appointees at Kilbirnie (1567), Dunlop (1567) and Perceton (1570), Alexander Hamilton, John Hamilton and Francis Adamson, had all been students at St Andrews university in the 1550s. They are examples of the new men, university-trained and often from outside the parish, who became increasingly characteristic of the reformed ministry. James Lumsden who became the first reader at Stewarton (1567) was probably related to (perhaps the son of) the pre-Reformation curate of Stewarton, sir Alexander Lumsden. At Dreghorn the exhorter was sir Gavin Naismith (1567), a notary from Bothwell in Lanarkshire who had become a burgess of Irvine. At Kilmarnock the earliest appointee, sir John Muir (1561), was called 'minister', serving the parish for five years before the arrival of the better-known Mr Robert Wilkie. Sir Rankin Davidson, former chaplain and notary who became exhorter at Loudoun (1567), which he combined with the parish of Galston in Kyle, was recommended for service by the reforming lairds of the Irvine valley at the general assembly of December 1560. Kilmaurs was first served by sir John Howie (1567), the working vicar, a chaplain and notary who had long been closely associated with the affairs of the earls of Glencairn. He must have been old by contemporary standards when he took on his new charge, but had had long experience serving the inhabitants of Glencairn's home parish.

Over in Kyle the first charges were in the hands of conforming clergy in 13 out of the bailiary's 21 parishes. At the burgh of Irvine the working vicar and one-time Ayr chaplain sir Thomas Andrew became reader (1561). Of the seven parishes in the Stewart heartland belonging to Paisley abbey, Dundonald was served by the ex-prior of the Irvine Carmelites (whose monastery actually stood in Dundonald parish), Robert Burn, as reader (1567); the former local chaplain Adam Wallace was exhorter at the quasi-parochial chapel of Crosbie; sir John Wylie, former preceptor of the pilgrimage chapel of Our Lady of Kyle at Monkton, his home parish, and curate of Monkton in 1557, became 'minister' or reader there (1563); sir Robert Leggat, having assisted at Ayr during the transition year 1559, returned to Prestwick (where he had long been curate) as reader probably after 1560 although the first record of him as reader is in 1563; George Cochrane, former organist and master of the song school at Ayr, became reader at St Quivox (1567); sir Thomas Boyd became reader at Riccarton (1571); and David Wallace, a former chaplain, became reader at Craigie (1574). The remaining three parishes of Kylestewart, annexed to Fail, were Symington where Thomas Carrington became reader, Barnweil where sir John Miller, former chaplain and vicar of Symington, became exhorter, and Galston which was served by Rankin Davidson jointly with Loudoun in Cunninghame; they are probably the 'ministers' who are said to have been paid in all three parishes from 1561. Ayr as we have seen was served by a protestant pastor from 1559, first by Mr Christopher Goodman, assisted by the schoolmaster John Orr. They were followed by Robert Acheson (1559) and James Dalrymple (1568), a former chorister in the burgh kirk who was one of those recommended to the general assembly in 1560.

Besides Ayr itself there were nine parishes in southern or King' Kyle. Of those on the Carrick border, Alloway, Coylton, Dalmellington and Dalrymple, James Ramsay, probably the former curate, became reader at

Alloway (1567), James Davidson, called at different times minister, exhorter and reader, was appointed to Coylton (1569), Leonard Clerk became 'minister' at Dalmellington (1559) and George Feane became reader at Dalrymple (1570). The two Kyle parishes that supported canonries in Glasgow cathedral, Tarbolton and Cumnock, got pastors who had connections with reforming lairds. Sir David Curll, who became reader at Tarbolton (? 1564), was chaplain of the chapel of St Katherine at Kilbarchan in Renfrewshire, in the patronage of Chalmers of Gadgirth to whose son he granted a charter of the chapel lands in 1564, dated at Tarbolton where he may by then have been reader. In his earlier years Curll was a witness to the transactions of Cunningham of Caprington and the earls of Glencairn and was probably an Ayrshireman although holding a Renfrewshire chaplainry, not an unusual circumstance. Adam Landells, who had charge as exhorter of Cummock (1567) with Ochiltree and Auchinleck, was another of those recommended to the general assembly by the Kyle lairds in 1560. Born in Ochiltree in 1507, he had long been associated as a chaplain and notary with the transactions of Lord Ochiltree himself, and Glencairn and his kinsmen. Robert Hamilton, who can probably be identified as another St Andrews student of the 1550s, became minister of Ochiltree (1562) in conjunction with the huge parish of Mauchline (1562).

Of the eight extensive parishes of Carrick, Kennedy of Bargany's home parish of Dailly was served by John Cunningham (before 1567) who later moved to Ballantrae (1571); Leonard Clerk, already mentioned, after a spell at Dalmellington became reader at Kirkmichael (1567); John McQuhorne became exhorter (1568) and later minister at Straiton; Hugh Kennedy became reader at Kirkoswald (c. 1572); Mr James Greg, possibly vicar of Dunsyre in Lanarkshire, became minister at Colmonell (1568); Alexander Davidson, possibly a Davidson of Greenan, became reader at Maybole and its associated chapel of Kirkbride a little later (1571) and Mr James Young became reader at Girvan (1574).

Numbers and dates alone do not complete the picture of Ayrshire's early reformed ministry. Local evidence can record an appointment earlier than its appearance on an official list, and this filling-out of the picture will go on as records continue to be searched. The earliest local practice in some areas was probably derived from that of the privy and household kirks of the late 1550s which relied on locally available ability to read the common prayers and scriptures, expound the latter and from time to time dispense the reformed sacraments. It was probably familiarity with this kind of ministry that caused the earliest protestant appointees to be called 'minister' in a general sense, even although the same individuals were designated exhorter or reader in official lists when these were later compiled. In this way we have references to sir John Maxwell, minister at West Kilbride, sir John Muir, minister at Kilmarnock, Rankin Davidson, former chaplain and minister at Galston, sir John Wylie, former preceptor of the chapel of Our Lady of Kyle and minister at Monkton, and Leonard Clerk, minister at Dalmellington. As we saw, even the Ayr schoolmaster John Orr, as the minister's assistant, was expected to dispense the sacraments in his absence. We will close our minds to the evolutionary nature of early Scottish protestantism if we rely entirely on the chronology and terminology of official lists or dismiss these earlier designations and practices as merely a preliminary to the period when firm guidelines were set from above by the general assembly or government. Certainly the assembly was to take a firm line with 'unqualified' and 'unfit' local appointees, but that is not to say that initially reforming lairds and burgesses and other parishioners were unable to find the ministry they wanted. John Lind, minister at Irvine, whom the assembly pronounced unfit in 1565 appears reinstated in 1573.[10]

Local documentary references sometimes illuminate this early stage. The earliest official reference to a protestant cleric at Dalmellington is that to John McConnel as reader in 1571, but Leonard Clerk is called minister on 19 November 1559 when in Ayr burgh court he accepted for safekeeping a sum of money bequeathed by James Steel in Ochiltree to his son John. Leonard's kinsman (probably brother), Robert Clerk burgess of Ayr, stood surety that the money would eventually be handed over to the young man. The oversman of Steel's testament who put the money in the minister's hands was the Ochiltree notary Adam Landells who was himself soon to be recommended for service in the new church. Landells and Clerk would be personally acquainted within the early-protestant community of Kyle on the eve of the Reformation settlement. The earliest official reference to Landells as exhorter in neighbouring Cumnock and Auchinleck parishes is in the 1567 Register of Ministers but the fact of his long association with the reforming lairds of Kyle makes it likely that he began his service before then.

The question of financial support in the 1560s, even after the arrangement of the Thirds of Benefices came into operation, must often have fallen on leading parishioners, many of whom were as it happened tacksmen of teinds.[11] At the general assembly of 1565 the lairds of Carnell, Sornbeg and Dreghorn from Kylestewart petitioned 'for support of a ministrie for their kirkis of Riccarton and Dundonald', promising to contribute whatever was laid down by the assembly and to ensure that the incumbents did not desert their charges for want of financial support.[12] While we could say that by asking the assembly to set the amount of stipend the lairds ensured that they would not have to pay more than was judged necessary, at the same time their willingness to carry on supporting the ministry indicates a concern for the parish service.

An early expedient in providing cover for the parishes was to put one capable man in charge of more than one kirk, an arrangement which foreshadowed the grouping of parishes under one minister, assisted by readers, introduced by the earl of Morton's administration in the mid-1570s. John Cunningham, for example, who was appointed minister at Dailly before 1567, was appointed that same year to baptise and marry in Kirkmichael parish. Rankin Davidson was exhorter at Loudoun and Galston by 1567, and Adam Landells exhorter at Cumnock, Ochiltree and Auchinleck by 1567, at Ochiltree as assistant to the minister. Gavin Naismith, exhorter at Dreghorn (1567), had charge also of Kilmaurs.

At the same time there would appear to have been sufficient numbers, even in the 1560s, to provide two appointees in some parishes.[13] At Irvine the vicar Thomas Andrew was reader from at least 1561 to 1586, acting as assistant to a succession of ministers. As exhorter at Galston, Rankin Davidson assisted the minister John Barron; Davidson himself was called 'minister' at the time of Barron's arrival. Glencairn's home parish of Kilmaurs was particularly well served in the later 1560s. The elderly former parish priest sir John Howie maintained the reader's service until 1571, assisting in turn the minister, Mr Archibald Crawford (1567–69), and the exhorter Gavin Naismith, (1568–71) who also had charge of Dreghorn. Howie, who was already in the parish, probably began his service at the Reformation. Even Kirkmichael in the more religiously conservative Carrick had both an exhorter and a reader by 1567. The exhorter, John Cunningham, who also had charge of Dailly, was admitted to baptise and marry in Kirkmichael parish that year, as already mentioned. The reader Leonard Clerk, who already had between seven and eight years' experience in the reformed kirk, had moved south from Dalmellington

The centrality of preaching in the reformed church, aimed at both conversions and a deeper understanding of the faith, is reflected in the appointment of exhorters who in default of a full-time minister were charged with preaching to the congregation, catechising and in some cases teaching the children of the parish. Taking early designations at face value, there were exhorters in 10 and ministers in 18 Ayrshire parishes by 1569, which meant that in these 28 parishes preaching might be heard fairly frequently; five of them were in Carrick, 11 in Kyle and 12 in Cunninghame. Although the ability of some men initially called ministers was later reviewed by the higher church authorities, there were some promotions over the years. John Hamilton was called successively exhorter, then (when that office was phased out) reader and finally minister at Dunlop where he served till 1608; James Davidson was reader, then exhorter at Coylton, and finally minister at Dalmellington; John McQuhorne was exhorter and then minister at Straiton; and Gavin Naismith was exhorter and then minister of the linked charges of Dreghorn and Kilmaurs.

Those who were found able to be ministers soon after 1560 came from a variety of backgrounds which in themselves illustrate those influences that culminated in their acceptance of protestantism. James Walker, usually called 'sir' but occasionally 'Mr', who became minister at Stevenston (1561) was as we saw earlier a cleric in the circle of the earls of Glencairn. William

The people's church: Symington parish church. Dating from the twelfth century, this is the oldest Ayrshire parish church still in use. The Norman work was revealed during restoration early this century.

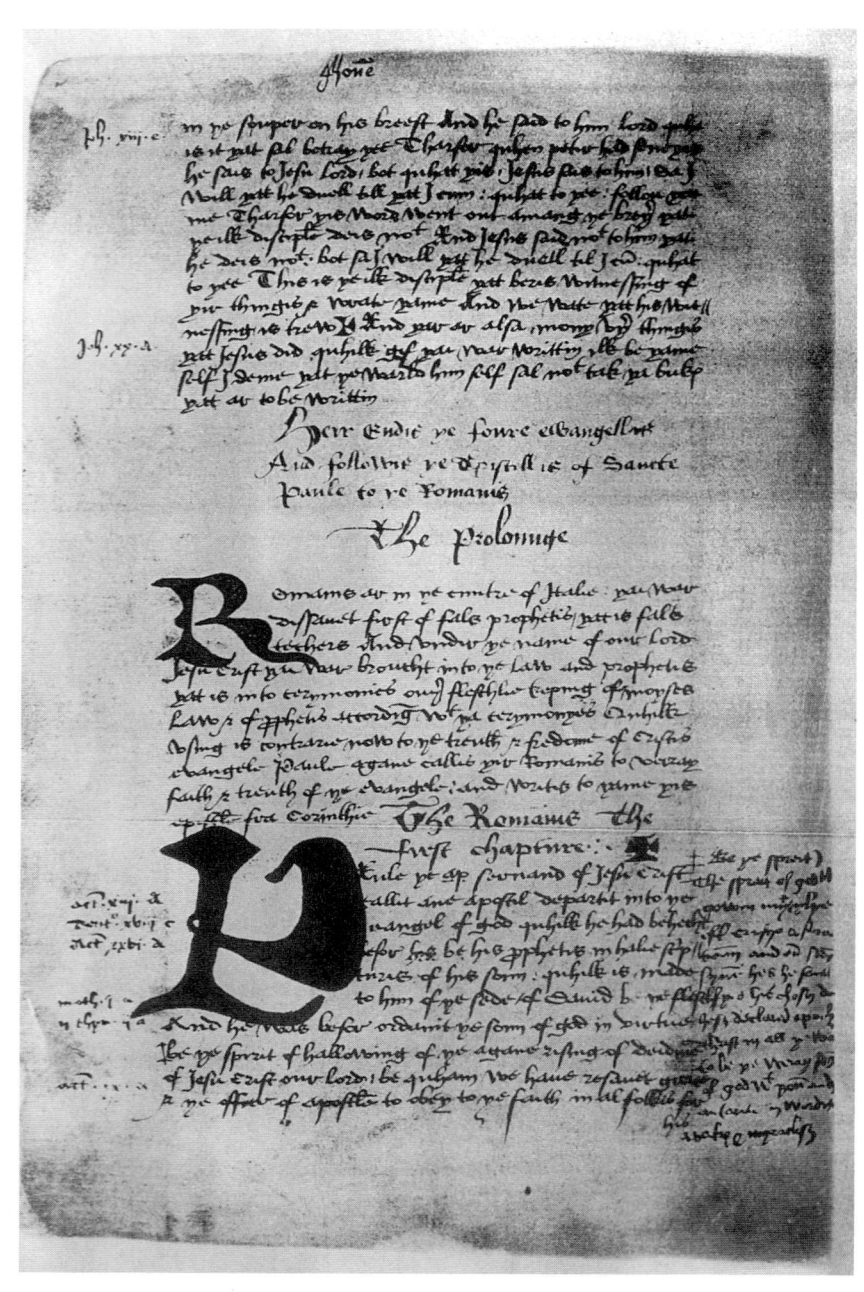

Scottish Lollardy: a page from Murdoch's Nisbet's Scots version, c.1520s, of an English translation of the New Testament which is itself based on that of John Wycliffe. *(Courtesy of the Scottish Text Society.)*

'A receptacle of God's servants': the Tower of Bar, Galston, home of the radical reformer, John Lockhart, where he gave hospitality to both George Wishart (1545) and John Knox (1556). *(Courtesy of the Carnegie Library, Ayr, and the Royal Commission on the Ancient and Historical Monuments of Scotland.)*

Lay leadership: Dean Castle, Kilmarnock, home of Robert 5th Lord Boyd who, with Alexander, Earl of Glencairn, led the Congregation of Cunninghame. (As engraved for Francis Grose, *Antiquities of Scotland, 1789-91*.)

Transformation: the Abbey Green, Kilwinning. Alexander Wreitton (1578-1605), second minister of Kilwinning, lived in the house in the centre of this view (gable to the camera), which survived until the late 1940s. An inscription above the door read: *Sine te domine cuncta nil - God is the builder Prasit be He*. Some idea of the extent of the former abbey church may be judged by the position of the tower (an early nineteenth century replacement for one of the twin western towers) and the surviving gable of the south transept on the right. (*Courtesy of the Royal Commission on the Ancient and Historical Monuments of Scotland.*)

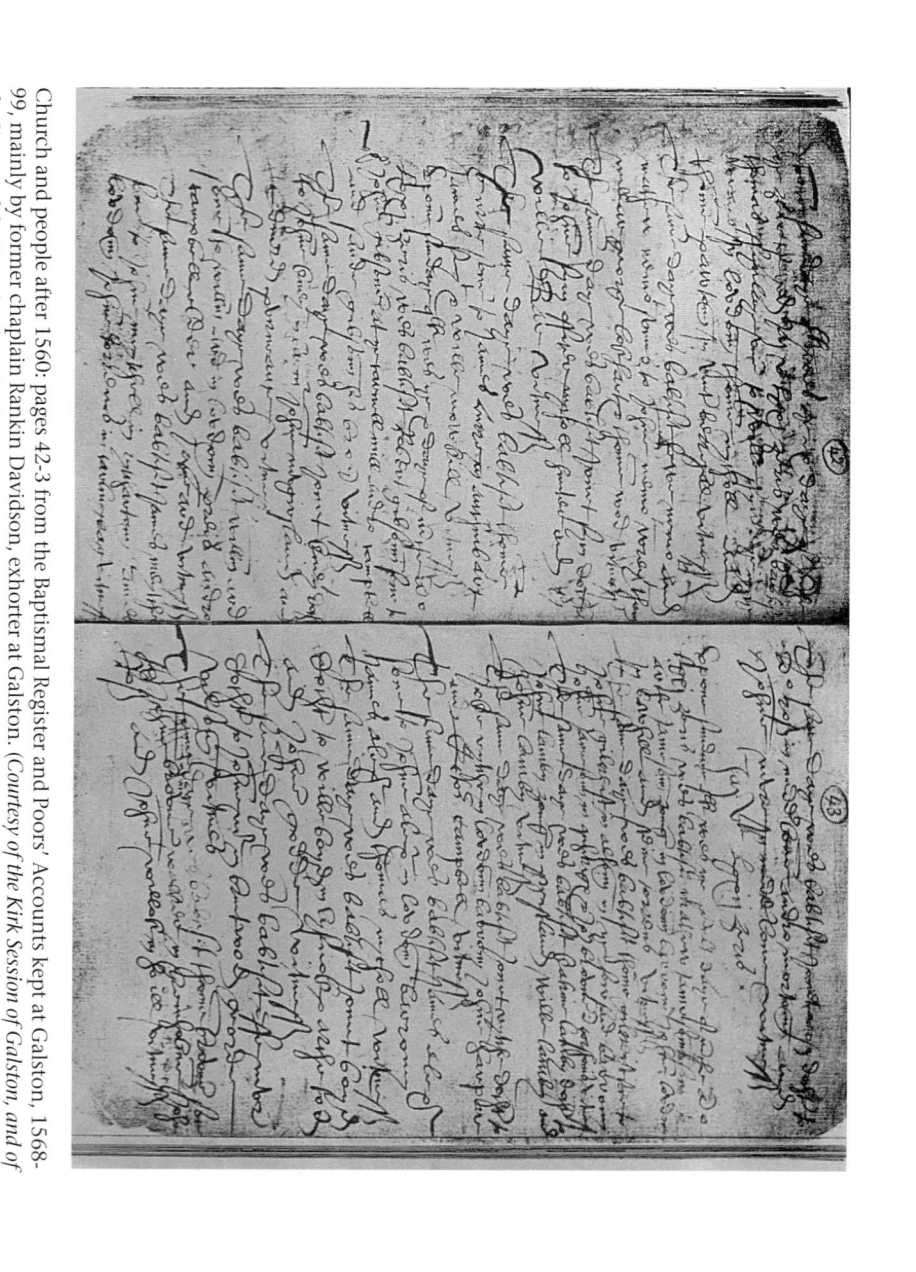

Church and people after 1560: pages 42-3 from the Baptismal Register and Poors' Accounts kept at Galston, 1568-99, mainly by former chaplain Rankin Davidson, exhorter at Galston. (*Courtesy of the Kirk Session of Galston, and of the Keeper of the Records of Scotland.*)

The new era: Monkredding House, built 1602-38. It was probably begun by Andrew Niven, son of Thomas Niven, a tenant of Kilwinning abbey who between 1539 and 1545 feued Monkredding and neighbouring lands. Thomas was killed at Pinkie (1547). Andrew supported the Congregation and subscribed the Band of Ayr as a young man in 1562. (*Courtesy of the Royal Commission on the Ancient and Historical Monuments of Scotland.*)

The old order: the cloister at Crossraguel Abbey, near Kirkoswald, whose last abbot, Quintin Kennedy, was the sole public apologist for the Roman Catholic faith in Ayrshire. A handful of surviving monks practised the Catholic rites at marriages and baptisms for local people until the end of the century. (*Courtesy of Historic Scotland.*)

Kirkpatrick, ex-monk of Kilwinning abbey who became minister there (1563), belonged to a strongly protestant merchant and shipowning family in Ayr with links to the Kirkpatricks of Closeburn in Dumfriesshire. The academic and European connections of Mr Christopher Goodman who was invited to become first minister at Ayr are well known and are eloquent of the burgh's links with leading reformers through the protestant gentry of the Kyle hinterland. Mr Robert Hamilton, minister at Ochiltree and Mauchline (1562), was a recent graduate of St Andrews. John Muir at Kilmarnock (1561) had had earlier associations as a chaplain and notary with Lord Boyd. John Cunningham, minister at Dailly 'for divers yeris' before 1567, is more obscure but his surname suggests a connection with the widespread kindred of Glencairn. Mr James Greg, minister at Colmonell (1568), is believed to have been vicar of Dunsyre in Lanarkshire at the Reformation. The antecedents of John Lind, the minister at Irvine who was suspended in 1565, are not known but his surname is found in Irvine itself and in the neighbouring parish of Dreghorn where Laurence Lyn (or Lind) was reader in 1574.

Any attempt to make provision for the new ministry from the revenues of the old church was bound to cut across many vested interests: those of the government which for almost a century had regarded tapping into the church's wealth as a legitimate means of supplementing crown revenue; lay tacksmen who had long counted on the teinds as part of their annual income; and the existing benefice-holders, legatees of a system whose material resources had come to be regarded not as fuel for spiritual energy but as real property. The new church inherited the effects of the deficit of its predecessor, the result of allowing the parochial resources to seep away into secular pockets. It is to their credit that so many ministers, exhorters and readers were sufficiently committed to carry on in circumstances of hardship a service which their well-endowed predecessors the beneficed clergy had so largely neglected. It is also understandable that some gave up the struggle.

The Book of Discipline, while putting forward a moral argument for the ministers' rights to the teinds, made no practical suggestions as to how this might be accomplished. Even had it been possible to overcome clerical and secular opposition, it is doubtful whether the contemporary administration would have been capable of the enormous task of transferring the revenue from the old to the new regime. At the end of 1561 the arrangement of the Thirds of Benefices was devised by which the existing benefice-holders kept two-thirds of their revenues for life and paid the remaining third as a tax which was divided between the crown and the ministry. It was a compromise arrangement, loaded in favour of the crown and the survivors of the old establishment, symptomatic of the compromising nature of secular and ecclesiastical policy during Queen Mary's personal reign. It put the business of administration in the hands of crown officials, not the church, and it gave religious conservatives a glimmer of hope in that it left the old ecclesiastical structure intact in the property-holding form in which they recognised it. The Thirds were difficult to administer, the authority of its officials difficult to enforce, the procedures subject to repeated reorganisation over the first decade. The inroads of the crown into the kirk's share of the Thirds provoked complaints on behalf of the tardily-paid ministers. John Knox remarked that 'the gaird and the effaris of the [royal] kytcheing wer so gryping that the ministeris stipendis could nocht be payit', and Queen Mary's extravagant and injudicious use of the funds to make gifts, pay pensions and subsidise the expenses of the royal household is well documented.[14] At the same time many benefice-holders and tacksmen – some of them from Ayrshire – were at the horn for non-payment of their Thirds for years.

Due to the defective nature of the accounts of the Collector of the Thirds there is little information for Ayrshire before 1568. To begin with certain benefice-holders were 'allowed' their Third, that is given a tax rebate; they included sir Thomas Andrew the vicar and reader of Irvine, sir John Howie the vicar and reader of Kilmaurs and sir James Walker the vicar and minister of Stevenston. In the first accounting year, beginning November 1561, £130 was paid from the Third of Fail for stipends to the ministers of the monastery's appropriated parishes of Barnweil, Symington and Galston. For the year 1562 the total amount paid towards Ayrshire stipends was said to be £1493 17s 9$^{1}/_{2}$d.[15]

Certain attempts to improve the ministers' situation proposed in 1567, when the anomaly of a Catholic sovereign involved in provision for the reformed church was removed, failed to take effect, but reorganisation by the regent Morton after the end of the civil war brought improvement. There was a price to pay, however, in the opening up of the argument about the very nature of the ministry, between those who adhered to the ideal of 1560 of a minister to every parish, and those who accepted the pragmatic solution of Morton's administration to the problem not only of the shortage of ministers but of the funds with which to pay them.[16] The solution was to put a fully qualified minister in a position of supervision over several parishes, with a reader in each parish under his charge. Although something like this arrangement had existed in some areas in the early days of the reformed church in Ayrshire, there seems to have been some opposition there to the policy when introduced by the regent in the early 1570s. At least, some of the ministers most opposed to it, such as John Knox and John Davidson, had close links with Ayrshire. Indeed, when Davidson fell foul of the administration for writing a pamphlet against the measure he fled to Kyle to the lairds of Carnell and Kinzencleuch. Davidson's argument was that to be a true minister a man must both preach to and visit his flock, knowing each member of his congregation personally for the purposes of both encouragement and discipline. To turn up occasionally and preach a sermon to people whom he did not know intimately was no better, he argued, than the old impersonal performance, 'evin as the Preistis thair Matynis said'.

Whatever the opposition in Ayrshire may have amounted to, Cunninghame, Kyle and Carrick were subject to Morton's programme as elsewhere. The sheriffdom was divided into 16 groups of four parishes with a minister in charge of each group. By 1576 there were 58 clergy for the 44 Ayrshire parishes 16 ministers assisted by 42 readers. Some of the ministers had been promoted from reader since 1567. Stipends on the whole had increased. By 1576 these came from a variety of sources, but very largely from allocations from the Thirds, including those of the abbeys to which so many Ayrshire parishes were annexed. There had been an attempt to apply the principle that ministers and readers should be paid from the 'first and readiest duties of the kirkis and parishes where they serve'. Twenty-four of the 58 clergy in 1576 were paid from the Third of the parish they served. Twelve others (four ministers and eight readers) had by the early 1570s come into possession of the actual parochial benefice itself as had been advocated in December 1566. Also in the early 1570s there were 42 allocations to serving Ayrshire clergy directly from the Thirds of the abbacies of Kilwinning, Paisley, Melrose, Fail, North Berwick nunnery and the priory of Whithorn. One or two ministers and readers had possession of chaplainries (which by now simply represented income) on the good offices of local patrons.

When we compare the position of the serving parish clergy in Ayrshire in 1576 with that of their predecessors just prior to the Reformation, it appears that on the whole and in spite of piecemeal provision they were better provided for and the parishes better served. The man actually responsible for the 'cure' preached regularly in his 'home' parish church and periodically in the others under his charge, unlike the former absentee benefice-holder. He was paid a much higher stipend than his pre-Reformation counterpart, the curate. Even many of the post-Reformation deputies, as we might call the readers to continue the analogy, were also better paid than the curates had been.[17] Their recommended minimum stipend was £6 6s 8d more than that of a curate (though not all received as much), and since theirs was not a full-time service they might add to their income by working as notaries, teachers and clerks. Many readers as well as ministers came into possession of the parochial benefices as time went on, an addition to income that had eluded most curates.

By the time the second generation of protestant clergy was serving the Ayrshire parishes in the last decades of the century things appear to have been more difficult. While the total number of ministers had risen, the total number of clergy had dropped. In 1590 there were 39 clergy compared with 58 in 1576, but the number of ministers had risen from 16 to 23. By then one of the difficulties of staffing may have been that people's expectations had risen. While in the early years the church may have welcomed willing if only moderately-qualified volunteers, as time went on the desired standard rose, demanding a fully trained and fully qualified ministry, which took longer to find. The aim was an educated workforce, trained in theology and carefully examined before appointment, a situation which was worlds away from the intellectual and training standards of the pre-Reformation working parish clergy and which, with all its deficiences, might have been envied by the reformist orthodox clergy who were concerned about parochial clerical standards in the 1550s.

Ministers' stipends, however, continued to rise. In 1591 a real step forward was taken in this respect in the bailiary of Cunninghame when 11 benefices (parsonages and vicarages) were disjoined from the abbacy of Kilwinning. With one exception these benefices were granted to the serving clergy of the parishes concerned, and so after hundreds of years' deprivation the revenues returned to the parishes for which they had originally been intended. Since the ministers of the remaining Cunninghame kirks already enjoyed the parochial benefices associated with their charges, the ministry of the northernmost bailiary was at last suitably provided for. In 1601 there was a minister in every Cunninghame parish.

The prosperity of the ministers of Kyle was more varied. Some of them still had the problem of collecting their stipends from different sources. All but one of the remaining groupings of Ayrshire parishes at the end of the century were in Kyle. The scale of stipends in the bailiary ranged from the £22 with victual of the minister of the united parishes of Craigie-Riccarton, to the comfortable £200 enjoyed by Mr Peter Primrose at Mauchline, albeit the largest parish in Ayrshire. In Carrick the position was even less satisfactory at the end of the century, although with the exception of Maybole and its dependent kirk of Kirkbride, groupings had ceased. Mr James Inglis at Dailly survived on an allowance of 14 bolls of meal, or their money equivalent. Mr Patrick Anderson at Kirkoswald whose income amounted to 19 bolls of meal and £13 6s 8d eventually left his charge for Ireland, 'for lack of stipend'.[18]

Yet, in spite of difficulties and imperfections there had been a radical change in the social commitment of the kirk since 1560, in that the imbalance of wealth at the top and responsibility at the bottom had been readjusted. The top-ranking office-bearers of the church, whatever designations they went under, were working clergy, able to preach and charged with active oversight and discipline of their colleagues. The laity sat in the church courts, an important amplification of lay participation in the people's church.

The goal of all effort, difficult though it was to achieve, was unalterably the provision of a qualified, resident and adequately endowed parish ministry. The difficulties had been perceived from the beginning. As the authors of the Book of Discipline put it:

> We are not ignorant that the rarity of godly and learned men shall seem to some a just reason why that so strait and sharp examination should not be taken universally [i.e. before ministers were admitted] ... The chiefest remedy left to your Honours and to us, in all this rarity of true ministers, is fervent prayer unto God that it will please his mercy to thrust out faithful workmen into this his harvest; and next, that your Honours, with consent of the Kirk, are bound by your authority to compel such men as have gifts and graces able to edify the Kirk of God that they bestow them where greatest necessity shall be known ...[19]

It was the eternal conflict between principle and expedient. Preachers and politicians rarely agreed on these matters and a clash was bound to come.

CHAPTER NINE

The People's Church After 1560

As the new religious establishment expanded, the fabric of the old gradually disappeared as the pre-Reformation clergy died off and their benefices passed to the reformed ministry. Attachment to the old faith itself, in so far as this can be detected in surviving records, was also dying out by the late 1570s for want of officiating priests, although in the later 1580s and 1590s there are signs that in parts of Ayrshire and in Dumfriesshire, as elsewhere in Scotland, residual recusancy gained some confidence from the presence of Jesuit activists and other priests from overseas.[1]

Archbishop James Beaton of Glasgow sailed for France with the departing French army in the autumn of 1560, leaving the clergy of his archdiocese to their own devices in facing the landslide. To a great extent his place was taken by Archbishop John Hamilton of St Andrews, whose family's territorial hegemony and his own ecclesiastical base at Paisley abbey gave him natural headquarters in the south-west. He could report to the pope in the 1550s that the archdiocese of Glasgow was riddled with heresy. His sole determined supporter in Ayrshire – where most of the beneficed clergy seem to have kept their heads down – was Abbot Quintin Kennedy of Crossraguel who was in turn backed by the monks of his abbey, a handful of minor clerics in his patronage and his conservative Kennedy kinsmen led by his nephew the 4th earl of Cassillis.

The first general assembly, which met at about the same time as a convocation of hopeful catholic magnates met at Dunbar, called for a crackdown on the persistent saying of the proscribed mass. Among those places named as trouble spots were Eglinton castle in Cunninghame where the earl's chaplains officiated for his household; Cambuskeith near Kilmarnock, also in Cunninghame, home of William Hamilton of Cambuskeith, a member of Chatelherault's religiously divided clan, who was then a young man under age; and a group of parish kirks in Carrick where it was claimed that mass was still said openly for the parishioners under the protection of Cassillis and the abbot of Crossraguel – Maybole, Kirkoswald, Girvan and Dailly, and Kirkmichael which was appropriated to the priory at Whithorn of which the catholic Malcolm Fleming was prior.[2] To fill this vacuum Mr George Hay was commissioned by the assembly in 1562 to visit these 'unplanted' kirks, where for a month he 'preached with great fruit'. Nevertheless, the Kennedy country remained a flashpoint in efforts to maintain uniformity and it was not until 1566 when Cassillis married a sister of Lord Glamis that according to Knox he made a show of 'reforming his kirks'.[3]

The People's Church After 1560

The rising of the Gordons in the autumn of 1562, which took the queen to the north-east, created an uneasy feeling among those on the lookout for signs of papistry. Apprehension may have increased in the south-west when about the same time 'the Bishop of St Andrews and Abbot of Crossraguel kept secret convention ... in Paisley, to whom resorted divers papists ...'[4] Knox who reported this visited Ayrshire himself about the time George Hay was preaching in Carrick, taking the opportunity to alert the nobles and gentlemen of Ayrshire to the possibility of a papist plot, and exhorting them 'to put themselves in such order that they might be able to serve the authority, and yet not to suffer the enemies of God's truth to have the upper hand'.

It was during this spell in Ayrshire that Knox had his celebrated four days' disputation in Maybole with Abbot Quintin Kennedy on the doctrine of the mass.[5] That autumn there met in Ayr (whose town council sent wine to the disputants at Maybole) a large gathering of the nobles, barons and gentlemen of Cunninghame, Kyle and Carrick. On 4 September, 'after exhortationis made and conference had', 77 of them subscribed a bond pledging themselves to

> maintain and assist the preaching of [Christ's] holy Evangel, now of his mercy offered unto this Realm; and also ... maintain the ministers of the same, against all persons, power, and authority that will oppose themselves to the doctrine proponed, and by us received.

They promised assistance to 'the whole body of Protestants within this Realme, in all lawful and just actions against all persons'.[6]

Besides the veterans who had subscribed the public bonds of the 1557-60 crisis, Glencairn, Boyd and Ochiltree, the Ayr bond was subscribed by many of those lairds and gentlemen of the Ayrshire Congregation who had acted with them in those years, including Gadgirth, Carnell, Hessilhead, Dreghorn, Bar, Caprington, Stair, Craigie, Campbell of Loudoun, Cunninghamehead, Leffnoris and Kinzeancleuch, and some who put their names to such a public declaration for the first time, such as Fergushill of that Ilk, a neighbour of the recusant earl of Eglinton, Kerr of Kersland, Hunter of Hunterston, Dunbar of Blantyre and Reid of Barskimming, with a clutch of gentlemen from the Carrick-Kyle border and even four Kennedy lairds from Cassillis' home country. The signatories who were headed by Mr Michael Wallace, provost of Ayr, also included four Ayr burgesses, and new men like Andrew Niven of Monkredding, son of a tenant-turned-feuar of Kilwinning abbey and now a prosperous bonnet laird, as the new men were called. In geographical and social terms the gathering was extraordinarily wide. Taking Knox's warning to heart, they prepared to confront what might prove to be a backlash from the old establishment, of the kind almost to be expected in the wake of a revolution.

An attempt by the archbishop to set the Crawfords and Reids against one another and so split protestant solidarity in Kyle was foiled 'by the labours of some indifferent [i.e. neutral] men who favoured peace'.[7] The backlash when it came took the form of a public celebration of mass at Easter 1563.[8] Although not negligible, the demonstration was limited geographically to those areas under the direct influence of those who appear to have orchestrated it: the archbishop, the abbot of Crossraguel and the prior of Whithorn. Even in Kennedy territory it was felt necessary to give the ceremony armed protection, and the effect lasted little beyond the event itself, in Ayrshire at least. The effort resulted in the trial of the archbishop and 47 others in May 1563, when the jury of 15 included some of those Ayrshire lairds who had subscribed the bond of Ayr 18 months earlier.

When the Queen tried to enlist the help of Knox in persuading the gentlemen of the west not to punish the accused 'for using themselves in their religion as pleased them', Knox reminded her that it was necessary to punish according to the law. His gloss on the outcome of the trial was that the culprits were jailed (fairly lightly as it happened) in order to mollify the protestants into not pressing the Queen with religious questions at the imminent parliament. Most of the clergy who took part in the Easter demonstration were formerly associated with the cathedral and other churches in Glasgow and with Paisley abbey and some of its dependant churches in Renfrewshire. Mass had been celebrated by these priests in the parish churches of Sanquhar, Neilston, Rutherglen and Cathcart, and in certain unconsecrated locations such as the houses of two Glasgow burgesses and that of Robert McNair in Provan, as well as in the archbishop's lodging at Paisley abbey.

In Ayrshire the demonstration was arranged to take place in the collegiate church of Maybole and in the parish church of Kirkoswald near Crossraguel. The clergy involved were three monks of that abbey, Gilbert Kennedy, Michael Dewar and Adam Maxwell; a chaplain sir William Allanson and sir Thomas Montgomery, vicar of Kirkmichael (a parish annexed to Whithorn priory), who, along with sir William Telfer, vicar of Cruggleton, assisted the prior of Whithorn to say mass; sir John Dunlop, vicar of Dalmellington (where the parishioners were at that time refusing to pay his teinds), sir Thomas Muir and sir James Kennedy, all of whom assisted at mass at Maybole or Kirkoswald. David Kennedy, brother of Kennedy of Brunstane, and Hugh Kennedy of Blairquhennachy had collected the armed guard of some 200 persons who protected the proceedings at Maybole and Kirkoswald between 8 and 11 April. Other laymen accused of assisting were George Kennedy of Barskeoch and William Hamilton, tutor of Cambuskeith.

Between 31 July and 9 August 1563 reformed and recusant gentry alike welcomed Queen Mary on her progress down the Ayrshire coast, some of them no doubt with reservations about her hospitality in catholic households where mass would be said for her convenience, others avoiding as best they could their 'unfriends' with whom they were at feud or embroiled in legal disputes.[9] On the surface, however, in the royal presence there was a kind of sociable truce which even stretched to a gathering at Dunure castle which included members of the recusant Cassillis kindred and the staunchly protestant Wallaces of Carnell. This was a minor historic occasion when the queen in her role of Prince and Steward of Scotland personally received the resignation of land in Kylestewart, by two Kennedy heiresses, and granted it to the son of the laird of Carnell. The sight of the queen and her retinue that autumn must have lived long in the folk memory of the inhabitants of Ayrshire's coastal parishes. Her first hosts were catholics, the aged Lord Semple who entertained her at the castle of Southannan near Largs, after she had crossed the Firth of Clyde from Dunoon, and the earl of Eglinton at his castle near Irvine. There are no extant relevant records for Ayr, where the queen arrived in the evening of 2 August, but she may have been the guest of the sheriff, Sir Matthew Campbell of Loudoun, at his town house. She spent two days with Cassillis at Dunure, thence on to the next Kennedy stronghold of Ardmillan, and then to Ardstinchar where she stayed with the protestant Thomas Kennedy, younger of Bargany, and his father the laird before riding down Glenapp out of Ayrshire into Galloway.

Two years later Glencairn, Boyd and Ochiltree, with the lairds of Cunninghamhead, Bar, Carnell, Dreghorn and Kersland, joined the earl of Moray in the abortive rising against Mary's marriage to Darnley known as the Chase-about-Raid. If, as Moray protested, their action was in defence of the 'true religion', the presence of these seasoned Ayrshire campaigners for reform is to be expected. But many Ayrshire people had cause to resent the Hamiltons (who naturally opposed the marriage) and the Ayrshire contingent, although numbering about 1000 men, was more modest than the turn-out of the Congregation in 1559–60.

The alignments of the civil war, as we know crossed religious barriers.[10] No fewer than 114 Ayrshire names, it has been calculated, including those of many protestant lairds, can be listed among the queen's supporters, many of whom were forfeited or escheated, or pardoned, for fighting for her at Langside or identifying with her party thereafter. It does not qualify their lifelong adherence to the protestant faith that men like Lord Boyd, Thomas Kennedy of Bargany and Sir Matthew Campbell of Loudoun stood by the queen and were in favour of her restoration in some form. The regard of many in Ayrshire for constituted authority, although in Mary's case this meant some compromise of the reformed kirk's ideal of uniformity, must partly account for their loyalty to her in peace and war. It may be that there were in Ayrshire, as has been suggested, some moderate reformers – not so much moderate in their beliefs as amenable in trying to find a peaceable means of co-existence with (in their terms) a less than perfect government. That there were shades of opinion in this respect is suggested by the taunt of the radical Robert Campbell of Kinzeancleuch, the personal friend of Knox, offered to his countryman Lord Ochiltree when they met at court soon after the queen's homecoming:

> My Lord, now ye are come and almost the last of the rest; and I perceive by your anger, that the fire-edge is not off you yet, but I fear, that after that the holy water of the court be sprinkled upon you, that ye shall become temperate as the rest. For I have been here now five days, and at the first I heard every man say, 'Let us hang the priest'; but after that they had been twice or thrice in the Abbey, all that fervency was past. I think there be some enchantment whereby men are bewitched.[11]

Nevertheless, the tone of the 1562 band of Ayr indicates that in strictly religious matters the subscribers were determined to eradicate all signs of the old faith and maintain the authority of the new kirk locally through its ministers.

The revolution of 1567 began a period of consolidation in the position of the reformed church and consequently of increased pressure on those who still declined to conform to it. Attempts were made to translate the authority of the church into practical terms. The holding of public office was to be confined to those whose orthodoxy was assured, a rule which was to apply not only to officers of the crown and burgh officials but to members of the legal profession, to university staffs and other teachers, and to notaries, many of whom had been in holy orders before 1560. It was evident that church and government were working together in a way that had not previously been possible, with some instances of the death penalty being meted out for the saying of mass.

The most decisive step taken by government in the 1570s to reduce the amount of recusancy and at the same time obtain the benefices of nonconforming clergy for the ministry was the act of 1573 which required all benefice-holders to subscribe to the Confession of Faith. The religious policy of the regencies appears on the whole to have increased the pressure of the penal laws. By the late 1570s what remained of the organism of the old church was losing cohesion as a religious force, and it is doubtful whether indigenous catholicism would have revived but for the reinforcement provided by the Jesuits and other missionary priests. As an organised force, at no time was it in a position to mount a sustained attack on the new regime.

There are scattered instances of adherence to the old faith in Ayrshire in these decades. Catholic practice continued to be fostered in the earl of Eglinton's household where his chaplains also performed the occasional marriage ceremony according to the old rite, about which the general assembly heard complaints in March 1572.[12] The offenders were said to be a Mr Robert Cunningham, sir John Mure 'living at Kilmarnock' who was still described as 'a papist and perverter of the truth' in March 1588, John Mason in Eglinton and sir Jasper Montgomerie there, a former legal guardian of the earl, a priest who was among those accused of killing a servant of the vicar of Ardrossan in 1568.

The popish scares of the late 1580s resulted in a detailed report to the general assembly in March 1588 in which some Ayrshire troublemakers were named;[13] others, like the heretics of Catholic times, may simply have evaded detection. Those named included John Lockhart burgess of Ayr, who is said to have refused to subscribe the Confession or to come to communion; as John Davidson remarked in his book against his former friend Abbot Quintin Kennedy, 'mony faderis and sonnis is separatit . . . in thir our days' in matters of religion.[14] John Kennedy of Breckloch and Thomas Kennedy, tutor of the 5th earl of Cassillis, were reported as papists. David Barclay of Ladyland in Kilbirnie parish who was said to have 'lately come home from Flanders apostate, reasoning against the truth', was later implicated in the alleged catholic plot of 'the Spanish blanks'. His son Hugh, who was pursued by the minister of Paisley and others for his 'defection from the faith' in 1597, is said to have been drowned in the scuffle surrounding his arrest, but a Hugh Barclay of Ladyland was accused of sheltering an Italian priest in 1601.[15] Family ties landed some Ayrshire ministers in trouble in 1610 when Mr John Young, minister of Beith, Mr William Fullarton, minister of Dreghorn, Mr Alexander Scrymgeour, minister at Irvine, and Mr Alexander Campbell, minister of Ardrossan, were accused of having communicated with 'trafficking priests' visiting the district. These turned out to be Mr Campbell's brother John, a Capuchin friar, and the brother-in-law of Mr Young, 'ane known trafficking papist'.[16] The roster of Ayrshire recusants is modest, considering that the ecclesiastical authorities of Kyle and Cunninghame, at least, might have been expected to be particularly vigilant. The list is modest, that is, in so far as transgressors were reported to the general assembly. The lack of early kirk session minutes prevents our knowing how many people may have taken heed of a local warning.

While conscientious objection may have motivated some of the pre-Reformation clergy – beneficed or not – to decline to take office in the reformed church, it is just as likely that the non-resident parsons and vicars, whose connection with the parishes meant little more than the collection of their teinds or tack-duty, simply did not consider their talents to lie in that direction. Clergy with local family connections often went on living in the parishes after 1560, including sir Thomas Eccles, vicar and curate of Colmonell, Mr John Dunbar, parson of Cumnock, Andrew Mitchell, curate of Mauchline, sir William Hume, curate of Auchinleck, sir Duncan MacLelland, curate of Maybole, Mr William Boswell, vicar of Straiton, and sir Rolland MacNeill, vicar of Girvan. After 1560 these men continued to act as notaries, witnessed legal transactions and in one or two cases granted feu charters of the parochial kirklands to local lairds and relatives. Sir Alan Porterfield, vicar of Ardrossan, brother to Mr John Porterfield of that Ilk, went to live in Glasgow in the 1560s where he married Florence Cunningham from a burgess family and bought various pieces of property in the city. In 1562 he gave a feu charter of the kirklands of Ardrossan to his nephew Gilbert Porterfield[17] and in 1568 demitted the vicarage in favour of another kinsman, Mr John Porterfield, minister of Dumbarton and later of Ayr.[18]

There were some latecomers to the ranks of the reformed ministry. One of these was sir William Allanson, a chaplain who was accused of taking part in the public celebration of mass in 1563 but who, having apparently come to terms with the kirk after the test act of 1573, became reader at Dailly. Another was Andrew Gray, a prebendary of Maybole collegiate church whom Cassillis called his 'weilbelovit servitor' in 1563, when he granted Gray a pension of £100 'with his honest sustentatioun, hors and boy daylie and yeirlie'. The pension was confirmed 20 years later in return for Gray's 'good service over the last 20 yeris'.[19] When Cassillis eventually got round to planting the kirks in his territory, Gray was made reader at Colmonell.

The remaining monks of Crossraguel and Kilwinning abbeys lived out their lives in their chambers and yards, in possession of their portions. Sir James Fergusson in his book *The White Hind* gives a picture of the last years of those at Crossraguel: Michael Dewar, who admitted rather than welcomed the post-Reformation commendator Alan Stewart in 1565, John Bryce who successfully sued the earl of Cassillis in the court of session for over £700 arrears of his portion in 1602 and thereafter retired to Dumfries, Adam Maxwell who was cited before the privy council in 1590 for saying mass, and Gilbert Kennedy who lived on in the abbey precincts fostering the old faith among the local population as long as he was able.[20] At Kilwinning, as we saw, two monks joined the reformed ministry: Alexander Henderson as exhorter at Ardrossan and Stewarton and then reader at Kilmaurs, and William Kirkpatrick as minister at Kilwinning, with supervision of Beith and Dunlop after 1574.[21] For some years William had as his neighbours at the Greenfoot of Kilwinning, where the monks' chambers stood, several of his former monastic colleagues, including Alan Stein who disponed his chamber and yard to his servant James Bennet in 1564, reserving the use of them for his lifetime, and made his will in 1569. The last surviving member of the Kilwinning convent was James Mitchell the former sub-prior, who took custody of the abbey seal, producing it for use on the commendator's charters until the 1590s.

Legislation awarded the friars an annual pension of £16, to be paid by the town councils out of the rents of their former property and lands which were granted by the crown to those burghs in which the friaries had formerly stood. This arrangement may have helped to lessen any bitterness still felt by survivors of the Beggars' Summons. David Allanson, 'auld freir Allansoun', who regularly collected his pension from Ayr town council until 1618, must have been one of the last survivors of the pre-Reformation religious establishment in Ayrshire. He may or may not be the David Allanson who was reader at Barnweil between 1576 and 1580; Allanson was a common Ayrshire surname.[22] Two other Ayrshire friars took office in the reformed church: Robert Gaw, from Fail, who became reader at nearby Barnweil in 1574, and the Ayr Dominican Henry Smith who became reader at Glasserton in Wigtownshire.

The threat of 'popery' in the background made those who adhered most strictly to the ideals of 1560 sensitive to any suggestion that the church's organisation might take on any of what they regarded as the characteristics of the old regime. The establishment of the Scottish Reformation took the outward form of a revolt against the government. This circumstance, in which the reform legislation was passed in absence of the sovereigns and in defiance of their wishes, appeared to provide the new church with an opportunity for self-determination, the chance to implement a blueprint which would render its organisation radically different from that of its predecessor. The opportunity proved to be an illusion. For reasons that were largely outwith the church's power to remedy, the provision for and polity of the reformed church became from 1561 onwards a question of expedient and compromise in which the shortfall in personnel and funds, exacerbated by political instability, made it impossible to achieve the ideal of the 1560 reformers with its focus on the parish service.

Underneath the practical difficulties lay a difference of principle between the religious and political leaders over the role of the ministry, the source of authority in the church and the extent to which supervision of the clergy was felt to be an important issue. At the beginning 'a thing most expedient for this time' was hit upon in the office of the superintendents, who were both visitors and preachers, 'planters' of kirks and upbuilders of the faith, subject to both the good opinion of local congregations and the authority of the general assembly. Their numbers were filled out in the first decade or so by the handful of pre-Reformation bishops who became protestants.

The contest for the control of the kirk's destiny reached a crisis with the clash between kirk and state over the emergence of the presbyterian solution to the question of supervision and authority. The trouble began with ecclesiastical opposition to the practical erastianism of the Regent Morton which in 1572, with the convention of Leith, resurrected the office of bishop, and culminated in the confrontation between James VI and the more radical ministers in the 1580s over the king's preference for an episcopal system of church government as spelled out in the so-called Black Acts of 1584 and the proposals of Archbishop Patrick Adamson of St Andrews.[23]

The controversy split the church between those who regarded episcopacy in any form as having no place in 'the best reformed kirks', and those who believed in the advantages of a reformed episcopate, or were at least prepared to acquiesce in the king's plans. It has been claimed that the older ministers who had came through the crisis of 1559–60 and who could remember the participation of the conforming bishops may on the whole have been favourably disposed to the return of the bishops in 1572 and to the king's episcopal programme. At the same time it has been demonstrated that a large number of these veterans participated in the preparation of the Second Book of Discipline (completed in 1578) which denied scriptural warrant for the kind of bishops the king had in mind.

The debate about whether ultimate authority in the church should lie with church courts (i.e. the general assembly) or bishops can look like an argument for committee or personal rule. But it was more than that. King James's preference for bishops, whom he could appoint, reward, punish and dismiss was his solution to the problem of how the crown might check the ambitions of the church. Having been stolen a march on, as it were, in 1560, government made a determined effort in the post-civil war years to head off the ecclesiastical columns in their march towards self-determination. The Black Acts of 1584, as they were called by those who opposed them, affirmed the king's supremacy over 'all civil and spiritual estates'.

Several points should be made about this state of affairs. Firstly, the struggle for supremacy between church and state did not begin in the late sixteenth century, but was inherited from the middle ages, when the din of battle between the two forces makes the most acrimonious exchanges between James VI and the ministers sound like a mere noisy business meeting. In Scotland, since the late fifteenth century, the state had won some notable victories over the church which had resolved themselves into financial tribute from the latter. Secondly, the idea of presbytery, which was advanced by the opponents of episcopacy, was not sprung on anyone but grew out of the practice of holding a district 'exercise' of ministers, which had already been found beneficial in those areas where it was practised. Thirdly, the support which presbytery did receive was not given for mere doctrinaire reasons, but because it seemed that it might help to ease certain problems, especially that of supervision.

Clergy and laity participated in these debates in Ayrshire where the presbyteries of Ayr and Irvine were set up in 1581; the former to include the parishes of Kyle and Carrick, the latter those of Cunninghame. Four ministers, John Young of Irvine, James Dalrymple of Ayr, Peter Primrose of Mauchline and John Inglis of Ochiltree, with four laymen, the lairds of Bargany, Bar, Carnell and Hessilhead, attended the convention of Leith in 1572 where a compromise was reached between the church and the Regent Morton's administration whereby, in order to relieve the church's financial needs, ministers were to be given access to the revenues of the bishoprics as these fell vacant. Such was the strength of the habitual association of title and property that those ministers who acquired episcopal revenues found themselves with the title of bishop as well. This is paralleled by the way in which the post-Reformation grantees of the revenues of vicarages and chaplainries were legally entitled to call themselves – and in legal documents did call themselves – vicar or chaplain of X, although these functions no longer existed.

However, there were those who interpreted these developments as an attempt to integrate into the structure of the new church the episcopal stratum of the old. The general assembly recognised the Leith solution as of only temporary convenience in the tortuous and long-drawn-out business of acquiring the old church's 'greater benefices' (bishoprics and abbacies) for the use of the ministry, and deplored the use of accompanying titles. The protestant laity, seeing financial benefits to family and friends, were prepared to exploit these resources as they had done before 1560, through the system of appointments. The earl of Glencairn put forward the name of Mr John Porterfield, then minister of Kilmaronock, for the archbishopric of Glasgow in 1571 – the fact that Porterfield was described as his 'servant' shows how the old tradition of personal patronage continued into the post-Reformation era. John Porterfield's apparently abortive nomination was followed by two successive Ayrshire appointments to the archbishopric: those of Mr John Boyd of Trochrig and Robert Montgomerie of the Hessilhead family. In spite of the Cunninghams' radical protestantism they managed to hang on to the commendatorship of Kilwinning abbey in the 1580s, even although William 5th earl of Glencairn had been one of the Ruthven raiders in 1582.

Tensions during the conflict over the role of the presbyteries were felt in the burgh of Ayr. The easygoing minister John Porterfield (who was remembered for practising archery on Sunday afternoons, and as the friend of 'divers great men') caused no problem for the government in the early 1580s over the business of the bishops. In August 1584, however, information sent to Walsingham suggests that Ayr town council may have used rent-a-crowd methods to let the visiting archbishop Robert Montgomerie know that he was not welcome. On arriving at the burgh with his brother, Lord Semple, the Masters of Eglinton and Seton and about 80 horsemen he was met

> upon the bridge by a number of lads, boys and women, who followed him to his lodging with outcries of 'atheist dogge, schismatique and excommunicat beast onworthy to breath or beare life, much lesse to be sene in companie of Christians'; and were hardly withheld from stoning him out of the town. After he had dined, he went notwithstanding to the church where he broke open the doors, the keys being refused him; and having sent for the magistrates they refused to come to him, but sent him privately an admonition in writing, which being laid on the desk of the pulpit before him while he was at prayer, troubled his patience when he perused, the persons who laid it there retiring without note. This kind entreaty made him shorten his invective sermon, and departing the town the same night he went to Irvine.[24]

In March 1585, in response to the royal demand for subscription to the Black Acts, Ayr presbytery, defiantly meeting, sent such a heavily qualified response that the ministers concerned had their stipends stopped. Mr David Hume of Argettie informed Mr James Carmichael minister of Haddington that

> The Presbytery of Ayr subscribed the Acts with comments:- 'The first act of parliament made anno 1584 we approve. The 23rd and 24th we damne, as divilish': (I mean the 23rd and 24th that appertain to the state of religion). They have caused their notar subscribe with them, and instruments tane to the effect that they have subscribed no otherwise. For this cause their stipends are tane from them, and the king is to ride to that countrey; what will be the end the Lord knows.[25]

In an attempt to quash revolt by the civic authorities the earl of Arran, son of Lord Ochiltree and architect of the Black Acts, had his brother Sir William Stewart of Monkton appointed provost of Ayr, in whose honour the town council spent considerable sums on a banquet and civic breakfast in the accounting year 1585–86. However, about the same time they entertained the ministers of Ayr presbytery when they held their meetings in the burgh, while these were still proscribed. The determined opposition to the king's policies mounted at the turn of the century by the Ayr ministers John Welsh and George Dunbar lies outwith the scope of this present study. Suffice it to say that the Ayrshire communities drawn into these and the greater conflicts of the seventeenth century were no strangers to the experience of being caught up in debates and events of national importance affecting their social and religious life.

'Back to the parish' might have been a slogan of the Reformation. Provision for a resident ministry was one of its strongest ideals. The basic problem of finding the minister a suitable home, however, proved to be about as difficult as guaranteeing his stipend and, like the greater problem, that of securing a manse encountered the barrier of local vested interests.[26] Like the problem of revenue, that of accommodation was inherited from the old kirk, in that the ancient perquisites of manse and glebe (on which the crops supplied the incumbent's larder and the pasture represented his travelling expenses) had not gone with the job but with the benefice. Neither the pre-Reformation curate nor post-Reformation minister or reader had guarantee of possession. That right belonged to the benefice-holder. In pre-Reformation times the latter would sometimes make formal arrangements for his paid deputy to have the use of the manse and glebe, but just as often he would lease or feu it to some other occupier. In 1560, therefore, the minister or reader might find himself unable to dislodge whoever was already there. The problem continued after 1560, for in an attempt to narrow the gap between their incomes and the rising cost of living benefice-holders continued to feu their parochial kirklands including the manse and glebe. The situation was a little better in towns where it was customary to rent lodgings for the minister and reader, although in some cases the accommodation may have been less than adequate.

Although as early as July 1562 the general assembly had petitioned the queen and council for the 'manses, yards and glebes justly pertaining to the ministers without which it is impossible unto them quietly to serve their charges', it was not until the summer of 1563 that parliament took a hand in the matter. On 4 June it was enacted that no-one should feu or set long leases of their manses or glebes without licence from the queen in writing and that those appointed to serve the kirks should have the principal manse of the parson or vicar 'or as much as shall be thought sufficient'. Alternatively, the benefice-holder, tenant or feuar was to build a house and attach a reasonable piece of land to it. For several years there were attempts to apply this unsatisfactory act, with many disputes between ministers and the occupants of the manses and glebes.

Feu charters of parochial kirklands granted about this time sometimes reserved the use of manse and glebe. A charter by Mr Archibald Crawford, vicar of West Kilbride, referred to the manse, glebe and yards then occupied by the reader John Maxwell; as Maxwell had formerly been the curate, he may already have had permission to live there. In 1565 when George Brounside, vicar of Perceton, feued the vicarage lands to the local laird William Barclay of Perceton he reserved 'an honest chamber and one acre to be inhabited by the minister or vicar of the parish church', a far from clear-cut arrangement. When David Crichton, vicar of Ochiltree, feued the kirklands to Lord Ochiltree, also in 1565, it was stated that the grant should in no way 'prejudice the order of parliament [of 1563] anent the enjoyment of manses and glebes by ministers of the Word'.

It was not until January 1573 that parliament could be got to clarify the act, when it was decided that the diplomatic business of allocating the manses and glebes to the ministers locally should be done by the bishop, superintendent or commissioner, whichever operated in the region. The minister would be given possession after he had handed a testimonial to the privy council proving that the designation of his manse and glebe had been duly carried out. Occupiers would then be called upon to surrender the property to the minister within 10 days. The manse should be the most commodious house nearest to the kirk, and the glebe, also near the kirk, should consist of the time-honoured four acres. In passing this legislation parliament was effectively cutting across the heritable rights of feuars in favour of the ministers (presumably on the ground that these assets should not have been alienated in the first place), and needless to say the process of designation often led to disputes and even quarrels on the spot. Mr Robert Wilkie, minister of Kilmarnock, had some difficulty in removing the subtenants of the leaseholder of his glebe, William Crawford, kinsman of the vicar Mr Archibald Crawford. Crawford's argument was that at the time when the archbishop of Glasgow had designated it, corn was growing on the glebe, making it impossible to walk across it and measure it accurately, so that the four acres were 'but guessit'. He lost his case when it was put to Mr Wilkie's oath as to whether or not corn had been growing on the glebe at the time of the archbishop's visit, who swore that it had not.[27]

One reason for urgency in finding a suitable manse, as indeed stipend, was the protestant recognition of the pastor's family. There had sometimes been children in the manse and curate's house before 1560, unacknowledged in law – unless their father could afford to pay for letters of legitimation, which many did – their presence prohibited by the provincial councils of the church and their material provision from 'the patrimony of Christ' similarly forbidden.[28] Yet, the fact that the sons of chaplains, curates and the beneficed clergy also became priests (by frequent papal dispensations), practised as notaries, were merchants and craftsmen, acted as executors (sometimes to a parent), witnessed legal transactions and are found in the followings of nobles and lairds, and that their daughters married townsmen, lairds and tenant-farmers shows that the offspring of the pre-Reformation clergy were not ghettoised. The fact that the vicar of Kilbarchan could allow the curate's daughter to have the house next the kirk which her father had built, where she and her tradesman husband set up home, suggests that in practice they were no more ostracised by the clergy than by the laity. Clerical celibacy – the non-marriage of the clergy – which became a characteristic of the western church, was imposed on the secular clergy by Pope Gregory VII (Hildebrand) in the late eleventh century, thus extending to the seculars the standard adopted by the religious orders. This ruling accompanied a period of increasing clericalisation of the church and a deepening separation in outward respects between clergy and laity. Clearly, in the last decades of the undivided church, in Scotland as elsewhere, there was considerable relaxation of the rule in practice and a measure of apparent dissent from it, ranging from the denunciations of heretics to the tacit secession of many of the clergy themselves. Secession, silent though it had to be for fear of a charge of heresy, rather than profligacy may have been responsible for the situation which provoked the charge of hypocrisy in personal standards levelled at the late-medieval church.

The marriage of the clergy was not only accepted but advocated by the sixteenth-century reformers, for whom the pastor's family – 'the school for character', as Luther called it – was the supreme example of Christian family life. The Scottish reformers saw the minister, his wife and children as a normal Christian family who were prepared to make additional sacrifices in the service of God.[29] For this reason stipends must take account of family responsibilities, including the education, apprenticeship and marriage portions of sons and daughters, with enough 'whereupon to keep an house and be sustained honestly in all things necessary'. Since most ministers served rural parishes, the First Book of Discipline called for their children to be given access to the facilities of the nearest towns for the purposes of education and work.

Although in early days ministers' wives had no formal role outside their households, they and their children were expected to set an example of Christian character and godly living, which extended even to the quiet and modest appearance of their dress, standards also enjoined on the ministers themselves. The memorial to John Hamilton, exhorter and later minister of Dunlop for almost 40 years, and his wife Janet Denham, expresses the ideal well and is probably the earliest public tribute to a minister's wife:

> Heir lyes the bodies of Hanis Hamilton, sonne of Archibald Hamilton of Raploch . . . and of Janet Denham his wife, daughter of James Denham, laird of West Sheilde. They lived maryed together 45 yeeres, during which tyme the said Hans served the cure at this Church. They were much beloved of all that knew them, and especially of the parishioners. They had six sonnes, James, Archibald, Gavin, John, William and Patrick, and on[e] daughter, Jean, maryed to William Muire of Glanders-toune.
>
> > The dust of two lyes in the arte-full frame,
> > Whose birth them honor'd from an honored name,·
> > A painefull pastor, and his spotles wife,
> > Whose devout statues embleme here there life . . .[30]

It is noteworthy that the minister is praised for his labours, his wife for her character, not having a formal role, and that respectable lineage as well as exemplary life contributed to the reputation of the minister and his wife.

Largely, although not entirely, drawn from the social background that had produced most of the beneficed clergy, the new presbyter was usually of higher social standing than the old parish priest. The second generation of ministers, equipped with their university degrees and belonging to an increasingly hereditary profession, moved even further away from the origins of their parishioners; but this subject needs fuller investigation before generalisations can be made. The men in Ayrshire's first post-Reformation charges, however, were from varied backgrounds, drawn as some of them were from the lower ranks of the pre-Reformation clergy, although the association of even some of these with the households of reforming lairds and, in many cases, their responsibilities as notaries and clerks gave them a certain standing with the lairds, small proprietors and burgesses into whose families they married.

Alison Brown, the wife of Gavin Naismith, exhorter and then minister at Dreghorn, was probably the daughter of an Irvine burgess. Since Gavin belonged to Bothwell in Lanarkshire, he probably acquired his burgess-ship of Irvine by her right on their marriage. Margaret Smollet, first wife of Mr John Porterfield who came to Ayr from Dumbarton in 1580, was probably from one of the landed Smollet families in the Lennox. Porterfield himself belonged to the family of a minor laird. Mr Robert Wilkie, minister of Kilmarnock, may have met his wife Helen Lockhart during his earlier charge in Loudoun parish which lay next door to that of Galston, home of many Lockhart families.

Janet Cochrane, wife of James Dalrymple the former chorister in St John's kirk and minister at Ayr, may have been the sister or daughter of his former colleague George Cochrane, organist and master of the song school at Ayr, who became reader at St Quivox. Helen Wilson, wife of Adam Landells, the chaplain and notary who became exhorter at Cumnock and Auchinleck, may have come from a comparatively humble background, while Jean Barclay, wife of Mr Alexander Hamilton, minister at Kilbirnie, may have belonged to the family of the Barclays of Ladyland in that parish.

The greatest change in lyfestyle must surely have been that of the two Kilwinning monks, Alexander Henderson and William Kirkpatrick. Alexander Henderson, whose name first appears as a member of the Kilwinning convent in 1551, may have been one of the younger monks. Although he never became a minister, he served three parishes as exhorter and reader for a total of over 30 years, the last being Kilmaurs where he went in 1574 on the death of sir John Howie. He was still alive in 1598. He married, but his wife's name has not been discovered. In spite of retaining his monk's portion and acquiring the vicarage of Kilmaurs he did have financial difficulties. In 1584 he complained to the privy council of the drop in value of the vicarage, due to the loss of the vicarage lands, asking to have the amount of his tax adjusted accordingly, and in 1588 he sued the commendator of Kilwinning, Alexander Cunningham, for arrears of his monk's portion which in the same year was allocated to his son David, then a student at St Andrews university. In 1598 David himself became minister of Kilmaurs where he was long remembered as an energetic if somewhat eccentric pastor. His manse with a biblical inscription over the door long stood at the Townhead of Kilmaurs.[31]

William Kirkpatrick married Alison Campbell, daughter of James Campbell of Stevenston, whose barony marched with land in Stevenston parish held by Glencairn. On 11 August 1567 the minister and his wife received the substantial gift of a pension worth 20 bolls of victual, 12 stones of cheese and £20 in money from Gavin Hamilton, commendator of Kilwinning, and in 1568 they acquired the chamber and yard of one of the former monks in addition to William's own, setting up house at the Greenfoot of Kilwinning in the abbey precincts. The problem of living space was eased by boarding out some of their children with a parishioner in Byres at the west end of Kilwinning town. However, even if the laird's daughter had to rear her three children, Martha, Marion and William, in a makeshift manse, the family were comparatively well-off, with the minister's stipend of £100, his monk's portion and the commendator's pension. Like colleagues elsewhere, he was able to lend money, including £100 on one occasion to his father-in-law, and he died a richer man than his brother John Kirkpatrick the Ayr merchant. A new manse, which survived until within living memory, was built in the Abbey Green for the second minister of Kilwinning, Alexander Wreitton. Wreitton's oldest son Alexander became the parish schoolmaster, while his younger sons John and Daniel went to Edinburgh to be apprenticed to the printer Andrew Hart. John Wreitton later set up his own printing business in the capital.

One unsettling element in life at the manse must have been the long-term prospects of the minister's family after his death. The problem confronted the compilers of the First Book of Discipline in 1560:

> ... provision must be made not only for their own sustentation during their lives but also for their wives and children after them. For we judge it a thing most contrarious to reason, godliness and equity, that the widow and children of him who in his life did faithfully serve the kirk of God, and for that cause did not carefully make provision for his family, should after his death be left comfortless of all provision.[32]

They added: 'Provision for the wives of ministers after their decease, to be remitted to the discretion of the kirk'. In this vital matter, practical difficulties rendered the kirk's performance far short of its intentions. It was not until 1743 that a fund was set up for the benefit of ministers' widows and children, a scheme which to its great credit was a pioneering measure in its field.[33] Meantime ministers themselves did what they could with available resources. Alexander Henderson's monastic portion, as we saw, provided his son with a student's allowance. William Kirkpatrick earmarked the sale of his own books, worth 40 merks, for his son William's education: 'I leve my sone William to be put to the schule [university] sasone as possibill is, with sum freindis that will tak him and his geir togidder...'

Many ministers' widows simply remarried, as many other women did. Alison Campbell, who was a comparatively young woman when her husband died in 1577, remarried twice. Like other widows, those of ministers had a claim to a share of their late husbands' property and income. In 1571 over £40 arrears of stipend due to Adam Landells, exhorter at Cumnock, Ochiltree and Auchinleck, was paid to his widow Helen Wilson by the collector of the Thirds.[34] Like many other people, however, including many women, ministers' widows found themselves having to pursue debtors in court in order to secure what was their due. In April 1590 Agnes Borthwick, the widow of Mr William Strang, minister at Irvine, sued the parishioners for half her late husband's arrears of stipend which he had assigned to her before he died.[35] In November of the same year Alison Brown, Gavin Naismith's widow, took the parishioners of Dreghorn to court for arrears of his vicarage dues.[36] When all else failed, and provided the widow lived on in the parish, she and her children had an obvious moral claim on the poor's roll. Ayr town council gave financial help to the widow and 'fatherless bairns' of the minister James Dalrymple who died in 1580, 'for the ardent luf shown by the said James to the said burgh'.[37] Even the efficient management of the household's economy might involve the minister's wife in litigation. In October 1595 Janet Campbell, the wife of Mr David Mylne, minister at Dundonald, sued Robert Henry in Irvine burgh court for his failure to return eight ells of blue cloth which she had left with him for fulling. When he admitted having it, she got him returned to gaol until the cloth was handed over.[38]

The loss of early kirk session records for Ayrshire parishes has deprived us of much that we might have learned of the first protestant congregations and the ministers' role in the local community, how regularly poor relief was paid and to whom, how congregational discipline was observed, and what standards of educational facilities were achieved. If we accept as justified the regrets and accusations levelled from time to time at the localities, including Ayrshire, by the general assembly, with regard both to the quality of the ministry and its effectiveness among the parishioners, we can only conclude that it was an uphill task. But then, no doubt, it had been equally uphill before 1560, according to the fulminations of the provincial councils, about whose local effectiveness we have just as little information. If the lamentations of the general assemblies about poor attendance, irreverent behaviour, ignorance of the faith, carelessness of ministers and 'universal coldness, want of zeal . . . contempt of the word and sacraments' are to be taken seriously, so too must those of the pre-Reformation church councils and synods when they deplored the casual behaviour in church, neglect of the sacraments, immorality, poor state of knowledge and personal moral failings of the clergy, and the reluctance of the 'faithful' to pay kirk dues, come to confession and partake of the mass, at least at Easter, or to conduct themselves properly when they did come. The truth is surely that both before and after 1560 the church carried many 'passengers', who found religious discipline and obligations irksome. At any time people were probably most attached to those ceremonies surrounding the crises of life, the 'rites of passage' of baptism, marriage and burial, which certainly feature prominently in the evidence for lingering catholicism after 1560. Where the pre-Reformation church scored in maintaining an outward level of lay piety was in its genius for absorbing by Christianising those popular, essentially pagan customs such as well-visiting, bonfires and seasonal local festivals which were banned completely by its successor. In fact the latter found these seasonal activities among the most difficult 'faults' to eradicate.

In the burghs the role of the magistrates in ordering and maintaining divine service was as clear to everyone as it had been in pre-Reformation times. The bailies and town council were as ready to lay down rules for the minister and readers as they had been for the curate and burgh chaplains. In August 1583 Irvine town council made a contract with its minister Mr William Strang who had previously served at Kirkliston and had been in Irvine since at least June of that year. He was contracted 'to do the work of a minister', preaching twice publicly on Sundays and once on Wednesdays and Fridays, 'as neid requyris'. For their part the council in name of the burgesses promised to subject themselves to the discipline of Christ's kirk as established in the realm, to choose elders to meet weekly with the minister and to make good any deficiency in his stipend. They also agreed to repair the kirk and kirkyard and to provide him with a suitable house and yard.[39] In the 1590s Strang's successor taught the pupils of Irvine grammar school for which he was paid £40 a year.[40] In 1595 the minister of Irvine, Mr Alexander Scrymgeour, was awarded 100 merks and commended by the council for not diminishing his income by setting tacks of his glebe and kirklands.[41] Town councils also took the initiative in acquiring a minister. When James Dalrymple who had served Ayr as chorister and then minister for over 20 years died in 1580, the council sent two colleagues to Paisley 'to confer with Mr Thomas Smeaton to be minister of this burgh then being desolat of ane pastor'. In the event they got Mr John Porterfield from Dumbarton, to whom they reimbursed his removal expenses and on whose behalf they petitioned the privy council for the parsonage and vicarage of Alloway.[42]

The First Book of Discipline made a distinction, in laying down lines for congregational worship and observance, between that which was 'utterly necessary', that is preaching, the sacraments, the common prayers, catechising and discipline, and that which was 'profitable but not of mere necessity', such as the singing of psalms in worship, the particular passages of scripture to be read and the frequency of services.[43] The practical framework for the conduct of essential services was left to be determined by local circumstance.

Glimpses of the early reformed congregations may be gleaned from various sources. Baptismal registers for the sixteenth century are rare. In that of Galston, kept mainly by Rankin Davidson and dated 1568 to 1599, the regular entries of baptisms and occasional references to the payment of poor relief illustrate his responsibilities as assistant to a succession of ministers; he described himself in the register as 'Rankin Davidson, exhorter at the kirk of Galston and baptiser of the bairns'. Attempts at romantic verse in the margins of his book suggest that the comparatively carefree mood of his chaplaincy days had not entirely disappeared.[44] In enforcing congregational discipline the kirk burdened itself with a problem. While admitting that even in a congregation which showed 'the certain and infallible signs of the true kirk' it would not be the case that 'every particular person joined with such a company be an elect member of Jesus Christ', the kirk session nevertheless tried to bring to 'unfeigned repentance' every parishioner whose transgressions compromised the godly character of the company.[45] Their difficulty was the inevitable result of having chosen a territorial (i.e. parish) rather than voluntary basis for congregational membership. The reformers claimed that in the pre-Reformation church, which had operated on the same geographical basis, congregational discipline had broken down. It might have been replied that before 1560 the more manageable practice was that personal sins were privately confessed — except that the late-medieval church appears to have had more difficulty in inculcating resort to confession than its successor had in-bringing culprits to the stool of repentance. The magnitude of this perennial problem is illustrated in the increasingly disproportionate amount of the kirk sessions' time which was taken up with disciplinary matters, evident in the church records from the seventeenth century onwards.

However, the kirk never gave up the struggle, in which it was no respecter of persons. In 1567 the minister and kirk session of Mauchline complained to the general assembly that one of their elders, Sir William Hamilton of Sanquhar, persisted in extending hospitality to another elder, John Spottiswood, whom they had excommunicated for adultery. The assembly backed the kirk session, warning Sir William that if he did not abandon his attitude to the kirk's censure, it would fall upon himself in turn.[46] In March 1570 it was the turn of a parishioner to complain to the assembly, when Thomas Smith in Ochiltree, probably a smith to trade, objected to being debarred from the Lord's Table for having removed horse shoes on the Sunday afternoon, 'when there was neither prayers nor preaching'.[47] The assembly took his part, ordering his reinstatement, which may suggest that in the early days the spiritual exercises on Sunday rather than Sunday itself may have been the focus of observance, although the First Book of Discipline had emphasised the need to observe the Lord's Day.

The protestant service was above all participatory in character, with its focus on the congregation itself, the face-to-face delivery of the vital part of the service, the sermon, reading from the scriptures and of the prayers in a familiar language, congregational singing and the communal experience of the Lord's Supper at which communicants initially sat round the table and partook of both the bread and the wine in an atmosphere which had exchanged mystery for immediacy. Although music was a spontaneous form of expression in Scottish culture, most singing in churches before the Reformation had been the business of the officiating clergy and their assistants. After 1560, although psalm-singing was optional, it was encouraged in practice, men and women being told 'to exercise themselves in the Psalms, that when the church conveneth and does sing, they may be the more able together with common heart and voice to praise God'.[48] One cannot help wondering if the popular 'gude and godly ballatis' continued to be sung in less formal surroundings as a more robust expression of religious feelings in song. In 1564 the general assembly ordained that every minister, exhorter and reader should have one of the recently printed psalm books for use at the reading of the prayers and administration of the sacraments.[49] In 1592 Irvine town council paid Alexander Henderson 20s 'for singing the psalms to the kirk at communion', presumably precenting, and Ayr kirk also had a precentor.[50] Psalm books found their way also into private ownership, so that families who could afford them might practise their singing at home as recommended. That owned by the Ayr merchant William Hunter in 1569 was valued at five shillings.[51]

The ceremonies accompanying the several rites of passage were simplified and shorn of all symbolic features. The extent to which people appear to have accepted, and even expressed a preference for, these simple forms in connection with burial – the rite of passage in respect of which people feel at their most vulnerable – may suggest that in time the desire for the old familiar symbolic adjuncts withered away from lack of usage. A second generation of protestants would be unfamiliar with them in any case. Some people were still buried inside the church according to the requests in wills and the funeral was, and remained, the occasion *par excellence* in Scotland where things were seen to be done decently and in order and every possible mark of respect and respectability was almost paraded. This did not begin with the Reformation, however; in 1550 Agnes Arnot of Kilmarnock parish, while she left no money for special prayers or commemoration by the priests, set aside £10 for the expenses of the 'deid lyke walking, furth bryngin' and compulsory 'corsepresand'.[52] Sir Hugh Kennedy of Girvanmains who died in 1578 asked his executors to have gowns of black 'dule claith' made for six poor boys 'to convey me to the sepulture' each of whom was to be given two shillings, with 40 shillings 'to a minister for exhortatioun making at my burial'. He asked to be buried in the collegiate kirk of Maybole in his family burial place at the south end of the former high altar.[53] Lord Boyd's wishes in 1590 were more overtly protestant with regard to his funeral. After committing his soul to God 'to be savit through the death and blud of Jesus Christ his son', he asked to be buried in the parish kirk of Kilmarnock 'in the sepulchre of my forebears ... to be careit hidder bot [without] onie order, bot onlie betwix twa hors and ane black claith abone ane kist, bot [without] onie farder ceremonie'.[54]

Emphasis in reformed teaching was on the individual believer's intellectual grasp of the tenets of the faith (according to capacity), hence the importance of catechising, a process which the late-medieval church had itself used and had actively promoted in the late 1550s as an antidote to exposure to heresy. Since the message of salvation was believed to be fully conveyed in scripture, in the meaning of Christ's death, scripture was expounded to those who were then expected to improve their own understanding of it, and so develop their Christian character. This is not to say that early protestantism lacked its own fervency and piety, but this was differently expressed from formerly. Protestant lay piety was taught to draw its strength not from repeated actions but from cumulative understanding which would inculcate an assurance, rather than simply a hope, of salvation. This assurance comes out in the preambles to many wills where the testator made a confession of faith in word or writing before disposing of his or her worldly goods. Emphasis in these confessions is usually on personal assurance of salvation through faith in the unique sacrifice of Christ's death, anticipation of the joys of heaven immediately after death (the conscious elimination of purgatory is important) and the prospect of the resurrection of the body.

In January 1574 Elizabeth Corry, widow of Robert Cathcart of Carlton in Carrick, made her verbal confession before her minister, friends and servants:

> Considering herself approaching the end of her pilgrimage and to be dissolvit of this erthlie mansioun, hoiping assuritlie to be transportit to the eternall habitatioun quhair Christ hes obtenit ane eternal possessioun for his elect. Not douting bot God of his frie mercie hes pardonit her synnis accepting for the same the onlie sacrifice of Christis blude.[55]

Being in the third person, the words are a transcript by the writer of the testament. On the other hand, the words of John Wallace of Craigie spoken on his deathbed in 1570 and unaltered by the writer of the testament convey an impression of familiarity with the truths behind them, slightly garbled as they are into a brief sentence by a sick man: 'I leve my saule to almyghtie God and to be merciful intil it, in his passioun and bluid sched'.[56] In still different circumstances Annabelle Cunningham, widow of Sir James Chalmers of Gadgirth, wrote her own will in 1569: 'I do commend my spirit to Jesus Christ my onlie saviour and redeemer, in quhome and by quhome I luke for eternall joy and felicitie'.[57]

The personal experience and acquaintance with the language of the bible which enabled the men and women of the first generation of Ayrshire protestants to express their faith in this way was not entirely acquired in the kirk seats or laird's loft 'under' the minister. The First Book of Discipline did not stop at public catechising and regular church attendance in advocating ways in which parishioners might gain a knowledge of their faith. This had to be nurtured at home as well. The generation of Annabelle Cunningham and John Wallace, who died in the 1560s and 1570s, may have learned their first lessons in the protestant faith in the family circle and privy kirks. It was therefore natural for them to implement the exhortation of their spiritual mentors that

> Every Master of household must be commanded either to instruct, or else cause [to] be instructed, his children, servants and family in the principles of the Christian religion; without the knowledge whereof ought none to be admitted to the Table of the Lord Jesus.[58]

Robert Campbell of Kinzeancleuch, whom Annabelle Cunningham made one of the overseers of her will, was commended by his friend the minister Mr John Davidson for the regularity of family worship in his household, where after supper he even catechised the poor who sought shelter under his roof:

> Also his servants he did call:
> And every Sabboth him before,
> To give a reckoning there but more
> O chiefe heades of Religion,
> So they got great instruction.[59]

It was for instruction in such circumstances that substantial householders were told to obtain a bible; it was unlikely that humbler families could afford, or read, one themselves. Those who took the lead in local society were in this way expected to inculcate religious knowledge and good conduct just as by other means they were expected to maintain law and order in the Christian commonwealth. Robert Campbell of Kinzencleuch, who with likeminded friends had once reminded Mary of Guise of his local responsibilities in spiritual as in temporal matters, seems to have combined his roles literally by catechising his servants when they appeared before him to give an account of their week's work.

The transformation of the people's church in Ayrshire and beyond involved a revolution in the relationship of clergy and laity. The revolution not only removed clerical privilege by transforming the clergy into members of ordinary society, burdened with responsibilities on its behalf, but claimed to give every lay believer a priestly role in the spiritual sphere: unmediated access to God, equal rights with other believers in the Christian community and personal responsibility for grasping the means of salvation as revealed in scripture. It was towards these ends that the lay programme of reform had as its priorities the provision of preachers and free access to the bible as the means of disseminating the protestant message. Since beliefs lead to practice and to outward forms of worship, the reform programme developed a practical side which reflected its doctrines: the removal from church buildings of the visual representation of the traditional channels of efficacy, such as images of the Virgin Mary and the saints; the substitution of the pulpit for the altar as the focus of the congregation's attention; the communal character of the communion; the abolition of the church's calendar; the functions of elders and deacons.

We may wonder how people coped with these as with other changes in religious life. But then, the Reformation was not imposed on them suddenly in 1560. The Scottish reform movement, although ratified late by the standards of most other protestant countries, was a gradual, evolutionary, at times deceptively low-key, process, and we need to take it at its own pace if we are to evaluate the way in which it may have created a climate for change in a period of over 30 years: the speculative 1530s which, although marked by the flight of many who might have become the movement's religious leaders, also saw the transmission of their ideas to the laity, a number of whom were among those put to death for heresy in that decade; the combative, iconoclastic 1540s when the laity led attempts at practical reform and openly supported public protestant preaching, while the possibility of using political means to put Scotland in the protestant camp first appeared on the horizon; the underground growth of the 1550s which gave increasing cohesion to local dissenting groups who were exhorted by preachers like Knox and Willock to secede from catholic worship, focusing their objections to traditional religion on the mass; the confrontational later 1550s which saw the failure of both dialogue and attempts at internal reform, and culminated in the protestant party's withdrawal of their civil obedience, leading to the revolution of 1559–60.

Not only had reformation taken some time, but the content of the message of salvation – as distinct from what should be done about the institutional church – was still the familiar one of the efficacy of the Passion of Christ, a theme which had permeated the outward expressions of lay piety in the late-medieval period. Indeed, the surge in pious activity can itself be seen as the laity's answer to their disillusionment with the institutional church which, having become self-sufficient, self-justifying and preoccupied with secular concerns, appeared to have forgotten that other people were its first responsibility. The familiarity of the Passion story and its relevance to the worries about sin and guilt, which loomed large in the minds of late-medieval people, would be reassuring to the average parishioner in the midst of so many practical changes. The difference now was (and it may have taken some time for it to become clear to most people) that instead of being taught to perform pious acts through which they might show themselves worthy of the grace offered to them in the sacraments, people were told that in the sight of God there was nothing they could do to help themselves, that all had been done on their behalf by Christ their substitute, and that assurance of the salvation which resulted from that historic fact came from believing the revelation contained in scripture. To those who accepted this message the traditional channels of efficacy were not only of no effect but misleading to the believer, and all recourse to them must be abandoned. They also saw the clergy as a stumbling block in the way of lay spiritual self-determination, and their activities as intruding in areas of ordinary life that were properly a layperson's own business: Adam Wallace believed it was incumbent on every man and woman to seek out their own salvation and to determine for themselves what constituted a 'true minister'; John Lockhart felt that the clergy should be banned from political life; the laird of Gadgirth deplored their grip of his and his tenants' economic circumstances; and Robert Campbell of Kinzeancleuch reminded the civil authority that he had a responsibility towards the religious as well as secular wellbeing of the local community. Not all would understand, or if they understood would accept, this relocation of spiritual responsibility, personal and communal, which stemmed ultimately from accentuation of the doctrine of the priesthood of all believers. If there were many mechanical practitioners before 1560, there would be many passive listeners afterwards. The sources that remain to us from the early days of the Reformed kirk in Scotland simply will not bear categorical conclusions as to whether the people, in those areas where the Reformation was undoubtedly delivered, determinedly resisted or took wholeheartedly to the new faith and its outward observances. This does not excuse us, however, from giving thoughtful consideration to the religious revolution in its own right or from making an attempt to empathise with those who lived through it.

The most momentous act of lay initiative was the part played in the 1559–60 revolution by the self-styled Lords of the Congregation. This was no last-minute grasping of the helm by a party of political opportunists. Given the hereditary background of these men, their social relations, political histories and normal preoccupation with private wars and property interests, the wonder is that they acted together at all. A fairly recent description of them as 'disparate – but nonetheless highly committed' is a good one.[60] For whatever personal reasons – and these varied – they were as committed to the success of the revolution as those like-minded lesser people on whose behalf they took charge. They were the lords, the natural leaders and spokesmen for 'the Congregation', the protestant community throughout Scotland. To a greater or lesser degree they had long felt a need for improvement in the quality of the service provided by the church and for a re-evaluation of their own place in it. Not a few of them, including some from Ayrshire, were second-generation protestants whose families had been involved in religious protest since the 1530s. They readily adopted the role of godly magistrates, charged to promote and defend the true kirk, which John Knox had outlined for them in his letters of exhortation. The most prominent of them had taken part in the dialogue with the religious and civil powers in the mid-1550s, when with considerable skill they attempted to exonerate themselves from blame for whatever civil conflict or other disaster should follow the breakdown of the negotiations. Their official statements could be constructive as well as confrontational or defiant, such as the recommendations prepared for those household groups and civil authorities who wanted to implement protestant practice in the wake of the First Band of the Congregation of 1557. Their bid to secure the Reformation by political and military means was the culmination of their efforts and strategy.

Ayrshire, whose own political leaders made an important contribution to these efforts, gained a few 'firsts' in the history of late-medieval religious dissent: the first native Scots laypeople to be tried for heresy, the first attempt to transcribe the biblical text into Scots (prepared by a layman), the earliest recorded iconoclastic attack on church property in Scotland (led by a layman), and probably the earliest signs of the introduction of protestant worship by civic authorities (at Ayr). Yet the lay character of Ayrshire's Reformation was not unusual but was evident elsewhere in Scotland. What is perhaps more unusual is the extent to which the earlier stages of religious dissent developed in landward Ayrshire – and came to town, illustrated by Walter Stewart's protest in Ayr in 1533.

For want of sources, little can be discovered about the 'mutation of religion' in Irvine, but the fact that the burgh kirk was well provided with a protestant ministry, including the services of the former vicar, that the early ministers of at least two neighbouring parishes came from burgh families, and that the local magnate the earl of Eglinton, apart from his own consistent recusancy, does not seem to have intimidated the new religious regime, suggests that things settled down there fairly well. Landward reforming influences were felt in Ayr from an early stage and the burgh continued to have particularly close links with its rural hinterland. This was mainly due to the large number of landward families who had colonised the politically active burgess ranks and who continued to make the burgh a meeting place and focal point of reformed strategy throughout the 1540s and 1550s. It is noteworthy that although Ayr stood so near the Carrick border, it was the lairds and gentlemen of Kyle rather than Cassillis who made their mark on its public life. Ayr town council constantly presented a bold and at times uncompromising front to religious and civil authority and took a masterful line with its own religious establishment which before 1560 is said to have been costing the burgh about a third of its income. Even more so than with Irvine, the early ministers and readers for a number of neighbouring parishes, including that which held the burgh's dependent barony of Alloway, were supplied from burgh families and clergy who had previously served the burgh kirk.

Lastly, is the long timescale of Ayrshire's dissent as revealed by the accusations levelled at the Lollards of Kyle exceptional, with no parallel elsewhere in Scotland? Militating against this conclusion is the recorded phenomenon of lollardy in fifteenth-century Scotland. Admittedly, most though not all the allusions to it involve the activities of non-Scots who attempted to spread the lollard message, whose activities would appear to have been contained by the watchfulness of kirk and state. Yet the existence of the Ayrshire Lollards (they are said to have come from Cunninghame as well as Kyle) suggests that some of their efforts bore fruit in Scottish soil. The real difficulty is not the feasibility of the existence of pre-protestant religious dissent in Scotland but the dearth of sources of information. Had John Knox not done an oral history exercise among his Ayrshire friends, eked out with such fragmentary documentation as they could scramble together for him, we would have known nothing at all about the Lollards of Ayrshire. We would thus have been deprived of an important insight into the nature of Ayrshire's contribution to the layman's history of the Scottish Reformation.

Notes

CHAPTER ONE

1. J. Strawhorn and K. Andrew, *Discovering Ayrshire* (Edinburgh, 1988), 1.
2. *Military Report on the districts of Carrick, Kyle and Cunninghame . . . between the years 1563 and 1566*, ed.R.B. Armstrong, in *Archaeological and Historical Collections relating to the Counties of Ayr and Wigton*, iv (1884), 17.
3. M.H.B. Sanderson, *Scottish Rural Society in the Sixteenth Century* (Edinburgh, 1982), 65, 97, 100, 126–7.
4. *Register of the Privy Seal*, ed. M. Livingstone and others, 8 vols (Edinburgh, 1908–82), 2: 2152 (hereafter, *RSS* (printed); RSS (manuscript)).
5. M.H.B. Sanderson, *The Mauchline Account Books of Melrose abbey, 1527–8*, (AANHS, 1975), 89, 92–3.
6. A. Graham, *Old Ayrshire Harbours* (AANHS, 1984), *passim*.
7. Edinburgh Commissariot, Register of Testaments (SRO) CC8/8/8, fo. 273v (hereafter, Edinburgh Testaments).
8. *Ibid.*, CC8/8/12, fo.121.
9. Register of Acts and Decreets (SRO), CS 7/19/1, part i, fo.209.
10. J. Bain and C. Rogers, eds., *The Diocesan Registers of Glasgow* (London, 1875), i, 375–6 (hereafter, *Diocesan Registers of Glasgow*).
11. Register of Acts and Decreets (SRO), CS7/10, fo.256v; case re. building of the Eglinton lodging, 1565.
12. Edinburgh Testaments, CC/8/8/6, fo.231v.
13. Register of Deeds (SRO), RD1/2, fo.280v.
14. *Ibid.*, RD1/6, fo.317.
15. *Calendar of Papers relating to Scotland and Mary Queen of Scots, 1547–1603*, ed.J. Bain and others (1898–19), i, 26 (hereafter, *CSP Scot.*).
16. *Letters and Papers of Henry VIII (London, 1862–1910)*, xviii, part i, 366 (hereafter, *LP Henry VIII*).
17. Edinburgh Testaments, CC8/8/3, fo.256.
18. R. Mackenzie, *A Scottish Renaissance Household; Sir William Hamilton and Newton Castle in 1559* (AANHS, 1990), *passim*.
19. J. Paterson, *History of the County of Ayr* (1847), i, part i, *passim*.
20. *LP Henry VIII*, xviii, i, 458.
21. (Grimmet) *Register of the Great Seal*, 3:945 (hereafter, *RMS*); (Eglinton), *Ibid.* 3:398; (Mure of Caldwell), *RSS*, 3:956.

CHAPTER TWO

1. I.B. Cowan, 'Patronage, Provision and Reservation, Pre-Reformation appointments to Scottish Benefices', in *The Renaissance and Reformation in Scotland: Essays in honour of Gordon Donaldson* (Edinburgh, 1983), 75–92.
2. *Charters of the Abbey of Crossraguel*, ed. F.C. Hunter Blair (Ayrshire and Wigtonshire Archaeological Association, 1886), i, 173 (hereafter, *Crossraguel Charters*).
3. Miscellaneous church records (SRO), CH 8/14.
4. Eglinton Muniments (SRO), GD 3: Inventory, volume vii, Bundle 24/3.
5. *RSS*, 3:2765.
6. *Ibid.*, 6:256.
7. D. McKay, 'Parish Life in Scotland, 1500–1560', in D. McRoberts, ed., *Essays on the Scottish Reformation, 1513–1625* (Glasgow, 1962), 93–6 (hereafter, McRoberts, *Essays on the Scottish Reformation*).
8. *Protocol Book of Gavin Ros, 1512–32*, eds J. Anderson and F.J. Grant (SRS, 1908), 725 (hereafter, *Gavin Ros*).
9. *Ibid.*, 726–8.
10. *Ibid.*, 975.
11. *Ibid.*, 555.
12. *Diocesan Registers of Glasgow*, i, 305–6, 270–1.
13. J. Durkan, 'Education in the Century of the Reformation', in McRoberts, *Essays on the Scottish Reformation*, 148.
14. *Gavin Ros, 414*.
15. *Ibid.*, 660.
16. A. McKenzie, *An Ancient Church* (Ayr, 1935), 37.
17. *Ayr Burgh Accounts, 1534–1624*, ed. G. Pryde (SHS, 1937), *passim*.
18. *Muniments of the Royal Burgh of Irvine*, 2 volumes (Ayrshire and Wigtonshire Archaeological Association, 1890–1), i, 194–203 (hereafter, *Muniments of Irvine*).
19. Register of Acts and Decreets, CS7/32, fo.81v.
20. A. McKenzie, *op.cit.*, 37.
21. *Muniments of Irvine*, i, 161.
22. *Obit book of the Church of St John the Baptist, Ayr*, ed. J. Paterson (1848), 67 (Hereafter, *Ayr Obit Book*).
23. *Melrose Regality Records*, ed. C.S. Romanes (SHS, 1917), iii, 217–18.
24. M. Dilworth, 'The Commendator System in Scotland', in *Innes Review*, xxxvii (1986), 51–72.
25. M.H.B. Sanderson, *Scottish Rural Society in the Sixteenth Century* (Edinburgh, 1982), 26.
26. W. Fraser, *Memorials of the Montgomeries* (1859), ii, 136.
27. *Liber Sancte Marie de Mailros*, ed. C. Innes (Bannatyne Club, 1837), ii, 598.
28. The subject of appropriation is fully discussed in the Introduction to I.B. Cowan, *The Parishes of Medieval Scotland* (London, revised 1976).
29. G. Chalmers, *Caledonia* (1890), vi, 91.

30. *Ibid.*, 138.
31. *Ibid.*, 544.
32. *Crossraguel Charters*, ii, 96–7; Ailsa Mun. (SRO), GD25/1/550.
33. M.H.B. Sanderson, *Scottish Rural Society in the Sixteenth Century*, 158–60.
34. J. Gillespie, *Dundonald, A Contribution to Parochial History*, 2 vols (1939), ii, 161, on the Fullartons.
35. *Records of the Burgh of Prestwick*, ed. J. Fullarton (Maitland Club, 1834), 52.
36. *Statutes of the Scottish Church, 1225–1559*, ed. D. Patrick (SHS, 1907), 136–8 (hereafter, *Statutes of the Scottish Church*).

CHAPTER THREE

1. *Gavin Ros*, 654.
2. J. Durkan, 'Chaplains in Scotland in the Late Middle Ages', in *RSCHS*, xx (1979), 91–103 (hereafter, Durkan, 'Chaplains').
3. L. MacFarlane, 'Was the Scottish Church reformable by 1513?', in N. MacDougall, ed., *Church, Politics and Society, 1408–1929* (Edinburgh, 1983), 23–43.
4. *Diocesan Registers of Glasgow*, i, 346–7.
5. *Ibid.*, i, 340–1.
6. David Beaton's first preferment was the canonry of Cambuslang to which was attached the office of sacrist of Glasgow cathedral. Soon afterwards he acquired the chancellorship of Glasgow, with the parsonage of Campsie. He was then a university student. M.H.B. Sanderson, *Cardinal of Scotland* (Edinburgh, 1986), 13.
7. *Gavin Ros*, 366
8. *Diocesan Registers of Glasgow*, i, 500–1.
9. Durkan, 'Chaplains', 100–102.
10. *Ayr Burgh Accounts, passim*.
11. See M.H.B. Sanderson, *Mary Stewart's People: Life in Mary Stewart's Scotland* (Edinburgh, 1987), 149–65, for a fuller study of Leggat's career.
12. The parish of Dalry was also appropriated to the collegiate church of St Mary and St Anne, Glasgow.
13. J. Major, *History of Greater Britain* (SHS, 1892), 30.
14. The island of Meikle Cumbrae was actually in the sheriffdom of Bute.
15. For details of vicarage settlements, see I.B. Cowan, *The Parishes of Medieval Scotland*, Introduction.
16. G. Chalmers, *Caledonia* (1890), vi, 555, 509.
17. *Gavin Ros*, 705.
18. G. Chalmers, *Caledonia*, vi, 515–16.
19. *Gavin Ros*, 726.
20. (Rolland), *Ayr Obit Book*, 44, 46, 48. *Charters of the Royal Burgh of Ayr*, ed. W.S. Cooper (Ayrshire and Wigtonshire Archaeological Association, 1883), 96.

21. J. Bossy, *Christianity in the West, 1400–1700* (Oxford, 1985), 68–9.
22. *Gavin Ros*, 528.
23. *Ibid.*, 928.
24. *Ibid.*, 1294
25. *Ibid.*, 708
26. *Ibid.*, 975
27. *Ibid.*, 473–5
28. *Diocesan Registers of Glasgow*,i, 487–8
29. J.C.Lees, *The Abbey of Paisley* (Paisley, 1878), cxviii.
30. *Gavin Ros*, 90, 92, 249.
31. *Statutes of the Scottish Church*, 166.
32. Register of Acts and Decreets, CS 15/5,24 May 1557.
33. F.D. Bardgett, *Scotland Reformed: The Reformation in Angus and the Mearns* (Edinburgh, 1989), 37.
34. R.Pitcairn, *Ancient Criminal Trials in Scotland, 1488–1624* (Edinburgh, 1833), 1a, 136* (hereafter, *Ancient Criminal Trials*).
35. Edinburgh Testaments, CC8/8/6, fos 104v–5
36. *Works of Sir David Lindsay*, 3 vols (Scottish Text Society, 1931),ii,'Ane Satyre of the Thrie Estaitis',lines 2053–55.

CHAPTER FOUR

1. *The New Testament in Scots, being Purvey's Revision of Wycliffe's version turned into Scots by Murdoch Nisbet,c. 1520*, ed. T.G.Law (Scottish Text Society, 1901–5), i, Introduction includes extracts from Sergeant Nisbet's Narrative (hereafter, *Law*)
2. J. Knox, *History of the Reformation in Scotland*, ed. W.C. Dickinson (Edinburgh,1949), i, 8–11 (hereafter,*Knox*).
3. The main discussions of lollardy in Scotland will be found in: W.S.Reid, '– The Lollards in pre-Reformation Scotland', in *Church History*, xi (1942); J.A.F.Thompson,*The Later Lollards, 1414–1520* (Oxford, 1965); T.M.A. Macnab,'Bohemia and the Scottish Lollards', in *RSCHS*, v.(1935),10–22; same author, 'The Beginnings of Lollardy in Scotland', in *RSCHS*, xi (1955), 254–60.
4. *Liber S. Marie de Calchou*, ed. C.Innes (Bannatyne Club, 1846) Volume ii, 538, 539 (hereafter, *Liber de Calchou*).
5. Macnab, T.M.A., 'Bohemia and the Scottish Lollards', *passim*.
6. *Liber de Calchou*, 181, 189, 191, 192, 203; J.B.Greenshiels, *Annals of the Parish of Lesmahagow*, (1864), 44–9.
7. T.M.A. Macnab, 'Bohemia and the Scottish Lollards',14, citing Reginald Poole, in *English Historical Review*, i, 309–11.
8. W.S. Reid, 'The Lollards in pre-Reformation Scotland', 272.
9. *Ibid.*, 275.
10. *Ibid.*, 276
11. M.H.B. Sanderson, *The Mauchline Account Books of Melrose Abbey*, 93.

12. *Liber de Calchou*, Volume ii, 480.
13. Portland Muniments (SRO), GD 163, Box 1.
14. D. Calderwood, *History of the Kirk of Scotland*, eds. T. Thomson and D. Laing (Wodrow Society, 1842–9), i, 54 (hereafter, Calderwood, *History*). W.S. Reid, *op.cit.*, 282; A.F. Scott-Pearson, 'Alesius and the English Reformation', in *RSCHS*, x, (1950) 57–87 H. Maxwell, *History of Dumfries and Galloway*, (1900), 190–1.
15. W. McDowall, *History of Dumfries* (Edinburgh, 1873), 219; T.M.A. Macnab, 'The New Testament in Scots', in *RSCHS*, xi, (1955), 82–103.
16. *Law*, Introduction, vii–xvii
17. A. Hudson, *Lollards and their Books*, (London, 1985), 85–110. In commenting on the charges brought against Purvey at his own trial in 1401, the author notes that he went a good deal further than Wycliffe himself when stressing that each predestinate man is a priest' (*op.cit.*, 88). Asserting the priesthood of all believers was one of the Articles brought against the Ayrshire Lollards. The claim to be able to discern 'a true minister', voiced by the Ayrshireman Adam Wallace at his trial in 1550, echoes the English lollards' characteristic use of the term 'trewe prechoures' (*op.cit.*, 109).
18. J. Durkan, 'Some Local Heretics', in *TDGNHAS*, xxxvi, 74.
19. M. Aston, *Lollards and Reformers* (London, 1984), 96–7.
20. *Diocesan Registers of Glasgow*, i, 298.
21. D.E. Easson, 'The Lollards of Kyle', in *Juridical Review*, xlviii, 123–8.
22. *Diocesan Registers of Glasgow*, ii, 203.
23. *RSS*.1:1425.
24. *Gavin Ros*, 654.
25. *Knox*, ii, 57.
26. *Diocesan Registers of Glasgow*, i, 303.
27. Justiciary Records (SRO), JC1/2, fos 37v, 39v, 130.
28. *Diocesan Registers of Glasgow*, i, 545–7, 549–50.
29. *Ibid.*, 512–13.
30. *The Scots Peerage*, ed. J. Balfour-Paul. (1909–14), Volume iv, 565. (hereafter, *Scots Peerage*).
31. Edinburgh Testaments, CC8/8/13, fo.32; testament of Adam Fullarton's wife, Marjorie Roger. At the time of her death in March 1583 Adam owed money to the laird, Fullarton of Dreghorn, making it seem likely that he belonged to that branch of the Fullarton family.
32. T. Pont, *Cunninghame Topographised, 1604–8*, ed. J.S. Dobbie (1876), 12, 108–10. D. Calderwood, *History*, iii, 621.
33. M. Aston, *op.cit.*, 232.

CHAPTER FIVE

1. For provisional list of persons accused of heresy or believed to have had protestant sympathies or associations, 1528–46, see M.H.B. Sanderson, *Cardinal of Scotland*, 270–84.

2. Calderwood, *History*, i, 104.
3. *Scots Peerage*, vi, 511–12.
4. *The St. Andrews Formulare*, eds G. Donaldson and C. Macrae (Stair Society, 1944), Volume ii, 59.
5. *Accounts of the Lord Treasurer of Scotland*, ed. J. Balfour Paul and others, vi (1903), 313.
6. G. Donaldson, *All the Queen's Men: Power and Politics in Mary Stewart's Scotland* (London, 1983), 11.
7. *LP, Henry VIII*, xii, part i, 703.
8. *Knox*, i, 27–8.
9. *Scots Peerage*, iv, 232–4
10. I.B. Cowan and D.E. Easson, *Medieval Religious Houses, Scotland* (2nd edn, London, 1976).
11. F.D. Bardgett, *op.cit.*, 56–7.
12. A. Ross, 'Notes on the Religious Orders in pre-Reformation Scotland', in McRoberts, *Essays on the Scottish Reformation*, 185–240, *passim*. J. Durkan, 'Scottish Evangelicals in the patronage of Thomas Cromwell', in *RSCHS*, xxi (1982), *passim*. J. Kirk, 'The Religion of Early Scottish Protestants', in *Studies in Church History, Subsidia 8, Humanism and Reform, Essays in Honour of James K. Cameron*, ed. J. Kirk (Oxford, 1991), 361–411.
13. A. Ross, 'Notes on the Religious Orders', *passim*.
14. *Ibid.*, 204n.
15. *Knox*, i, 19–21.
16. *Acts of the Lords of Council in Public Affairs, 1501–4*, ed. R.K. Hannay (London, 1932), 422.
17. D. Shaw, 'John Willock', in *Reformation and Revolution*, ed. D.Shaw (Edinburgh, 1967), 42–69. J. Durkan, 'Scottish reformers, the less than golden legend', in *Innes Review*, xlv, part i, (1994), 8–10.
18. *Ibid*.
19. *Register of Ministers, Elders and Deacons of the Christian Congregation of St Andrews*, ed. D.H. Fleming (SHS, 1889–90), 89–104 (hereafter, *St Andrews Kirk Session Register*).
20. *CSP Scot*, i, 34.
21. *Knox*, ii, 333–35.
22. *Scots Peerage*, ii, 468–71; *Knox*, i, 13.
23. Examples culled from documents in Portland Muniments, Box 1.
24. P. Lorimer, *Patrick Hamilton* (Edinburgh, 1857), 215.
25. *LP Henry VIII*, xviii, part i, 494.
26. M.H.B. Sanderson, *Cardinal of Scotland*, 148–58, for a fuller account of these events.
27. *Acts of the Parliaments of Scotland*, eds. T. Thomson and C. Innes (London, 1814–75), ii, 410–15, 424–5.
28. *Ayr Burgh Accounts*, 90.
29. *LP Henry VIII*, xviii, part i, 140.

30. See M. Merriman, 'The Assured Scots', in *SHR*, xlvii (1968), 10–34.
31. *LP Henry VIII*, xvii, 1193.
32. *Ibid.*, xviii, part i, 174.
33. This aspect of Anglo-Scottish relations is discussed in K. Brown, 'The Price of Friendship: the "Well-Affected" and English Economic Clientage in Scotland before 1603', in R. Mason, ed., *Scotland and England* (Edinburgh, 1987), 139–62.
34. This subject has been much studied by historians in recent years. See R. Mason, 'Covenant and Commonwealth: the language of politics in Reformation Scotland', in N. Macdougall, ed., *Church, Politics and Society in Scotland, 1408–1929* (Edinburgh, 1983), 97–126; R. Mason, 'Scotching the Brut: politics, history and national myth in 16th century Britain', in R. Mason, ed., *Scotland and England* (Edinburgh, 1987), 60–84; R. Mason, 'Chivalry and Citizenship: aspects of national identity in Renaissance Scotland', in R. Mason and N. Macdougall, eds., *People and Power in Scotland, Essays in honour of T.C. Smout* (Edinburgh, 1992); R. Mason, 'The Scottish Reformation and the Origins of Anglo-British imperialism', in R. Mason, ed., *Scots and Britons: Scottish Political Thought and the Union of 1603* (Cambridge, 1994), 161–86; M.Merriman, 'James Henrisoun and "Great Britain": British Union and the Scottish Commonwealth', in R. Mason, ed., *Scotland and England* (Edinburgh, 1987), 85–112; A.H. Williamson, 'Scotland, antichrist and the invention of Great Britain', in J. Dwyer, R. Mason and A. Murdoch, eds., *New Perspectives on the Politics and Culture of Early Modern Scotland* (Edinburgh, 1982), 34–58; J.E.A. Dawson, 'Anglo-Scottish Protestant Culture and integration in sixteenth-century Britain', in S.G. Ellis and S. Barber, eds., *Conquest and Union, Fashioning the British State, 1485–1725* (London, 1995),
35. *Acts of the Parliaments of Scotland*, ii, 431–2, 443.
36. Ayr Burgh Accounts, manuscript volume in Carnegie Library, Ayr: former SRO number, B6/25/1, fo. 32v.
37. *Knox*, i, 51.
38. *Ibid; RSS* 3:962.
39. M.H.B. Sanderson, *Cardinal of Scotland*, 185–8.
40. *LP Henry VIII*, xx, part i, 210.

CHAPTER SIX

1. A.I. Cameron, ed., *The Scottish Correspondence of Mary of Lorraine* (SHS, 1927), 133.
2. *Ibid.*
3. *Royal Commission on Historical Manuscripts, Papers of the Marquis of Salisbury*, i (London, 1883), 59.
4. F.D. Bardgett, *op. cit.*, 33
5. For George Wishart's visit to Ayrshire, see *Knox*, i, 61–2.
6. For a modern assessment of Wishart and his impact, see J. Durkan, 'Scottish

Evangelicals', and the same author's 'Scottish Reformers, the less than golden legend', 2–7.
7. *Knox*, i, 61.
8. *Acts of the Lords of Council in Public Affairs*, 416.
9. On the career of Mr Robert Lockhart, see I.A. Muirhead, 'M. Robert Lockhart', in *Innes Review*, xxii, part ii (1971), 85–100.
10. *Liber de Mailros*, ii, 598.
11. Reference to Rankin of Shiel in *Knox*, i, 62.
12. *Ayr Burgh Accounts*, 95–6.
13. *Register of the Privy Council*, i, 28–9.
14. *Ancient Criminal Trials*, i, part i, 353.
15. J. Durkan, 'Some Local Heretics', 73–4.
16. *Knox* i, 114–16.
17. *Melrose Regality Records*, Volume iii, 180.
18. *Statutes of the Scottish Church*, 84–134.
19. T. Winning, 'Church Councils in sixteenth century Scotland', in McRoberts, *Essays on the Scottish Reformation*, 333–4.
20. *Ibid.*, 334.
21. J. Stuart, ed., *Records of the Monastery of Kinloss* (Edinburgh, 1872).
22. *Statutes of the Scottish Church*, 135–82.
23. A.F. Mitchell, *The Catechism set forth by Archbishop Hamilton (1552): together with the Two-penny Faith (1559)* (Edinburgh, 1882); see also W.C. Dickinson, G. Donaldson and I.A. Milne, eds. *A Source Book of Scottish History*, ii (Edinburgh, 1958), 149–50.
24. European influences on attempts at internal reform of the pre-Reformation Scottish church are discussed in J. K. Cameron, '"Catholic Reform" in Germany and in the pre-1560 Church in Scotland', in *RSCHS*, xx (1979), 105–117. For efforts of Archbishop James Beaton of Glasgow to implement the decrees of the 1559 Council, see *Melrose Regality Records*, iii, 167–87.
25. Cameron, '"Catholic Reform" . . .', 115; there is strong evidence that the actual 'author' was the English exile, the Dominican Richard Marshall.
26. *Scottish Correspondence of Mary of Lorraine*, 427.
27. *Acts of the Parliaments of Scotland*, ii, 499–500.
28. *Ibid.*, 485, 488–9.
29. *Knox*, i, 85–6.
30. *Ibid.*, i, 118–123, for narrative of Knox's visit to Scotland in 1555–6.
31. *Ibid.*, i, 120–1.
32. *CSP Scot.*, i, 12.
33. Register of Deeds, RD1/1, fo.252v.
34. *Knox*, i, 121.
35. John Davidson, 'A Memorial of the Life of Two Worthy Christians, Robert Campbell of Kinzeancleuch and his wife, Elizabeth Campbell', printed in C. Rogers, *Three Scottish Reformers* (Edinburgh, 1874), 100–131 (hereafter, Davidson's 'Life of . . . Robert Campbell').

36. *Ayr Burgh Accounts*, 96, 104, 106, 108, 111, 120, 122.
37. *Ibid.*, 124–7.
38. *LP Henry VIII*, xix, part i, 809.
39. F.D. Bardgett, *op. cit.*, 48–53.
40. *Knox*, i, 122–3.

CHAPTER SEVEN

1. D. Laing, ed., *The Works of John Knox* (Wodrow Society, 1864), vi, 78.
2. *Knox.*, 131–6.
3. *Ibid.*, 136.
4. *Ibid.*, 137–8.
5. *Ibid.*, 246–54, for their correspondence.
6. *Ibid.*, 148.
7. *Ibid.*, 126.
8. J.E.A. Dawson, 'The Scottish Reformation and the Theatre of Martyrdom', in *Studies in Church History, Subsidia*, Volume 10 (Oxford, 1997) 268–70.
9. *Knox*, i, 148–52.
10. *Ibid.*, 152.
11. D. Hay Fleming, *Mary Queen of Scots*, (1897), 22–4; Prince Labanoff, *Lettres et Mémoires de Marie, Reine d'Ecosse*, 7 vols. (1844), i, 50–6.
12. *Knox*, i, 154–8. The date is given (without authority) as 5 December 1558 in *Foreign Calendar, Elizabeth*, i, 66.
13. *Source Book of Scottish History*, ii, 163–7.
14. Winning, 'Church Councils', 348.
15. *Knox.*, i, 159.
16. Register of Acts and Decreets, CS 7/30, 23 January 1564/5.
17. For a fuller study of the career of sir Robert Leggat, see M.H.B. Sanderson, *Mary Stewart's People*, 149–64.
18. Ayr Burgh Court Book, 1549–60 (Carnegie Library, Ayr), fo.32v.
19. *Ibid.*, fo.23v.
20. Register of Acts and Decreets, CS7/32, 6 July 1564.
21. Ayr Burgh Court Book, 1549–60, fos. 16, 31v, 52.
22. *Ibid.*, fo.15v.
23. *Statutes of the Scottish Church*, 156ff for statutes of the 1559 council.
24. Text reproduced in *Knox*, ii, Appendix V, 255–6.
25. For a Note on the significance of 'Flitting Friday', see G. Donaldson, 'Flitting Friday, The Beggars' Summons and Knox's sermon at Perth', in *SHR*, xxxix (1960), 175–6.
26. For the correspondence between Willock and Kennedy, see *Wodrow Miscellany*, i (1844), 265–77.
27. *Ayr Obit Book, passim.*
28. *Charters of the Friars Preachers of Ayr*, ed. R.W. Cochran-Patrick (Ayrshire and Wigtonshire Archeological Association, 1881), *passim* (hereafter, *Ayr Dominican Charters*).

29. Information gleaned while researching for a paper on 'The evidence for Personal Belief in Sixteenth Century Scotland', *forthcoming*.
30. W.M. Bryce, *The Scottish Grey Friars* (Edinburgh, 1909), i, 358.
31. Davidson's 'Life of . . . Robert Campbell', 108.
32. *Ayr Burgh Accounts*, 130.
33. *Ibid.*, 30.
34. Ayr Burgh Court Book, 1549–60, fo.15v.
35. On Catholic recusancy, see M.H.B. Sanderson, 'Catholic Recusancy in Sixteenth Century Scotland', in *Innes Review*, xxi, part ii (1970), 87–107.
36. Ayr Burgh Court Book, 1549–60, fo.53v.
37. *Ancient Criminal Trials*, i, part i, 407*
38. *Knox*, i, 171, 175.
39. *Ibid.*, 164.
40. *Ibid.*, 178.
41. A. Teulet, *Relations politiques de la France et de l'Espagne avec l'Ecosse* (Paris, 1862), i, 319.
42. *Knox*, i, 264.
43. T. Rhymer, *Foedera* (London, 1704–35), xv, 569–71.
44. *Knox*, i, 314–16.
45. *Foedera*, xv, 593–7.
46. Morton Muniments (SRO), GD 150/2234.
47. J.E.A. Dawson, 'Anglo-Scottish Protestant Culture', 113–14.

CHAPTER EIGHT

1. For the proceedings of the 'Reformation Parliament', see *Acts of the Parliaments of Scotland*, ii, 525–6. See also, for biographical information on individual Ayrshire commissioners and others attending that parliament, M.D. Young, ed., *The Parliaments of Scotland, Burgh and Shire Commissioners* (Edinburgh, 1993), ii, *passim*, and ii, 761, 809–10, for special lists and analysis.
2. *Ayr Burgh Accounts*, 31, 33.
3. *CSP Scot.*, i, 880, 885–6.
4. The text of the First Book of Discipline is printed in *Knox*, Volume ii, 280–324.
5. *CSP Scot.*, i, 885.
6. E. Percy, *John Knox*, 105.
7. *Acts and Proceedings of Kirk of Scotland from the year 1560*, eds T. Thomson and C. Innes, 3 Volumes (Bannatyne and Maitland Clubs, 1839–45), i, 4. Usually referred to as *The Buik of the Universal Kirk* (hereafter, *BUK*).
8. *Knox*, ii, 324.
9. Details of the appointments of all ministers, exhorters and readers, 1559–1600, with biographical information on many of them will be found in the Appendix, below. For the historical context of the provision of ministers, J. Kirk, *Patterns of Reform, Continuity and Change in the Reformation Kirk* (Edinburgh, 1989) especially, Ch. 4, 'Recruitment to the Ministry at the

Reformation', 96–153.
10. *BUK*, i,61; Edinburgh Register of Testaments, CC8/8/4, fo.87v.
11. For a discussion of the operation of the Thirds arrangement, see G. Donaldson, ed., *The Thirds of Benefices, 1561–72* (Scottish History Society, 1949), vii–xxxix (hereafter, *Thirds*).
12. *BUK*, i, 61.
13. Details of appointments in Appendix, below.
14. *Knox*, ii, 103; *Thirds,* xxv.
15. *Ibid.*, 152.
16. This issue is discussed in F.D. Bardgett, 'Four Parische Kirkis to Ane Preicheir', in *RSCHS*, xxii (1986), 195–209.
17. On stipends, see Introduction to *Thirds*, and The First Book of Discipline, in *Knox*, ii, 289–90.
18. H. Scott, *Fasti*, iii, 46
19. *Knox*, ii, 286–7

CHAPTER NINE

1. M.H.B. Sanderson, 'Catholic recusancy', 87–107.
2. *BUK*, i, 5–6.
3. *Knox*, ii, 189.
4. *Ibid.*, ii, 54–5.
5. *Ibid.*, ii, 57.
6. *Ibid.*, ii, 55–6.
7. *Ibid.*, ii, 57.
8. *Ibid.*, ii, 70–1, 76–7; R. Pitcairn, *Ancient Criminal Trials*, i, 427–30; *CSP Scot.*, ii, 70–1, 76–7.
9. J. Fergusson, *The White Hind*, 41–53, for a full account of the Queen's Ayrshire progress.
10. This is fully discussed in G. Donaldson, *All the Queen's Men*, especially Ch. 6, 83–116.
11. *Knox*, ii, 12.
12. *Ancient Criminal Trials*, i, 30.
13. *BUK*, ii, 703–27.
14. *Wodrow Miscellany*, i, 187.
15. *BUK*, ii, 722; iii, 803.
16. *Register of the Privy Council*, viii, 405, 421, 719, 732, 845.
17. Reg. of Abbreviates of feu charters of kirklands (SRO), E14/2, f. 299.
18. *RSS* 6: 256.
19. Register of Deeds, RD1/5, fo. 415v; *RMS* 4: 1846.
20. J. Ferguson, *The White Hind*, 54–66.
21. M.H.B. Sanderson, 'Kilwinning at the time of the Reformation and its first Minister William Kirkpatrick', in *Ayrshire Archaeological and Natural History Collections*, X (1972), 102–26, on Alexander Henderson and William Kirkpatrick.

22. Last reference, *Ayr Burgh Accounts*, 267.
23. For different interpretations of these developments, see G. Donaldson, *The Scottish Reformation* (Cambridge, 1960), Chs. 3 and 4; M. Lynch, 'Calvinism in Scotland, 1559–1638', in M. Prestwich, ed., *International Calvinism, 1541–1715* (London, 1985), 225–55; J. Kirk, *Patterns of Reform*, Chs. 5, 6 and 9.
24. *CSP Scot.*, vii, 279.
25. *Wodrow Miscellany*, i, 433.
26. M.H.B. Sanderson, 'Manse and Glebe in the Sixteenth Century', in *RSCHS*, xix (1975), 81–92.
27. *Ibid.*, 90–1.
28. M.H.B. Sanderson, *Cardinal of Scotland*, Ch. 3, 30–42.
29. *Knox*, ii, 288–9, for passages on the minister's household in the First Book of Discipline.
30. The Memorial is illustrated and described, with text of the inscription, in *Archaeological Collections of Ayr and Wigton*, iv (1884), 41–3.
31. D. McNaught, *Kilmaurs Parish and Burgh* (Paisley, 1912), 150.
32. *Knox*, ii, 288.
33. A.I. Dunlop, ed., *The Scottish Ministers' Widows' Fund, 1743–1993* (Edinburgh, 1992).
34. *Thirds*, 264.
35. Diligence Records, Ayr Register of Hornings (SRO), DI 125/1, fo.13.
36. *Ibid.*, DI 125/1, fo.106.
37. Ayr Town Council Minutes, 1549–60 (Carnegie Library, Ayr), former SRO ref. B6/11/1/1,f.6.
38. Irvine Burgh Records, Council Minutes (SRO), B37/12/1,fo.19.
39. *Muniments of Irvine*, i, 221.
40. Irvine Burgh Records, B37/12/1, fo.3.
41. *Ibid.*, fo.8.
42. *Ayr Burgh Accounts*, 145–6.
43. *Knox*, ii, 312.
44. These marginalia include various versions of the lines, 'I think it is ane plesand thing, ane bonny las to cum upon'.
45. *Knox*, ii, 306–8.
46. *BUK*, i, 98–9
47. *Ibid.*, i 159. For the First Book of Discipline on Sunday observance, *Knox*, ii, 312.
48. *Ibid.*, ii, 314.
49. *BUK*, i, 54.
50. Irvine Burgh Records, B37/12/3, fo.3; *Ayr Burgh Accounts*, 218.
51. Edinburgh Testaments, CC8/8/2, fo.116.
52. Glasgow Testaments, CC9/7/1, fo.93v.
53. Edinburgh Testaments, CC8/8/6, fo.230v.
54. *Ibid.*, CC8/8/2, fo.238.

55. *Ibid.*, CC8/8/3, fo.117v.
56. *Ibid.*, CC8/8/3, fo.171v.
57. *Ibid.*, CC8/8/7 17 February 1579/80
58. *Knox*, ii, 314.
59. Davidson's 'Life of . . . Robert Campbell', 114.
60. R. Mason, 'Covenant and Commonweal: the language of politics in Reformation Scotland', in N. Macdougall, ed., *Church, Politics and Society in Scotland, 1408–1929* (Edinburgh, 1983), 105.

Appendix

Revised Fasti of Ministers, Exhorters and Readers in Ayrshire, 1559–1600

This *Fasti* includes incumbents who were, or who may have been, in office in 1600, but one of the sources used is the Register of Assignation of Stipends (E47) which includes the year 1601. The information, which itself fills out the lists in Hew Scott's *Fasti Ecclesiae Scoticanae* (Edin. 1915–) Volumes iii and viii, is not complete but should provide a basis to which new data may be added. Biographical details, which have been kept to a minimum, illustrate the antecedents of personnel in the early Reformed ministry. Information taken from Scott's *Fasti*, for which no source is given in that publication, or where the source given is obscure, has simply been referenced '*Fasti*'. All information in Scott's *Fasti* up to 1574 has been checked against that in Charles H. Haws, *Scottish Parish Clergy at the Reformation* (Scottish Record Society, 1972).

Parishes are listed in alphabetical order for ease of reference. The letter (A) or (I) after the names denotes the presbytery of Ayr or Irvine, after 1581. With regard to dates of service, it has to be remembered that the relevant sources do not refer to every year from 1559 to 1600. The *Register of Ministers* (Reg.Min.) and *Wodrow Miscellany*[1] (Wod.Misc.) refer to the period 1567–76, with gaps. The Register of Assignation of Stipends (Reg.Assig) records incumbents in the years, 1576, '78, '80, '85–86, '88–89, '90, '91, '93–97, '99 and 1601. When supplying dates of service it has been assumed, unless otherwise indicated, that incumbents in charge in two of the above dates were in office in the intervening year(s). In many cases parishes linked in groups in 1574 (as indicated by the reference to *Wod.Misc.*) remained so until nearly the end of the century. The only benefice-holders included are serving Ministers, Exhorters and Readers. Designations are given exactly as in the record concerned, usually without gloss. The significance of the early general use of the title Minister is discussed in Chapter 8, above.

ALLOWAY (A). JAMES RAMSAY, Reader, 1567-c.80 (*Reg.Min.*,39; *Wod. Misc.*,386; Reg.Assig., E47/1–2). Stipend paid by the Minister of Ayr. May have been former curate of A; on 5 Sept.1569 subscribed will of an A. parishioner who called him 'curat of my paroche kirk', perhaps out of habit (Edin.Tests, CC8/8/6,f.105). Gr. pars.and vic. of A. 1573 (*Fasti* viii,211).

Appendix 159

JAMES DALRYMPLE, Minister (of Ayr) had oversight, 1574, 1576 (*Wod. Misc.*, 38; Reg.Assig.,E47/1).
THOMAS FALCONER, Reader, 1585–89 (Reg.Assig.,E47/3–4).
WILLIAM WALLACE, Reader, 1594–97 (Reg.Assig.,E47/6–7).
MR ADAM DENNY, Reader, 1599-at least 1601 (Reg.Assig.,E47/8).

ARDROSSAN (I) ALEXANDER HENDERSON, Exhorter, 1567–72 (*Reg.Min.*, 38; *Thirds*,263). Trans. to Stewarton, Lammas 1572. Biog. details under KILMAURS.
THOMAS BOYD, Reader, 1572–73 (*Reg.Min.*,38). Trans. from Riccarton. Trans. to Beith.
WILLIAM MONTGOMERIE, Exhorter, 1573–74 (*Reg.Min.*,38) Trans. to Stewarton.
SIR GEORGE BOYD, Reader, 1574–91 (*Wod.Misc.*,384; Reg.Assig.,E47/1–5). Trans. from Dalry.
ALEXANDER CALLANDER, Minister (at Largs) had oversight, 1574 (*Wod.Misc.*, 384).
MR ALEXANDER CAMPBELL, Minister, 1591-bef.1603 (Reg.Assig.,E47/5–8).

AUCHINLECK (A). ADAM LANDELLS, Exhorter, 1567-c.70 (*Reg.Min.*,39; *Thirds*, 264). Also had Cumnock and Ochiltree in charge. Biog. details under OCHILTREE.
JOHN GEMMILL, Reader, 1574-at least 1601 (*Wod.Misc.*,385; Reg.Assig.,E47/1–8).
MR JOHN INGLIS, Minister, 1574–?75 (*Wod.Misc.*,385). Trans. from and ret. to Ochiltree, 1576–77, with A. in charge (*Reg.Min.*, 85; Edin.Tests. CC8/8/5,f.345v). Minister of A. again in 1578–80, with O. in charge (Reg.Assig.,E47/1–2).
MR GEORGE WALKER was Minister by 1617. Son of John W. bailie in Newmilns (*Fasti*, iii,3).

AYR(A). Note: 'A preacher' was brought to Ayr in early 1559 who was probably John Willock, who preached in Ayr at Easter 1559 and left Ayrshire in late May with the Congregation of Kyle and Cunninghame when they marched to Perth (*Ayr Burgh Accounts*, 130). MR CHRISTOPHER GOODMAN, Minister, Nov. 1559–60 (*Fasti* iii,5; *Ayr Accounts*,30–1). Trans. to St Andrews.
JOHN ORR, Schoolmaster and Reader, Nov.1559–? (Ayr Burgh Court Book,f.53v).
ROBERT ACHESON, Minister,1559–60x62 (*Ayr Burgh Accounts*,33,134).
JAMES DALRYMPLE, Minister,1560–80 (*Reg.Min.*,39; *Thirds*,262; *Wod.Misc.*, 386; Reg.Assig.,E47/1–2). Former chorister and chaplain in St John's kirk, Ayr (*Ayr Burgh Accounts, passim*). Recommended to general assembly of 1560

for service in Reformed kirk (*BUK*,i,4). Entered at Beltane 1568. Pres. vic. A. 1571, dem. 1574 in fav. of Hugh Kennedy, Reader. Married Janet Cochrane; charity to her and their children,1581 (Ayr Council Minutes,B6/11/1/1,f.6). See also *Calderwood*, ii,45; Register of Acts and Decreets,xlviii,f.145).

HUGH KENNEDY, Reader,1574 (Reg.Pres.Ben.,i(4),18).

WILLIAM CAMPBELL, Reader,1576–79 (Reg.Assig.,E47/1–2).

JOHN PORTERFIELD, Minister,1580-c.1604 (Reg.Assig.,E47/2–8). Trans. from Dumbarton,1580. Pres. pars. A. 25 April 1581 and pars. A. 'secundo',22 Sept.1582. Brother of Porterfield of that Ilk. Student at St Andrews, 1539(?) (*Acta.Fac.Art.,St And.*). Wit. doc. earl of Glencairn at Finlayston, 1545 (Glencairn Mun., GD39/1/56). Pres. vic. Ardrossan, 1568, on dem. sir Allan Porterfield (*RSS* 6:256). Member of at least 11 general assemblies before 1597. As 'servant' of William 5th earl of Glencairn, nominated to the archbishopric of Glasgow in 1571, but the appointment was not operative (Watt, *Medieval Fasti*, 150). A commissioner appointed in 1589 for preservation of true religion in Kyle. Said to have been 'easy in his disposition, even going to bowbutts and archery on the Sabbath afternoons'. Married (1) Margaret Smollet; (2) Elizabeth Stewart, who survived him. See also *Calderwood*, ii, 501;iv, 566;v, 447.

MR NINIAN YOUNG, Reader,1580–93 (Reg.Assig.,E47/2–6).

MR JOHN WELSH, Minister, came to Ayr as assistant to John Porterfield in 1600. See also *Fasti*,iii, 5–7.

BALLANTRAE (Kirkcudbright Innertig) (A). JOHN CUNNINGHAM, Exhorter, 1571–74 (RSS, 6:1151; *Thirds*, 263; *Wod.Misc.*,387n.). Trans. to Dailly.

ALEXANDER KENNEDY, Reader, 1574–85 (*Wod.Misc.*,387 and n;Reg.Assig., E47/1–3).

MR JAMES GREG, Minister (of Colmonell) had oversight, 1574 (*Wod.Misc.*,387). No entries 1593–1601 in Reg.Assig.

BARNWEIL (A). UN-NAMED Minister in 1561 (*Thirds*, 95) may be the following:

SIR JAMES MILLER, Exhorter, 1566 (*Reg.Min.*,39). Trans. to Symington bef. 1574. Biog. details under SYMINGTON.

MR JOHN NISBET, Minister (of Tarbolton) had oversight, 1574 (*Wod. Misc.*,386).

ROBERT GAW, Reader,1574-bef.1585 (*Wod.Misc.*,386). Former friar of Fail,1544–58 (Register House charters (SRO), RH6/1353b, 1353c, 1741).

DAVID ALLANSON, Reader, 1576–80 (Reg.Assig., E47/1–2). Trans. to St Quivox by 1585. May be former Dominican friar of Ayr who was paid his pension by town until 1618 (*Ayr Burgh Accounts*, 267).

ROBERT CUNNINGHAM, Minister, c.1580 (*Fasti*, iii, 76). Married Jean Hunter, dau. Robert H. of Hunterston. She married (2) bef. 1608

Alexander Scrymgeour, Minister of Irvine. Their dau. Jean became heiress of Hunterston and married Patrick, s. Wm Hunter of Binberrie Yairds. (J. Paterson, *History of Ayr and Wigton*, iii, 347).
UNNAMED Reader, 1585, stipend paid from Third of Fail (Reg. Assig., E47/3/1, f. 42v).
ENTRY DELETED, 1586 (*Ibid.*, E47/3/2, f. 48v).

BEITH (I). WILLIAM KIRKPATRICK, Minister (of Kilwinning) had oversight, 1574 (*Wod. Misc., 384).*
SIR THOMAS BOYD, Reader, 1574–80 (*Wod. Misc., 384; Reg. Min.*, 85; Reg. Assig., E47/1–2). Former chaplain, (?)s. of Lord Boyd.
JOHN WALLACE, Reader, 1585–86, 'changit be the commissionaris advice', 26 Nov. 1586 (*Fasti*, iii, 81).
ROBERT MAXWELL, Reader, 1586–88 (Reg. Assig., E47/3–4).
MR JOHN YOUNG, Minister, 1589-bef.15 Feb.1610 (Reg.Assig., to 1601, E47/4–8). Brother of Andrew Y., servant of James VI. Had previously served as Minister at N. Berwick, Duns, Jedburgh and Irvine. One of the Visitors in Ayrshire in 1593. Called before privy council in 1610 for communing with 'a known trafficking papist', his brother-in-law a Capuchin friar. D. bef. 13 Aug. 1622. Married (1) Jean Wallace; (2) Margaret Campbell, who survived him. His s. George Minister of Mauchline.

COLMONELL (A). MR JAMES GREG, Minister, 1568–86 (*RSS*, 6:366; *Thirds*, 261; *Reg. Min.*, 40; *Wod. Misc.*, 387; Reg. Assig.,E47/1–2; Edin. Tests, CC8/8/15, f. 171). Poss. former vic. Dunsyre, Lanarkshire.
THOMAS FALCONER, Reader, 1568- by 1574 (Reg. Min.,40). Trans to Dailly by 1574.
ALLAN CATHCART, Reader, 1574 (*Wod.Misc.*, 387).
ANDREW GRAY, Reader, 1576–91 (Reg. Assig., E47/1–5). Former prebendary of Maybole collegiate church and parson of Kells in Galloway. Gr. pension by Cassillis 21 May 1566 for over 20 years' service (*RMS* 4:1846).
MR JAMES YOUNG, Minister, 1585–? (Reg. Assig., E47/3–8). Trans. from Dailly where he had been Reader.

COYLTON (A). JAMES DAVIDSON, Reader, 1569 (*Thirds*, 265). Exhorter, 1570–74 (*Reg.Min.*, 39). Trans. to Dalmellington as Minister.
JOHN CAMPBELL, Exhorter, 1574–80 (*Wod.Misc.*, 386; Reg. Assig., E47/1–2).
JAMES DAVIDSON (above) Minister (of Dalmellington) had oversight in 1574 (*Wod.Misc.*,386).
MR MATTHEW WYLIE, Minister (of Dalmellington) had oversight, 1578 (Reg. Assig., E47/1). Trans. to C. as Minister, 1581–90 (*Fasti.*, iii, 20). Had oversight of Dalmellington and Dalrymple, being called Minister of Dalrymple, 1582 (RSS xlix, f. 9v). Pres. to vic. Coylton, 1582 (Reg.Pres.

Ben., i,57) and wit. will there 18 Feb. 1584 (Edin.Tests., CC8/8/14, f. 258). Trans. back to Damellington in 1590.

MR WILLIAM WALLACE, Minister, 1598 (*Fasti.*, iii, 20). Trans. from Dalmellington.
Minister of Dalrymple had oversight of C. in 1601 (Reg. Assig., E47/8), see below.

CRAIGIE (A). SIR DAVID WALLACE, Reader, 1574–79 (*Wod.Misc.* 386; Reg. Assig., E47/1–2).
GEORGE CAMPBELL, Minister (of Dundonald) had oversight in 1574 (*Wod.Misc.*, 386).
MR DAVID MYLNE, Minister, 1576, with Riccarton also in charge (*Fasti*, iii, 22). Trans. from Kilwinning where he had been reader. Trans. to Dundonald same year. Biog. details under DUNDONALD.
LAURENCE DALGLEISH, Minister, 1580–?86 (Reg.Assig.,E47/2–3). He is entered in 1580 under Riccarton, of which he probably had joint charge. He is unnamed in the record for 1586.
'NA READARIS' in 1580. Reg. Assig. E47/2/2f.59v.
MR ALEXANDER FORSYTH, Minister, 1586–91 (*Fasti*, iii, 22; Reg. Assig., E47/4–5). Trans. from Dumfries. Pres. vic. Dundonald, 20 June 1587. Deposed post-14 Oct. 1590, but pres. to Abercrombie bef. 20 Oct. 1593 (*Fasti*, iii, 22).
MR NATHAN INGLIS, Minister, 1593-c. Feb. 1612 (Reg. Assig., to 1601, E47/6–8). Married Anne Eccles, dau. John E. of Kildonan; their son James, Minister of Dailly. Imprisoned in Dumbarton castle for attending the Aberdeen general assembly of 1605. D. c. 1612, aged 42 (*Fasti*, iii, 22).

CROSBIE (A). Quasi-parochial pre-Reformation chapel dependent on Dundonald parish. SIR ADAM WALLACE, Exhorter, 1567 (*Reg. Min.*, 39). Former chaplain in the area, 1548–58, and clerk of the bailiary court of Cunninghame (*RMS* 4:256; Reg. of Acts and Decreets, CS7/13, fos. 15, 183v; 17, f. 15; 33, f. 101v).
GEORGE CAMPBELL, Minister (of Dundonald) had oversight, 1574 (*Wod. Misc.*, 386).
ROBERT BURN, Reader, with Dundonald, 1574 (*Wod. Misc.*, 386). Biog. details under DUNDONALD.
DAVID HALL, Reader, with Dundonald, 1576 (Reg. Assig., E47/1).
THOMAS STEVENSON, Reader, with Dundonald, 1578 (Reg. Assig., E47/1).
MR DAVID MYLNE, Minister (of Dundonald), prob. had oversight, linked to Dundonald, from 1576–1617 (Reg. Assig. until 1601, E47/1–8).

CUMNOCK (A). ADAM LANDELLS, Exhorter, 1567–71 (*Reg. Min.*, 39). Also had charge of Auchinleck and Ochiltree. Biog. details under OCHILTREE.

MR JOHN INGLIS, Minister (of Ochiltree) had oversight, 1574 (Reg. Min. , 39).
MR JOHN RHIND, Minister, 1572-c. 76 (*Reg. Min.*, 39; *Wod. Misc.*, 385). Trans. from Kinglassie (Reader). D. bef. 22 May 1576 (*RSS* 7:613). Error: John Ramage named in *Fasti* iii, 215, as Reader at Cumnock, was Reader at Carmunnock in Lanarkshire.
GEORGE CAMPBELL, Minister, 1576–?78. Pres. to vic. C. on d. Mr John Rhind (Reg. Pres. Ben., i(4)43). Trans. from Dundonald.
MR WILLIAM HAMILTON OF BARDANOCH, Minister, 1578–95 (Reg. Assig., E47/1–6). Trans. to Dalry, Kirkcudbrightshire (*Fasti*, iii, 25).
JOHN DUNBAR, Reader, 1578–80 (Reg. Assig., E47/1–2).
ROBERT LOCKHART, Reader, 1589–90 (Reg. Assig., E47/4–5).
GEORGE DUNBAR OF POLLESCHE, Minister, 1599-c. 1607 (Reg. Assig., to 1601, E47/8/1–2; *Fasti*, iii, 25). Trans. to Ayr.

DAILLY (A). JOHN CUNNINGHAM, Minister, 'divers yeris before' 1567–1590 (Reg. of Acts and Decreets, CS7/45, fos. 453–4; *Reg. Min.*, 40; *Wod. Misc.*, 387; Reg. Assig., E47/1–4; *Fasti* iii, 28). Admitted 'to baptise and marry at Kirkmichael', 1567 (*Fasti*, iii, 41). Had also been Exhorter at Ballantrae, 1571 (q.v.). Adm. (?a second time) to D. in 1573 with oversight of Girvan and Kirkoswald. Trans. to Girvan.
MR JAMES GREG, Minister, 1568 (*RSS*, 6:366). Trans. to Colmonell that year; may have been a temporary arrangement while John Cunningham (above) took charge at Kirkmichael.
JOHN YOUNG, Reader, 1567–86 (*Reg. Min.*, 40; Reg. Assig., E47/1–3).
THOMAS FALCONER, Reader, 1574 (*Wod. Misc.*, 387).
SIR WILLIAM ALLANSON, Reader, 1576 (Reg. Assig., E47/1). Former chaplain in Carrick, 1537–53 (RMS 3:1714, 1716, 1804; *RMS*, 4:195, 198) and at St John's Kirk, Ayr, 1554 (Carlton of Killochan Mun. (SRO), GD117/44, 45). Vicar of Dailly, 1560. Prosecuted for taking part in the public celebration of mass in Carrick, Easter 1563 (Pitcairn, *Ancient Criminal Trials*, i, 427–30).
ALEXANDER BOYD, (?) Reader; pre-1591. Said to have been deprived of the vic. of D. for 'absence from his charge', 17 March 1591 (*Fasti*, viii, 216, citing 'Misc. Eccles. Documents' and RSS lxii, f. 35.
DAVID BARCLAY, Minister, 1590–99 (Reg. Assig., to 1597, E47/5–7). Pres. to vic. of D. on dep. Alexander Boyd (above), 16 April 1591 (RSS, lxii, f. 35). Trans. to Maybole.
BLANK in the record in 1597 and 1601 (Reg. Assig., E47/8/1–2).
MR JAMES INGLIS was Minister by 1605 (*Fasti*, iii, 28).

DALMELLINGTON (A). LEONARD CLERK, Minister, 29 Nov.1559–?c.1567 (Ayr Burgh Court Book, 1549–60, f. 56v). Prob. son of Leonard C. burgess and bailie of Ayr (*Gavin Ros*, nos. 196, 436) and nephew of a L.C., chaplain at Ayr, 1519 (*Gavin Ros*, no. 335). Trans. to Kirkmichael, 1567.

JOHN MACCONNELL, Reader, 1571–2 (*Reg. Min*; Reg. Pres. Ben., i(3), 24).

DAVID CATHCART, Reader, 1572–80 (*Reg. Min.* 40; *Wod. Misc.* 386; Reg. Assig., E47/1–2).

JAMES DAVIDSON, Minister, 1574-c. 78 (*Wod. Misc.*, 386; Unnamed minister in 1576, Reg. Assig., E47/1, f.60v). Had oversight of Dalrymple and Coylton, 1574.

MATTHEW WYLIE, Minister, 1578–89 (Reg. Assig., E47/1–4). Trans. to Coylton.

ENTRY BLANK, 1590 (Reg. Assig., E47/5/1, f. 62).

MR JOHN MCQUHORNE, 1591–95 (Reg. Assig., E47/5–6). Pres. vic. D. on d. David Cathcart, 20 Dec. 1591 (*RSS* lxiii, f. 87). Trans. to Maybole.

MR WILLIAM WALLACE, Minister, 1595–98 (Reg. Assig., E47/6–7). Trans. to Coylton.

JOHN ANDERSON, Minister, 1599- at least 1601 (Reg. Assig., E47/8).

DALRY (I). Prob. error: *Fasti*, iii, 84; John Hepburn referred to here is more likely to have been Minister of Dalry in Kirkcudbrightshire (where John Hepburn was parson, 1554–1566) than Dalry in Ayrshire.

SIR GEORGE BOYD, Exhorter, 1567-c. 74 (*Reg. Min.*, 38; *Thirds*,, 263). Trans. to Ardrossan.

MR ARCHIBALD CRAWFORD, Minister (of Stevenston) had oversight, 1574 (*Wod. Misc.* 385).

ANDREW BLAIR, Reader, 1574–91 (*Wod. Misc*, 385; Reg. Assig., E47/1–5).

MR ROBERT MAXWELL, Minister, 1591 (Reg. Assig., E47/5).

MR ARCHIBALD BLACKBURN, Minister, 1593–1601 (Reg. Assig., E47/6-8). Trans. from Baldernock. Trans. to Aberdeen.

DALRYMPLE (A). GEORGE FEANE, Reader, 1570–80 (*Reg. Min.*, 39; *Thirds* 265; *Wod. Misc.* 386; Reg. Assig., E47/1–2).

JAMES DAVIDSON, Minister (of Dalmellington) had oversight, 1574 *Wod. Misc.*, 386).

MATTHEW WYLIE, Minister, had oversight in 1578 while Minister of Dalmellington (Reg. Assig., E47/1). The oversight probably continued until he became Minister of Dalrymple, 1590–1618, with Coylton in charge (Reg. Assig., to 1601, E47/5–8).

DREGHORN (I). SIR GAVIN NAISMITH, Exhorter, 1567–74. Had charge also of Kilmaurs. Called Minister of D., 1574, when he held the vicarage of Dreghorn (*Reg. Min.*, 38; *Thirds*, 264; *Wod. Misc.*., 385; Reg. of Acts and Decreets, 48, f. 229; Reg. of Feu Charters of Kirklands, E14/2, f. 210). Born in Bothwell parish, Lanarkshire, 1534, became a notary, 12 June 1556 (Notarial

Records (SRO), NP2/1, f. 70), burgess of Irvine by 1564 (*Laing Charters*, 778). Trans. to Kilmaurs. Married Alison Brown, who sued parishioners of D. for arrears of his vic. dues in 1590 (Ayr Hornings, DI 125/1, f. 106). He died in 1589.
OFFICE OF READER, said to be vacant in 1574 (*Wod. Misc.*, 358), but see below:
LAURENCE LYN, Reader, 1574 (*Fasti*, iii, 87–89; Reg. Assig., E47/1–4).
WILLIAM FULLARTON, Minister, 1590–1620 (Reg. Assig., to 1610, E47/5–8). Trans. from Kilmaurs. Called before privy council 5 Feb. 1601 for intercommuning with 'a trafficking priest'. Son of John F. of Dreghorn. His son James became Minister at Beith (*Fasti*, iii, 87).

DUNDONALD (A). Note: request for 'support of a ministrie' by lairds of Carnell, Sornbeg and Dreghorn to general assembly, 26 June 1565 (*BUK*, i, 61).
ROBERT BURN, Reader, with Crosbie, 1567–74 (*Reg. Min.*, 39; *Thirds*, 265; *Wod. Misc.*, 386). Formerly prior of the Carmelite friary, Irvine. His surname occurs in Irvine burgh; Kentigern Burn had a tenement there in 1547 (*RMS* 4:96). He granted a feu charter of the friary lands to Fullarton of Dreghorn, 1558 (J. Gillespie, *The Parish of Dundonald*, i, 149).
GEORGE CAMPBELL, Minister, 1572–76. Also had Riccarton in charge, 1572–74, when it was excluded and Crosbie, Craigie and Symington added. Trans. to Cumnock (*Fasti*, iii, 35; *Wod. Misc.*, 386).
DAVID HALL, Reader, 1576, with Crosbie (Reg. Assig., E47/1).
DAVID MYLNE, Minister, 1576–1617, with charge of Crosbie and Symington (Reg. Assig., E47/1–8). Trans. from Craigie. Married Janet Campbell (d.1618, when Robert C., burgess of Ayr, was one of her executors). The Minister d.1617 (*Fasti*, iii, 35).
THOMAS STEVENSON, Reader, 1578–9, with Crosbie (Reg. Assig., E47/1–2).
JOHN FULLER, Reader, 1580, with Crosbie (Reg. Assig., E47/2).

DUNLOP (I). JOHN (HANS) HAMILTON, Exhorter, 1567. Reader, 1567–96; Minister, 1597–1606 (*Reg. Min.*, 38; *Thirds*, 261; *Wod. Misc.*, 384; *RSS*, 6: 826; Reg. Assig., to 1601, E47/1–8). Nat. s. Archibald H. of Raploch. Gr. vic. D., 1563. In 1606 'unable to continue'. Married Janet Denham, dau. James D. of West Shield. Memorial to them in an aisle at Dunlop parish kirk. Hamilton was called 'Reader' for most of his career but on his memorial is described as a Minister and a 'faithful pastor'. His example suggests that some men may have been designated Reader because of their standard of remuneration rather than ability, and that the Readers who served so many post-Reformation churches may have been perfectly able to preach, with the neighbouring Minister-with-oversight being called in to dispense the communion, which was in any case infrequent.

WILLIAM KIRKPATRICK, Minister (of Kilwinning) had oversight, 1574 and probably until his death in 1577 (*Wod. Misc.* 384). Biog. details under KILWINNING.

GALSTON (A). SIR RANKIN DAVIDSON, c.1561–97. Prob. the unnamed Minister at Galston in 1561 (*Thirds*, 95); Minister, 1563–68 (SRO Portland Mun., GD163 Box 10 Bundle 4; *RMS* 4: 2541; Bks of Assumption, Edin. Univ. Library, fo. 48). Exhorter at Galston (SRO CH2/1335/1). Called Reader, 1574, by which time exhorters were phased out (*Wod. Misc.*, 386) and until 1597 (Reg. Assig., E47/1–7). Former chaplain and notary; at Inch, Galloway, 1549–50, *Wigton Charters*, 315). Recommended for service to general assembly of 1560 (*BUK*, i, 4). Gr. vic. Dalmellington, 1569 (RSS, 5: 724). In 1567 also Exhorter at Loudoun (q.v.).
MR JOHN BARRON, Minister, 1563–67. Deserted by his English wife, Anne Goodacre, 1563. He d.1568 (*BUK*, i, 42; *Reg. Min.*, 39; *Fasti*, iii, 39).
MR PETER PRIMROSE, Minister (of Mauchline) had oversight, 1574 (*Wod. Misc.*, 386).
MR ALEXANDER WALLACE, Minister, c.1592–1641 (Reg. Assig, to 1601, E47/6–8). Married (1) Alison Stewart, wid. George Lockhart of Sempill, (2) Sibella Wallace (d. 1643) (*Fasti*, iii, 39).

GIRVAN (A). MR JAMES YOUNG, Reader, 1574–78 (*Wod. Misc.*, 387; (Reg. Assig., E47/1).
JAMES ROSS, Reader, 1578–85 (*Reg. Min.* 40; Reg. Assig., E47/1–3).
JOHN CUNNINGHAM, Minister (of Dailly) had oversight in 1574 and prob. continued so until he became Minister of Girvan in 1590 (*Wod. Misc.*, 387; Reg. Assig., E47/5–8). D.c. 1612. Note: said to have been Minister of Girvan as well as of Dailly 'divers yeris' before 1567 (Reg. of Acts and Decreets, CS7/45, fos 453–4).

IRVINE (I). SIR THOMAS ANDREW, Reader, 1561–86 (*Thirds*, 93; *Reg. Min.*, 37; *Wod. Misc.*, 386; Reg. Assig., E47/1–3). Former chaplain in St John's Kirk, Ayr, 1532–38 (*Ayr Burgh Accounts*, 27,77; *Gavin Ros*, 1268) and vicar of Irvine before 1560, which he retained (Chalmers, *Caledonia*, vi, 545; *Thirds*, 93,261). Raised action against occupants of his vic. kirklands, 1565 (Reg. of Acts and Decreets, CS7/36, f. 49v) Wrote wills of parishioners as vicar and Reader, 1572–3 (Edin. Tests. CC8/8/4, f. 87v, CC8/8/12, f. 138). Gave tack of teinds to Wm. Scott, burgess of Irvine, 1584 (RSS, 1, f. 169). Died by 30 Nov. 1586 (Reg. Pres. Ben., ii, 159).
JOHN LIND (Lyn), Minister; declared unfit by general assembly 26 June 1565 (*BUK*, i, 61), but witnessed testament of an Irvine burgess 24 March 1573, when he is designated Minister (Edin. Tests, CC8/8/4, f. 87v).

Appendix

ROBERT HAMILTON, Minister, 1567–78 (*Reg. Min.*, 37; *Calderwood*, ii, 370; RSS xlix, f. 34; Reg. of Deeds, RD1/8, f. 160; *RSS.* 6:19; *Fasti*, iii, 97). Trans. from Ochiltree. Prob. s. Robert H. of Preston. Married (wife's name unknown). Died 1578.
MR JOHN YOUNG, Minister, 1570–89 (*Reg. Min.*, 37; *Thirds*, 263; *Wod. Misc.*, 386; Reg. Assig., E47/1–4; Ayr Hornings, DI 125/1 f. 14v). Trans. from Jedburgh, 1570. Perceton in charge, 1578 (Reg. Assig., E47/1). At Leith Convention, 1572, and many general assemblies, 1572–81. Trans to Beith, *q.v.* for biog. details.
MR WILLIAM STRANG, Minister, 1583–88 (born 1547, died 2 Aug. 1588). Prob. assistant to Mr John Young, above. Trans. from Kirkliston. Married Agnes Borthwick (sis. Alex. B. of Nether Leneyher) who raised an action in burgh court, 11 April 1590, for part of his stipend assigned to her before his death (Ayr Hornings, DI 125/1, f. 13). See *Fasti*, iii, 97–8 for further biog. details, including his confession of faith.
MR WILLIAM FULLARTON, Reader, 1588–89 (Reg. Assig., E47/4).
MR ALEXANDER SCRYMGEOUR, Minister, 1589–1617 (Reg. Assig., E47/4–8; *Fasti*, iii, 98) Native of Dundee. Regent in Edin. university, 1586–88. Recommended to the Merse in 1588 but adm. to Irvine after 27 May 1589. Nominated by privy council 6 March 1590 as a commissioner for maintenance of the Reformed religion in Cunninghame. Attended five general assemblies after 1595. Called before the privy council in 1610 for intercommuning with a catholic priest. Died bef. 12 July 1617. Married (1) Agnes Campbell; (2) Jean Hunter, dau. Robert H. of Hunterston. See *Fasti*, iii, 98 for further biog. details.

KILBIRNIE (I). MR ARCHIBALD HAMILTON, Exhorter, 1567 (*Reg. Min.*, 37); Reader, 1568–70; forfeited with other Hamiltons in 1571; Reader, 1574–85 (*Thirds*, 261; *Wod. Misc.*, 385; Reg. Assig., E47/1–3). Died 7 Oct. 1586, having dem. office. Married Jean Barclay, who survived him and married (2) Mr John Heriot, below (Fasti. iii, 102).
ROBERT CRAWFORD, Reader, 1571, during forfeiture of above (*Reg. Min.*, 38; *RSS* 6:1275).
MR ARCHIBALD CRAWFORD. Minister (of Stevenston); had oversight, 1574 (*Wod. Misc.* 385).
MR JOHN HERIOT, Minister, 1586-c. 1630 (*Fasti*, iii, 102; Reg. Assig. E47/4–8). Pres. vic. K. 21 March 1580. Died bef. 25 Nov. 1630. Married Jean Barclay, wid. of Archibald Hamilton, above.

KILMARNOCK (I). SIR JOHN MUIR, Minister, 1561 – at least 20 April 1565 (*Fasti*, iii, 104; Reg. of Acts and Decreets, CS7/36, f. 26). Former chaplain, possibly curate of K. Notary of doc. of Lord Boyd and John Wallace of Craigie, 5 June 1557 (Boyd Papers (SRO), GD8/160). In 1565 as Minister

of K. charged with others for not producing protocol book of late Mr John Hamilton, vic. of K. (Reg. of Acts and Decreets, CS7/36, f. 26).
JOHN BOYD, Reader, 1567–80 (*Reg. Min.*, 37; Reg. Assig., E47/1–2).
MR ROBERT WILKIE, Minister (of Loudoun) had oversight, 1574 (*Wod. Misc.*, 385). Minister of K., 1580–1601 (Reg. Assig., E47/3–8; *Fasti*, iii, 104). Had Loudoun in charge. Married (1) Helen Lockhart (d. 2 Sept. 1586), and (2) Agnes Borthwick, wid. Mr William Strang, Minister of Irvine.
MR JOHN HERIOT, Reader, 1585–86 (Reg. Assig., E47/3). Trans. to Kilbirnie as Minister, *q.v.*
HUGH PONAR, Reader, 1586–89 (Reg. Assig., E47/4).

KILMAURS (I). SIR JOHN HOWIE, Reader, 1567–71 (*Reg. Min.*, 37; *Thirds*, 261; *RSS*, 6:2302; Fraser Charters (SRO), GD86/123,125; Register House Charters (SRO), RH6/1867–8). Former chaplain, vicar and parish priest of Kilmaurs. Chaplain, 1516 (*Gavin Ros*, 139); parish clerk of Crosbie, 1520 (*Ibid*, 423); wit. documents re earls of Glencairn and other Cunninghams, 1521–36 (Glencairn Mun. (SRO), GD39/1/33,5/256; *RMS*, 3:596; Fraser Charters (SRO), GD86/113). As vicar, occupant of the lands of Lambrochton, Kilmaurs, 1538–50 (*RMS*, 3:1847; Glencairn Mun., GD39/5/24; Reg. of Acts and Decreets, CS7/2, part ii, f. 307). Wit. redemption at Kilmaurs kirk, 1551 (Register House Charters, RH6/1517). His son legit. 1544 (*RSS*, 3: 824). His vic. granted on his d. in 1571 to Alexander Henderson, below.
MR ARCHIBALD CRAWFORD, Minister, 1567–69 (*Reg. Min.*, 37; *Thirds*, 262). Trans. to Stevenston.
SIR GAVIN NAISMITH, Exhorter, 1568–71 (*Thirds*, 264). Minister, 1574–88 (*Wod. Misc.*, 385; Reg. Assig., E47/1–4). Biog. details under DREGHORN.
ALEXANDER HENDERSON, Reader, 1576–97 (*Wod. Misc.*, 385; *Reg. Min.*, 85; *RSS*, 6:2302; Reg. Assig., E47/1–7). Trans. from Stewarton. Former monk of Kilwinning abbey, first mentioned there in 1551. Had first been Exhorter at Ardrossan where he occupied the manse next the church, moved to Stewarton as Reader in 1572. Gr. vic. K. on d. of sir John Howie, above, in 1571. Complained to privy council re drop in value of the vic. in 1588 (*RPC* 3:649). Same year his monk's portion granted to his s. David, then a student at St Andrews university, who became Minister of K. in 1598 see below. Alexander H. d. 1598 (*RSS* lxx, f. 6). Married, wife's name unknown. Children included Mr David (below), Mr Samuel H., Reader at St Giles', Edinburgh, Patrick, James, Alexander and Marion (Testament of Mr Samuel, d. 1609, Edin Tests, CC8/8/46, f. 135).
MR WILLIAM FULLARTON, Minister, 1589–90 (Reg. Assig., E47/8). Trans. from Largs. Trans. to Dreghorn.

Appendix

MR DAVID HENDERSON, son of Alex. H., above, Minister, 1598–1637 (Reg. Assig., E47/8; D. McNaught, *Kilmaurs Parish and Burgh*, 150).

KILWINNING (I). WILLIAM KIRKPATRICK, Minister, 1563–77. Beith and Dunlop also in his charge, 1574 (Soc. of Antiquaries of Scotland Collection (SRO), GD103/2/22,p. 2; *Reg. Min.*, 37; *Wod. Misc.*, 384; *Thirds*, 263; Reg. Assig., E47/1). See also, M.H.B. Sanderson, 'Kilwinning at the time of the Reformation and its first Minister, William Kirkpatrick', in *AANHS*, X, 102–126. Former monk of Kilwinning abbey, first mentioned there in 1545. Brother of John K., merchant and bailie, and Laurence Kirkpatrick, shipmaster, of Ayr, with links to the Kirkpatricks, of Closeburn. Married Alison Campbell, dau. George C. of Stevenston; children, William, Martha and Marion. William K., the Minister, d.1577 (Edin. Tests., CC8/8/26 July 1581).
MR DAVID MYLNE, Reader, 1574–(?)75 (*Wod. Misc.*, 384). Trans. to Craigie and Dundonald, 1576.
MR ALEXANDER WREITTON, Minister, 1578–1605 (Reg. Assig., E47/1–8). Married Helen Pirrie. Children: Alexander, schoolmaster of Kilwinning, to whom he left his books and a house in K., John and David, both apprenticed to Andrew Hart, printer, Edinburgh in 1613, John W. later becoming a printer himself, and Joshua.
ALEXANDER MITCHELL, Reader, 1578–(?)91 (Reg. Assig., until 1589, E47/1–4). His stipend for 1587–91, in arrears when he died, was said to have been wrongly intromitted with by Mr Wreitton, above (CC8/8/28, f.339).

KIRKBRIDE (A); Chapel dependent on Maybole.
THOMAS FALCONER, Reader, 1568–9 (*Reg. Min.*, 40; *Thirds*, 265).
ALEXANDER DAVIDSON, Reader, 1571 (*Reg. Min.*, 40; *Thirds*, 265).
MR MATTHEW (?MICHAEL) HAMILTON, Reader, with Maybole, 1574 (*Wod. Misc.*, 387).
JOHN MCQUHORNE, Minister (of Straiton) had oversight of K. and Maybole, 1574 (*Wod. Misc.*, 387).
UNITED WITH MAYBOLE 'soon after 1571' (*Fasti*, iii, 51).

KIRKMICHAEL (A). LEONARD CLERK, Reader, 1567 (*Reg. Min.*, 40). Trans. from Dalmellington. Biog. details under DALMELLINGTON.
JOHN CUNNINGHAM, Exhorter, 1567–70, adm. to baptise and marry (*Reg. Min.*, 40; *Thirds*, 263).
JOHN MCQUHORNE, Minister (Straiton) had oversight, 1574 (*Wod. Misc.*, 387). May have remained so, although charge said to be vacant in 1594 (Reg. Assig., E47/6/2, f.45v).
OFFICE OF READER VACANT, 1574 (*Wod., Misc.*, 387).

WILLIAM HUNTER, Reader, 1576–1601 (Reg. Assig., E47/1–8).
MR ROGER MELVILLE, Minister by 1601 (*Fasti*, iii, 44).

KIRK OF MUIR (A). This pre-Reformation chapel in the parish of Mauchline became quasi-parochial after 1560 and was erected as the parish of Muirkirk in 1631.
JAMES CAMPBELL, Reader, 1576- at least 1601 (Reg. Assig., E47/1–8).

KIRKOSWALD (A). HUGH KENNEDY, Reader, c.1572–1603 (*Reg. Min.*, 40; Reg. Assig., to 1601, E47/1–8). Trans. from St Quivox.
MR JAMES BOYD OF TROCHRIG, Minister, 1572–81 (*Fasti*, iii, 46). Prom. archbishop of Glasgow, 1573, resumed parochial duties 1577. D. 21 June 1581.
JOHN MCCAVEL (?MCCARREL), Reader, 1572–74 (*Fasti*, iii, 46; *Wod. Misc.*, 387).
JOHN CUNNINGHAM, Minister (of Dailly); had oversight, 1574 (*Wod. Misc.*, 387).
Note: In 1607 Patrick Anderson is said to have left this charge 'for lack of stipend' (*Fasti*, iii, 46).

LARGS (I). SIR DAVID NEILL, Exhorter, 1563–74 (*Thirds*, 264; *Reg. Min.*, 37), Reader, 1576–85 (Reg. Assig., E47/1–3; *Prot. Book John Mason*, 98). The office of Reader was said to be vacant in 1574 (*Wod. Misc.*, 384) but a complaint by Neill for non-payment of stipend for 1573–74 was acted upon, 12 July 1580 (*RSS*, 7: 1580). Called Minister of Largs, 25 June and 28 Nov. 1590 (Ayr Hornings DI 125/1, fos. 46, 107), but in the same case is also referred to as 'sometime reader at Largs and now indweller in Ayr' (*Ibid.*, f.59v). His name is deleted from the record in 1586 (Reg. Assig., E47/3/2, f.48). Former chaplain, notary and curate at Largs and Monkton. Continued to act as a notary in the Largs area, post-1560. He was related to families in Monkton and Ayr, he himself holding property in latter (*Kelburn Writs*, 16, 17, 54, 74; *Hunterston Writs*, 18, 23, 24; Reg. of Acts and Decreets, 3, f.350, 34, f.68; *Prot. Book John Mason*, 98, 99).
MR ALEXANDER CALLANDER, Minister, 1585 (Reg. Assig., E47/3).
MR WILLIAM FULLARTON, Minister, 1588–1601 (Reg. Assig., E47/4–8; Ayr Hornings (1589), DI 125/1, f.95).

LOUDOUN (I). SIR RANKIN DAVIDSON, Exhorter, with Galston, 1567–71 (*Reg. Min.*, 39; *Thirds*, 263), Biog. details under GALSTON.
MR ROBERT WILKIE, Minister, 1574–80, with Kilmarnock and Riccarton in charge (*Wod. Misc.*, 385; Reg. Assig., E47/1–7). Trans. to Kilmarnock, *q.v.* for biog. details.

Appendix

JAMES HALL, Reader, 1574–96 (*Wod. Misc.*, 385; Reg. Assig., E47/1–7).
MR JAMES LANDLESS (?LANDELS), Minister, 1594 (Reg. Assig., E47/6).
JAMES GREG, Minister, 1597–1635 (Reg. Assig., to 1601, E47/7–8). Son of James G., Minister of Colmonell. Biog. details, see *Fasti*, iii, 119.

MAUCHLINE (A). MR ROBERT HAMILTON, Minister of Ochiltree, also Minister here, 1562. Appointed to preach in 'the unplanted kirks of Carrick' (*BUK*, i, 17).
MR PETER PRIMROSE, Minister, 1567-bef. 13 Dec. 1617 (*Reg. Min.*, 39; *Wod. Misc.*, 386; Reg. Assig., to 1601, E47/1–8). Son of Duncan P., bailie of Culross, and Helen Smith. At Leith convention, 1572. Had Galston also in charge, 1574. Had lease of part of Mauchline mill, 1573 (Reg. of Deeds, RD1/12, f.40). Subscribed local testament, 1582 (Edin. Tests. CC8/8/13, f.311). Wit. charter of Lockhart of Bar, 1587 (*RMS*, 5: 1797). With others, on committee to deal with irregularities among the clergy of Ayrshire, and in 1589 on committee for preservation of Reformed religion in Kyle. Married, wife's name unknown. Son Peter became Minister of Crossmichael; dau. Margaret m. Wm. Spottiswood of Foular; son Henry, notary in Mauchline and Reader, see below; perhaps Duncan P., King's physician, may have been another son (*Calderwood*, iv, 570, v, 104, vii, 96, 106).
READERSHIP VACANT, 1576 (Reg. Assig., E47/1, f.60).
HENRY PRIMROSE, Reader, 1578–91 (Reg. Assig., E47/1–5). Son of Mr Peter P., above.
JOHN INGLIS, Minister (with Mr Peter Primrose, above), 1589 (Reg. of Acts and Decreets, xx, f.246).

MAYBOLE (A) ALEXANDER DAVIDSON, Reader, 1571, with Kirkbride (*Reg. Min.*, 40; *Thirds*, 265).
MR MATTHEW (OR MICHAEL) HAMILTON, Reader, 1572–90 (*Reg. Min.*, 40; *Wod. Misc.*, 387; Reg. Assig., E47/1–5). Subscribes testament of a parishioner, 14 April 1576 (Edin. Tests., CC8/8/4, f.212).
JOHN MCQUHORNE, Minister (of Straiton) had oversight, 1574 (*Wod. Misc.*, 387). Minister here, 1595–98 (Reg. Assig., E47/6–7). Trans. back to Straiton, 1598.
MR HUGH HAMILTON, Reader, 1591–94 (Reg. Assig., E47/5–6).
DAVID BARCLAY, Minister, 1599- at least 1609 (Reg. Assig., to 1601, E47/8). Trans. from Dailly. Trans. to Dumfries after 15 July 1605 (Reg. of Deeds, RD1/112, f.129).

MONKTON (A). JOHN WYLIE, Minister, 1563 (*Records of Prestwick*, 67). Reader, 1567–94, including Prestwick from 1574 (*Records of Prestwick*, 59, 67–8; *Reg. Min.*, 39; *Wod. Misc.*, 387; *Thirds*, 266; Reg. Assig., E47/1–6). Curate of Monkton, 1557 (Hamilton Mun. Box 4: 72). Brother of Andrew

W. in Monkton (*Records of Prestwick*, 67). Preceptor of the Chapel of Our Lady of Kyle RSS, L, fo. 73).
MR JOHN NISBET, Minister (at Tarbolton) had oversight, 1574 (*Wod. Misc.*, 386).
MR NINIAN YOUNG, Minister, 1593-c.97×98 (Reg. Assig., E47/6–7). Brother of Mr James Y., Minister of Colmonell. Gr. vic. M. 4 Jan. 1592 (RSS, lxiii, f.108).
MR CLAUD HAMILTON, Minister, c.1599–1613 (Reg. Assig., to 1601, E47/8). Elder son of John H. of Newton (*Fasti*, iii, 55).

OCHILTREE (A). MR ROBERT HAMILTON, Minister, also at Mauchline, 1562–66 (*BUK*, i, 17). Commissioned to preach 'in the unplanted kirks of Carrick'. Trans. to Irvine.
ADAM LANDELLS, Exhorter, with Cumnock and Auchinleck, 1567–71 (*Reg. Min.*, 39; *Thirds*, 264). Former chaplain and notary. Born in Ochiltree, 1507 (Notarial records (SRO) NP2/1, f.2). Notary and wit. on docs *re* Cunningham of Caprington, Lord Ochiltree and Glencairn, 1548–60 (Reg. of Acts and Decreets, CS7/6, f.434; NP 1/13, no.43; Register House charters, RH6/1538, 1810). Handed money to Leonard Clerk, Minister of Dalmellington, as oversman of a testament, at Ayr, 29 Nov. 1559 (Ayr Burgh Court Book, 1549–60, f.56v). Recommended for service in the Reformed kirk at general assembly of 1560 (*BUK* i, 4). Continued to act as a notary post-1560 (Fraser Charters, GD86/200). Arrears of his stipend paid to his widow, Helen Wilson, in 1571 (*Thirds*, 264).
MR JOHN INGLIS, Minister, 1567–1608, with Cumnock and Auchinleck in charge in 1567; Ochiltree in charge in 1574 and 1585 while Minister of Auchinleck (*Reg. Min.*, 39; *Thirds*, 263; *Wod. Misc.*, 385; Reg. Assig., E47/3). Minister at Ochiltree, 1586-at least 1608 (Reg. Assig., E47/3–8). Commissioner for preservation of Reformed religion in Kyle, 1589. Married Agnes Grosar. Biog. details on family, see *Fasti*, iii, 61.
JOHN MACCLANNOCHAN, Reader, 1574–78 (*Wod. Misc*, 385; Reg. Assig., E47/1).
JAMES GIBSON, Reader, 1579–86 (Reg. Assig., E47/2–3).
JOHN MURDOCH, Reader, 1588 (Reg. Assig., E47/4).
HENRY PRIMROSE, Reader, 1589, with Mauchline (Reg. Assig., E47/4).

PERCETON (I). MR FRANCIS ADAMSON, Reader, 1570–1 (*Reg. Min.*, 38; *Thirds*, 264). Student at St Andrews, 1566–67 (*Acta Fac. Art. St And.* ii, 426).
DAVID WHITE, Reader, 1572–89 (*Reg. Min.*, 38; *Wod. Misc*, 386; Reg. Assig., E47/2–4).
MR JOHN YOUNG, Minister (of Irvine) had oversight, 1574 (*Wod. Misc.*, 386).

Appendix 173

ROBERT MAXWELL, Minister, 1590–91 (Reg. Assig., E47/5). Trans. to Dalry.
MR JOHN BELL, was Minister by 1613 (*Fasti*, iii, 90).

PRESTWICK (A) (St Nicholas); combined with Monkton in the record from 1574.
SIR ROBERT LEGGAT, Reader, 1563–70 (*Records of Prestwick*, 48; Fraser Charters, GD86/128; *Thirds*, 266; *Reg. Min.*, 39). Former curate of Prestwick and vicar of Ayr. Clerk to Prestwick burgh court. Involved in the transition to Reformed practice in St John's kirk, Ayr, 1558–60. For fuller biog, see M.H.B.Sanderson, *Mary Stewart's People* (Edinburgh, 1987), 149–65.
MR JOHN NISBET, Minister (at Tarbolton) had oversight, 1574 (*Wod. Misc.*, 386).
SIR JOHN WYLIE, Reader (at Monkton), also Reader here, 1574 (*Wod. Misc.*, 386). Former chaplain and preceptor of the Chapel of our Lady of Kyle. Biog. details under MONKTON.

RICCARTON (A). United with Craigie 'some time after 1578' and disjoined again in 1648 (*Fasti*, iii, 63).
SIR THOMAS BOYD, Reader, 1571 (*Thirds*, 264). Trans to Beith by 1575. Biog. details under BEITH.
GEORGE CAMPBELL, Minister, 1572 (*Reg. Min.*, 39). Trans. to Dundonald by 1574.
MR ROBERT WILKIE, Minister (of Loudoun) had oversight, 1574 (*Wod. Misc.*, 385).
READERSHIP VACANT, 1574 (*Wod. Misc.*, 385).
NAME BLANK, 1576 (Reg. Assig., E47/1).
JOHN TURBAT, Reader, 1578 (Reg. Assig., E47/1).
NAME BLANK, Reader, 1579 (Reg. Assig., E47/2).
MR LAURENCE DALGLEISH, Minister (of Craigie) had charge, 1580 (Reg. Assig., E47/2).

ST QUIVOX (A). Sanquhar-in-Kyle.
SIR GEORGE COCHRANE, Reader, 1567–70 (*Reg. Min.*, 39). Former chaplain, organist and Master of the song school at St John's kirk, Ayr (*Ayr Burgh Accounts*, 114, 134). Gave up his post at magistrates' request, May 1559 (Ayr Burgh Court Book, 1549–60, f. 15v). D. Candlemas, 1570.
HUGH KENNEDY, Reader, 1572–74 (*Reg. Min.*, 39; *Wod. Misc.*, 387).
JOHN LEVERANCE, Minister, 1572 (Reg. of Acts and Decreets, CS7/49, f. 40; *Fasti*, viii, 224).
MR JOHN NISBET, Minister (of Tarbolton) had oversight, 1574 (*Wod. Misc.*, 386).

THOMAS FALCONER, Reader, 1576–80 (Reg. Assig., E47/1–2).
DAVID ALLANSON, Reader, 1585- at least 1601 (Reg. Assig., E47/3–8). Trans. from Barnweil. May or may not have been D.A., former Ayr Dominican; see under BARNWEIL

STEVENSTON (I). Note: According to *Fasti*, iii, 122, a Stephen Wilkinson, vic. of S., is said to have held office in the Reformed kirk in 1560. No reference given, and no other record of his appointment has been found.
MR (OR SIR) JAMES WALKER, Minister, 1561-c. 69 (*Reg. Min.*, 38; *Thirds*, 92, 150, 261; *BUK* i, 131; *Prot. Book, Nicholson*, 316; *RSS* 3: 3031, 6:661, 687). Former chaplain and vic. Stevenston, also pars. Inchcailoch and Killintag. Wit. many deeds *re* earls of Glencairn from 1537 onwards (*RMS* 3:1785, 4:372, 2115; Reg. of Acts and Decreets, CS7/3, f. 361, 372, CS7/13, f. 68, 190v; Bargany Mun. (SRO), GD109/321). Sat in general assembly, 1562. D. c. 1569.
MR ARCHIBALD CRAWFORD, Minister, Beltane 1569 – bef. 1603 (*Reg. Min.*, 38; *Thirds*, 262; *Wod. Misc.*, 385; Reg. Assig., to 1601 E47/1–8). Trans. from Kilmaurs. Dalry and Kilbirnie also in charge in 1574.
ALEXANDER MITCHELL, Reader, 1574–89, also at Kilwinning (*Wod. Misc.*, 385; Reg. Assig., E47/1–2; Edin. Tests., CC8/8/28, f. 339). See other biog. details under KILWINNING.

STEWARTON (I). JAMES LUMSDEN, Reader, 1567 (*Reg. Min.*, 67). Poss. related to pre-Reformation curate of S., sir Alexander L. James d. 1567.
ALEXANDER HENDERSON, Exhorter, 1571–2 (*Reg. Min.*, 37; *Thirds*, 263). Trans. to Kilmaurs, *q.v.* for biog. details.
SIR GAVIN NAISMITH, Minister, 1574–88 (*Wod. Misc.*, 385; *Fasti*, iii, 112). Biog. details under DREGHORN.
WILLIAM MONTGOMERIE, Reader, 1574–88 (*Wod. Misc.*, 385; Reg. Assig., E47/1–4). Called to St Cuthbert's, Edinburgh, 1586, but trans. not implemented. Still Reader in 1588 (Ayr Hornings DI 125/1, f. 93v).
ROBERT MONTGOMERIE, Minister, 1589-dem. 1607 (Reg. Assig., E47/4–8). Son of Wm. M. of Hessilhead, one of those thought 'apt to teach' by first general assembly, 1560. May have been settled in Cupar, 1562. Trans. Dunblane, 1567, and Stirling bef. Lammas, 1572. Prom. to archbishopric of Glasgow 1581, deposed by general assembly, but this interdicted by privy council, June 1582. Sentence removed 1587. Adm. Symington 1587. Trans. to Stewarton, 1589.

STRAITON (A). UNNAMED Minister, 1562. In that year the vic., sir William Boswell was obliged to pay 20 merks annually to a minister placed in the church by the reformers (PRO/31/9/33/51; Chalmers, *Caledonia*, vi, 536).
JOHN MCQUHORNE, Exhorter, bef. Beltane 1568; Minister 1568–97 (*Reg.*

Min., 40; *Thirds*, 263; *Wod. Misc.*, 387; Reg. Assig., E47/1–7; *Calderwood*, v, 570). In 1574 had charge also of Maybole, Kirkbride and Kirkmichael. D. bef. 30 May 1598.

SIR JOHN ANDERSON, Reader, 1576–89 (Reg. Assig., E47/1–4). Former chaplain, 1547 (*Wigton Charters*, no. 303).

MR JOHN MCQUHORNE, Minister, 1598–1645 (Reg. Assig., to 1601, E47/8). Son of J. McQ., above. Trans. from Maybole. For further biog. details, *Fasti*, iii, 71.

SYMINGTON (A). Un-named Minister referred to in 1561 (*Thirds*, 95 may be the following: THOMAS CARRINGTON, Reader, (?) 1561–67 (*Reg. Min.* 39).
GEORGE CAMPBELL, Minister (of Dundonald) had oversight, 1574 (*Wod. Misc.*, 386)

SIR JOHN MILLER, Reader, 1574–97 (*Wod. Misc.*, 386; Reg. Assig., E47/1–7). Former chaplain, notary and vic. of S., 1529–59 (*RMS* 3:828; 4:1732). Trans. from Barnweil where he was Reader. D. by 27 May 1598 (*RSS*, lxix, fos. 269–70).

ROBERT MONTGOMERIE, Minister, 1587–c. 1589 (*Fasti*, iii, 73). For biog. details, see under STEWARTON.

MR WILLIAM WALLACE, Minister, 1598 – at least 1626 (Reg. Assig. to 1601, E47/8).

TARBOLTON (A). SIR DAVID CURLL, Reader, (?) 1564–80; at Tarbolton, 12 Dec. 1564 (*RMS*, 4:1600; *Reg. Min.*, 39; *Thirds*, 265; Reg. Assig., E47/1–2). In 1580 he also had charge of Barnweil, St Quivox, Prestwick and Monkton (Reg. Assig., E47/2/2, f. 61). Former chaplain of the chapel of St Katherine, Kilbarchan, in patronage of Chalmers of Gadgirth, although may have been resident in Ayrshire. Gr. the chapel lands to son of Chalmers of Gadgirth, 1564. Wit. of docs. *re* Glencairn and other Cunninghams, 1543–52 (*RMS*, 3:2873; Caprington Mun. (SRO), GD 149/1/24). Recorded as Reader in 1573 and 1576 (Edin. Tests, CC8/8/3, f. 21; CC8/8/5, f. 41).

MR JOHN NISBET, Minister, 1574–1610 (*Wod. Misc.*, 386; Reg. Assig., to 1601, E47/1–8). Son of John N. of Rystubhill, East Lothian. Entered, May 1575, with Barnweil, St Quivox, Monkton and Prestwick also in charge. Married Margaret Dunbar (who survived him). Son William became Minister of Tarbolton, c. 1614.

WEST KILBRIDE (I). SIR JOHN MAXWELL, Minister, 1565 (Reg. of Deeds, RD 1/9, f. 97) and in 1566 (Soc. of Antiquaries Coll., GD 103/2/22, p. 29). Exhorter, 1567–71 (*Thirds*, 264; *Reg. Min.*, 37). Reader, 1574–80 (*Wod. Misc.*, 384; Reg. Assig., E47/1–2). Former priest and poss. curate of W.K.

ALEXANDER CALLANDER, Minister (of Largs) had oversight, 1574 (*Wod. Misc.*, 384).

GABRIEL CUNNINGHAM, Minister, 1585 (*Fasti*, iii, 127) but called Reader in record, 1585–86 (Reg. Assig., E47/3).

HUGH BOYD, Minister, 1588–93 (Reg. Assig., E47/4–6). Name deleted in 1594.

WILLIAM COOK, Minister (at Largs) served W.K., 1589 (Ayr Hornings, DI 125/1, f. 95).

MR JOHN HARPER, Minister, 1594-d. 1630 (Reg. Assig., to 1601, E47/6–8). Called before privy council in 1610 for harbouring papists. For further biog. details, see *Fasti*, iii, 128.

Bibliography

MANUSCRIPT SOURCES

Public and Legal Records

Acts of the Lords of Council (SRO:CS5)
Acts of the Lords of Council and Session (SRO:CS6)
Register of Acts and Decreets (SRO:CS7)
Justiciary Court Records (SRO:JC1)
Register of Deeds, First Series (SRO:RD1)
Register of Abbreviates of Feu Charters of Kirklands (SRO:E14)
Commissariot of Edinburgh, Register of Testaments (SRO:CC8/8)
Commisariot of Glasgow, Register of Testaments (SRO:CC9/7)
Protocol Book of John Crawford, 1541–50 (SRO:NP1/8)
Protocol Book of William McKerrell, 1585–1629 (SRO:NP1/44)
Ayr, Register of Hornings (SRO:DI 125)
Ayr Sheriff Court Records, Minute Book, 1515–20, 1556 (SRO:SC6/1/1)
Miscellaneous Church records (SRO:CH8)

Burgh Records

Ayr Burgh Court Book, 1549–60 (Carnegie Library, Ayr)
Ayr Council Minutes, 1580–89 (Carnegie Library, Ayr)
Irvine Council Minutes, 1593, 1606 (SRO:B37/12/1)

Church Records

Galston Kirk Session records: Register of Baptisms, with some accounts, 1568–99 (SRO: CH2/1335/1)

Private archives

Ailsa Muniments (SRO:GD25)
Bargany Muniments (SRO:GD109)
Bennan Writs (SRO:GD60)
Blair of Blair Muniments (SRO:GD167)
Boyd Muniments (SRO:GD8)
Cathcart of Carlton and Killochan Muniments (SRO:GD117)
Cathcart of Genoch and Knockdolian Muniments (SRO:GD180)
Cunningham of Caprington Muniments (SRO:GD149)
Cunningham of Craigends Muniments (SRO:GD148)

Cunningham of Thornton Muniments (SRO:GD21)
Findlay of Carnell Muniments (SRO:GD228)
Glencairn Muniments (SRO:GD 39)
Eglinton Muniments (SRO:GD3)
Leven and Melville Muniments (SRO:GD26)
Miscellaneous private collections (SRO:GD1)
Morton Muniments (SRO:GD150)
Portland Muniments (SRO:GD163)
Collection of Messrs Tods, Murray and Jamieson, W.S. (SRO:GD237)
Yule Colllection (SRO:GD90)

PRINTED PRIMARY SOURCES, INCLUDING LITERARY AND NARRATIVE SOURCES

Abstracts of Protocols of the Town Clerks of Glasgow, 1547–1600, ed. R. Renwick, 11 vols. (Glasgow, 1894–1900)
Accounts of the Lord High Treasurer of Scotland, ed. T. Dickson and others, 12 vols., 1472–1574 (Edinburgh, 1877–1970)
Acta Facultatis Artium Universitatis Sanctiandree, 1413–1588, ed. A.I. Dunlop (Scottish History Society, 1964)
Acts and Proceedings of the General Assemblies of the Kirk of Scotland from the year 1560, ed. T. Thomson, 3 vols. (Bannatyne and Maitland Clubs, 1839–45); referred to as *The Buik of the Universal Kirk (BUK)*
Acts of the Lords of Council in Public Affairs, 1501–04, ed. R.K. Hannay (Edinburgh, 1932)
Acts of the Parliaments of Scotland, ed. T. Thomson and C. Innes (Edinburgh, 1814–75), vol.2, 1424–1625
Ancient Criminal Trials in Scotland, ed. R. Pitcairn, 3 vols (Edinburgh, 1833)
Autobiography and Diary of Mr James Melville, 1556–1610, ed. R. Pitcairn (Wodrow Society, 1842)
Ayr Burgh Accounts, 1534–1624, ed. G. Pryde (Scottish History Society, 1937)
Books of Assumption of the Thirds of Benefics, ed. J. Kirk (Oxford, 1995)
Calderwood, David, *History of the Kirk of Scotland*, ed. T. Thomson and D. Laing, 8 vols (Wodrow Society, 1842–49)
Calendar of Letters and Papers, Foreign and Domestic, Henry VIII, ed. J.S. Brewer and others, 21 vols (London, 1864–1932)
Calendar of Documents relating to Scotland and Mary Queen of Scots, ed. J. Bain and others, 13 vols (Edinburgh, 1898–1969)
Catechism set forth by Archbishop Hamilton (1552); together with the Twopenny Faith (1559), ed. A.F. Mitchell (Edinburgh, 1882)
Charters of the Abbey of Crossraguel, ed. F.C. Hunter Blair, 2 vols. (Archaeological and Historical Collections of Ayr and Wigtown, 1886)
Charters of the Friars Preacher of Ayr, ed. R.W. Cochran Patrick (Archaeological and Historical Collections of Ayr and Wigtown, 1881)

Cunninghame Topographised, 1604–8, by Timothy Pont, ed. J.S. Dobie (Glasgow, 1876)

Davidson, J., *A Memorial of the life of two worthie Christians, Robert Campbell of Kinzeancleuch and his wife Elizabeth Campbell, printed in 1595*; in C. Rogers, *Three Scottish Reformers* (Edinburgh, 1874), 100–31

The Diocesan Registers of Glasgow, eds J. Bain and C. Rogers, 2 vols (Grampian Club, 1875)

Foedera, ed. T. Rhymer, vol. xv (London, 1704–35)

The First Book of Discipline, ed. J.K. Cameron (Edinburgh, 1972)

A Godly Exhortation as set forth by John Archbishop of St Andrews, commonly styled 'The Twopenny Faith', 1559; Bannatyne Club Miscellany iii (Edinburgh, 1855)

Some Family Papers of the Hunters of Hunterston, ed. M.S. Shaw (Scottish Record Society, 1925)

Knox, John, *History of the Reformation in Scotland*, ed. W. Croft Dickinson, 2 vols (Edinburgh, 1949)

Liber de Calchou, ed. C. Innes, 2 vols. (Bannatyne Club, 1846)

Liber de Mailros, ed. C. Innes, 2 vols. (Bannatyne Club, 1837)

Mair, John, *History of Greater Britain* (Scottish History Society, 1892)

Melrose Regality Records, ed. C.S. Romanes (Scottish History Society, 1917)

'Military Report on the districts of Carrick, Kyle and Cunninghame ... between the years 1563 and 1566', ed. R.B. Armstrong, in *Archaeological and Historical Collections* of Ayr and Wigtown, iv (1884), 17

Muniments of the Royal Burgh of Irvine, 2 vols. (Ayrshire and Wigtonshire Archaeological Association, 1890–1)

The New Testament in Scots, being Purvey's revision of Wycliffe's version, turned into Scots by Murdoch Nisbet, c.1520, ed. T.G. Law, 3 vols. (Scottish Text Society, 1901–05)

Obit Book of Ayr, ed. J. Paterson (Edinburgh, 1848)

Original Letters of Mr John Colville, 1582–1603, ed. D. Laing (Bannatyne Club, 1858)

Poetical Works of Sir David Lindsay, ed. D. Laing, 3 vols. (Scottish Text Society, 1879)

Protocol Book of Gavin Ros, ed. J. Anderson and F.J. Grant (Scottish Record Society, 1908)

Records of the Burgh of Prestwick, ed. John Fullarton (Maitland Club, 1834)

Register of the Ministers, Elders and Deacons of the Christian congregation of St Andrews, 1559–1600, ed. D. Hay Fleming, 2 vols. (Scottish History Society, 1889–90); usually known as the *St Andrews Kirk Session Register*

Register of Ministers, Exhorters and Readers and of their Stipends after the period of the Reformation (Maitland Club, 1830)

Register of the Great Seal of Scotland, ed. J. Maitland Thomson and others, Vols. 1–6, 1306–1608 (reprinted Edinburgh, 1984)

Register of the Privy Council of Scotland, ed. J. Hill Burton and D. Masson, Vols. 1–9, 1545–1613 (Edinburgh, 1877–89)

Register of the Privy Seal of Scotland, ed. M. Livingstone and others, Vols. 1–8, 1488–1584 (Edinburgh, 1908–82)

Royal Commission on Historical Manuscripts, Report on the Marquis of Salisbury's Muniments, vol.i (London, 1883)

The Scottish Correspondence of Mary of Lorraine, 1543–60, ed. A.I. Cameron (Scottish History Society, 1927)

The Second Book of Discipline, ed. J. Kirk (Edinburgh, 1980)

Statutes of the Scottish Church, ed. D. Patrick (Scottish History Society, 1907)

Stuart, J., ed., *Records of the Monastery of Kinloss* (Edinburgh, 1872)

Teulet, A., *Relations Politiques de la France et de L'Espagne avec L'Ecosse* (Paris, 1862)

Thirds of Benefices, 1561–72, ed. G. Donaldson (Scottish History Society, 1949)

Works of John Knox, ed. D. Laing, 6 vols. (Wodrow Society, 1864)

Wodrow Society Miscellany, i, ed. D. Laing (Wodrow Society, 1844); contains correspondence between John Willock and Quintin Kennedy, 1559

SECONDARY WORKS

Aston, M., *Lollards and Reformers* (London, 1984)

Balfour Paul, J., ed., *The Scots Peerage, 9 vols. (Edinburgh, 1909–14)*

Bardgett, F.D., 'Four Parische Kirkis to ane Preicheir', in *RSCHS*, xxii (1986), 195–209

Bardgett, F.D., 'The Monifieth Kirk Register', in *RSCHS*, xxiii, (1988), 175–95

Bardgett, F.D., *Scotland Reformed: The Reformation in Angus and the Mearns* (Edinburgh, 1989)

Bossy, J., *Christianity in the West, 1400–1700* (Oxford, 1985)

Broadie, A., *George Lokert of Ayr, Medieval Man of Ideas* (AANHS, 1987)

Bryce, W. Moir, *The Scottish Grey Friars* (Edinburgh, 1909)

Cameron, J.K., 'Aspects of the Lutheran Contribution to the Scottish Reformation', in *RSCHS*, xxii (1984), 1–13

Cameron, J.K., '"Catholic Reform" in Germany and in the pre-1560 Church in Scotland', in *RSCHS* xx (1979), 105–117

Chalmers, G., *Caledonia*, vol.vi (Paisley, 1890)

Cowan, I.B., *The Medieval Church in Scotland*, ed. J. Kirk (Edinburgh, 1995)

Cowan, I.B., *The Parishes of Medieval Scotland* (Scottish Record Society, 1967)

Cowan, I.B., 'Patronage, Provision and Reservation, Pre-Reformation Appointments to Scottish Benefices', in *The Renaissance and Reformation in Scotland, Essays in Honour of Gordon Donaldson*, ed. I.B. Cowan and D. Shaw (Edinburgh, 1983), 75–92

Cowan, I.B. and Shaw, D., eds., *The Renaissance and Reformation in Scotland, Essays in Honour of Gordon Donaldson* (Edinburgh, 1983).

Cowan, I.B., *The Scottish Reformation* (London, 1982)

Crichton, J. and others, *The Presbytery of Ayr, 1581–1981* (AANHS, 1981)

Bibliography

Dawson, J.E.A., 'Anglo-Scottish Protestant Culture and Integration in sixteenth-century Britain', in S.G. Ellis and S. Barber, eds., *Conquest and Union, Fashioning a British State, 1485–1725*, (London, 1995)

Dawson, J.E.A., 'The Face of Ane Perfyt Reformed Kyrk': St Andrews and the Early Scottish Reformation', in *Studies in Church History, Subsidia*, 8 (Oxford, 1991), 413–35

Dawson, J.E.A., 'The Scottish Reformation and the Theatre of Martyrdom', in *Studies in Church History, Subsidia*, 10 (Oxford, 1993), 259–70.

Dickens, A.G., *The English Reformation* (London, 1989)

Dickens, A.G., *Lollards and Protestants in the Diocese of York* (London, 1982)

Dickinson, W. Croft, Donaldson, G., and Milne, I., *A Source Book of Scottish History* (Edinburgh, 1958), vol.2

Dilworth, M., 'The Commendator System in Scotland', in *Innes Review*, xxxvii (1986), 51–72

Dilworth, M., *Scottish Monasteries in the Late Middle Ages* (Edinburgh, 1995)

Donaldson, G., *All The Queen's Men* (London, 1983)

Donaldson, G., *The Scottish Reformation* (Cambridge, 1960)

Durkan, J. 'Chaplains in Scotland in the Late Middle Ages', in *RSCHS*, xx (1979), 91–103

Durkan, J., 'Heresy in Scotland, the Second Phase, 1546–58', in *RSCHS*, xxiv (1992)

Durkan, J., 'Scottish Evangelicals in the Patronage of Thomas Cromwell', in *RSCHS*, xxi (1982), 127–56

Durkan, J., 'Scottish Reformers, the less than Golden Legend', in *Innes Review*, xlv (1994)

Durkan, J., 'Some Local Heretics', in *TDGNHAS*, xxxvi (1959), 67–77

Dwyer, J., Mason, R.A., and Murdoch, A., *New Perspectives on the Politics and Culture of Early Modern Scotland* (Edinburgh, 1982).

Easson, D.E., 'The Lollards of Kyle', in *The Juridical Review*, xlviii 123–8

Fergusson, J., *The White Hind* (London, 1963)

Finnie, E. 'The House of Hamilton, Patronage, Politics and the Church in the Reformation Period', in Innes Review, xxxvi (1985), 3–28.

Forbes-Leith, W,. ed., *Narratives of the Scottish Catholics under Mary Stuart and James V1* (Edinburgh, 1885).

Fraser, W., *Memorials of the Montgomeries, 2 vols (Edinburgh, 1859)*

Gillespie, J., *Dundonald Parish*, 2 vols, (Glasgow, 1939)

Graham, A., *Old Ayrshire Harbours* (*AANHS*, 1984)

Greenshiels, J.B., *Annals of the Parish of Lesmahagow* (Edinburgh, 1864)

Haws, C.H., 'The Diocese of St Andrews at the Reformation', in *RSCHS*, xviii (1973)

Haws, C.H., *Scottish Parish Clergy at the Reformation, 1540–1574* (Scottish Record Society, 1972)

Head, D.M.,' Henry VIII's Scottish Policy, a Reassassment', in *Scottish Historical Review*, lxi (1982)

Kirk, J., ed., *Humanism and Reform: The Church in Europe, England and Scotland, 1406-1643, Essays in Honour of James K. Cameron; Studies in Church History, Subsidia*, 8 (Oxford, 1991).

Kirk, J., 'Iconoclasm and Reform', in *RSCHS*, xxiv (1992)

Kirk, J.,'The Influence of Calvinism on the Scottish Reformation', in *RSCHS*, xviii (1974), 157-79

Kirk, J., *Patterns of Reform* (Edinburgh, 1989)

Kirk, J., 'The "Privy Kirks" and their Antecedents, The Hidden Face of Scottish Protestantism', in *Studies in Church History*, 23 (Oxford, 1986), 155-70

Kirk, J. 'The Religion of early Scottish Protestants', in *Humanism and Reform . . . Essays in Honour of James K. Cameron; Studies in Church History, Subsidia 8* (Oxford, 1991), 361-412

Kirk, J., 'The Scottish Reformation and the Reign of James VI, A Select Critical Bibliography', in *RSCHS*, xxiii (1987)

Lees, J.C. *The Abbey of Paisley* (Paisley, 1878)

Lynch, M., 'Calvinism in Scotland, 1559-1638', in M. Prestwich, ed., *International Calvinism, 1541-1715* (London, 1985), 225-55

Lynch, M., *Edinburgh and the Reformation* (Edinburgh, 1981)

MacFarlane, L., 'Was the Scottish Church Reformable by 1513?', in N. MacDougall, ed., *Church, Politics and Society, 1408-1929* (Edinburgh, 1983), 23-43

Mackenzie, A., *An Ancient Church; St John's, Ayr* (Ayr, 1935)

Mackenzie, R., *Ayr's Export Trade at the end of the 16th Century* (AANHS, 1988)

Mackenzie, R., *A Scottish Renaissance Household, Sir William Hamilton and Newton Castle in 1559* (AANHS, 1990)

McKay, D., 'The Induction of the Parish Clerk in Medieval Scotland', and 'Parish Life in Scotland, 1500-1560' both in D. MacRoberts, ed., *Essays on the Scottish Reformation, 1513-1625* (Glasgow, 1962)

MacNab, T.M., 'The Beginnings of Lollardy in Scotland', in *RSCHS*, xi (1953), 254-60

MacNab, T.M., 'Bohemia and the Scottish Lollards', in *RSCHS*, v (1935), 23-39

MacNab, T.M., 'The New Testament in Scots', in *RSCHS*, xi (1951), 82-103

McNaught, D., *Kilmaurs Parish and Burgh* (Paisley, 1912)

MacRoberts, D., ed., *Essays on the Scottish Reformation, 1513-1625* (Glasgow, 1962).

Mason, R., 'Chivalry and Citizenship: aspects of national identity in Renaissance Scotland', in R. Mason and N. Macdougall, eds, *People and Power in Scotland, Essays in Honour of T.C. Smout* (Edinburgh, 1992)

Mason, R., 'Covenant and Commonwealth: the language of politics in Reformation Scotland', in N. Macdougall, ed., *Church, Politics and Society in Scotland, 1408-1929* (Edinburgh, 1983), 97-126

Mason, R., 'Scotching the Brut: politics, history and national myth in 16th

century Britain', in R. Mason, ed., *Scotland and England* (Edinburgh, 1987), 60–84
Mason, R., ed., *Scotland and England* (Edinburgh, 1987)
Mason, R., ed., *Scots and Britons: Scottish Political Thought and the Union of 1603* (Cambridge, 1994)
Mason, R., 'The Scottish Reformation and the Origins of Anglo-British Imperialism', in R. Mason, ed., *Scots and Britons: Scottish Political Thought and the Union of 1603* (Cambridge, 1994), 161–86
Mason, R. and Macdougall, N., eds., *People and Power, Essays in Honour of T.C. Smout* (Edinburgh, 1992)
Maxwell, H., *History of Dumfries and Galloway* (Edinburgh, 1890)
Merriman, M., 'The Assured Scots', in *Scottish Historical Review*, xlvii (1968), 10–34
Moonan, L., 'Pavel Kravar and some writings once attributed to him', in *Innes Review*, xxvii (1976), 3–23
Muirhead, I.A., 'M. Robert Lokhart', in *Innes Review*, xxii (1971), 85–100
Muller, G., 'Protestant Theology in Scotland and Germany in early days of the Reformation', in *RSCHS*, xxii (1984), 103–117
O'Day, R., *The Debate on the English Reformation* (London, 1986)
Paterson, J., *History of the County of Ayr*, 2 vols (Ayr, 1847)
Percy, E., *John Knox* (London, 1937)
Plumb, D., 'The Social and Economic Spread of Rural Lollardy: a Reappraisal', in *Studies in Church History*, (Oxford, 1986), 111–129
Reid, W.S., 'The Lollards in pre-Reformation Scotland', in *Church History*, xi (1942), 269–83
Sanderson, M.H.B., *Cardinal of Scotland: David Beaton, c.1494–1546* (Edinburgh, 1986)
Sanderson, M.H.B., 'Catholic Recusancy in sixteenth-century Scotland', in *Innes Review* xxi (1970), 87–107
Sanderson, M.H.B., 'Kilwinning at the time of the Reformation, and its first Minister William Kirkpatrick', in *Collections of the Ayrshire Archaeological and Natural History Society*, x (Ayr, 1972), 102–26
Sanderson, M.H.B., 'Manse and Glebe in the sixteenth century', in *RSCHS*, xix (1975)
Sanderson, M.H.B., *The People of Sixteenth-Century Ayrshire* (AANHS, 1987)
Sanderson. M.H.B., *Mary Stewart's People, Life in Mary Stewart's Scotland* (Edinburgh, 1987)
Sanderson, M.H.B., *The Mauchline Account Books of Melrose Abbey* (AANHS, 1975)
Sanderson, M.H.B., *Scottish Rural Society in the Sixteenth Century* (Edinburgh, 1982)
Scott, H., ed., *Fasti Ecclesiae Scoticanae*, vols. iii and viii (1915–50)
Shaw, D., 'John Willock', in D. Shaw, ed., *Reformation and Revolution, Essays presented to Hugh Watt* (Edinburgh, 1967), 42–69

Shaw, D., ed., *Reformation and Revolution, Essays presented to Hugh Watt* (Edinburgh, 1967)

Shaw, D., 'Zwinglian Influences on the Scottish Reformation', in *RSCHS*, xxii (1985), 119-39

Strawhorn, J., *Ayrshire, the Story of a County* (AANHS, 1975)

Strawhorn, J., *The History of Ayr* (Edinburgh, 1989)

Strawhorn, J. and Andrew, K., *Discovering Ayrshire* (Edinburgh, 1988)

Thomson, J.A.F., *The Later Lollards, 1414-1520* (Oxford, 1965)

Mary B. Verschuur, 'Perth Craftsmen's Book; Some examples of the Interpretation and Utilization of Protestant Thought by Sixteenth-Century Scottish Townsmen', in *RSCHS*, xxiii (1988), 157-174

Williamson, A.H., 'A Patriotic Nobility?', *in Scottish Historical Review*, xlvii, (1968), 1-21

Williamson, A.H., 'Scotland, antichrist and the invention of Great Britain', in J. Dwyer, R. Mason and A. Murdoch, eds., *New Perspectives on the Politics and Culture of Early Modern Scotland* (Edinburgh, 1982)

Winning, T., 'Church Councils in Sixteenth-Century Scotland', in D. MacRoberts, ed., *Essays on the Scottish Reformation, 1513-1625* (Glasgow, 1962)

Wright, D., ed., *The Bible in Scottish Life and Literature*, (Edinburgh, 1988)

Index

Note. Covering numbers (eg. 24–6) may not necessarily denote continuous discussion of a subject, but simply references on consecutive pages. Places are in Ayrshire unless otherwise indicated.

Acheson, Robert, minister at Ayr, 111
Adamson, Francis, reader at Perceton, 110
—, Mr Patrick, archbishop of Glasgow, 127
—, Mr Stephen, chaplain, 15
Aikman, Francis, apothecary, 55
Aird, William, minister at St Cuthbert's, Edinburgh, 46
—, sir William, chaplain, 30
Allan (Alesius), Alexander, Augustinian canon, 52
Allanson, sir Adam, chaplain, 30
—, David, friar, 126–7
—, sir William, chaplain, reader at Dailly, 122, 126
Alloway, church and parish, 28–9, 122
Anderson, Mr Patrick, minister at Kirkoswald, 118
Andrew, sir Thomas, chaplain, vicar and later reader at Irvine, 16, 111, 114, 116
Angus, 6th earl of, Archibald, 62
Ardmillan castle, 123
Ardrossan, church and parish, 28, 29, 110
Ardstinchar castle, 123
Argyll, 4th earl of, Archibald, 68, 79, 84–5, 101, 103
—, earls of, 2, 8
Argyllshire, 3
Arth, William, friar, 53
Auchendrane, chapel, 28
Auchinleck, church and parish, 28–9, 112–13,
Auld, Thomas, parliamentary commissioner for Irvine, 58
—, sir Thomas, curate of Irvine, 22
Avondale (Lanarkshire), barony, 46, 49; parish, 50
Ayr, Band of (1562), 44, 121, 124;
burgh, 1, 2, 3–4, 7, 9, 26, 61, 65–8, 81, 90–2, 95–9, 106, 123, 129–30, 143–4; Dominicans, 95–6; Franciscans, 50, 61, 94, 96; parish, 29, 31, 111; presbytery, 128, 130; St John's kirk, 15–16, 22, 28, 30, 32, 68, 81, 90–2, 93–8; song school, 91, 111

Ballantrae, or Kirkcudbright-Innertig, church and parish, 28, 30
Balnaves, Mr Henry, 55–6, 101
Bankhead, sir William, curate of Riccarton and Loudoun, 32–3
Bannatyne, James, bailie of Ayr, 106
Barclay of Ladyland, David, 125
— — —, Hugh, 125
— of Perceton, William, 131
—, Jean, wife of Mr Alexander Hamilton, minister at Kilbirnie, 134
Barnweil, church and parish, 28–9, 111, 116, 127
Barron, John, minister at Galston, 114
Beaton, David, cardinal, archbishop of St Andrews, 48, 51, 55–6, 59–60, 65, 68, 103
—, James, archbishop of Glasgow, 83, 120
—, Robert, abbot of Melrose, 18
Beggars' Summons, The, 92–3, 126
Beith, barony, 4; church and parish, 28–9, 110
Bellenden of Auchnoull, Sir Thomas, 56
benefice system, 23–6
Berwick, Treaty of, 101
bible, (old and new testaments), 42–3, 48, 55, 60–1, 78, 137–9, 141, 143,
Black Acts, The, 127–8, 130
Blackadder, Robert, archbishop of Glasgow, 5, 43

Blair of that Ilk, John, 32
—, Humphrey, deacon, 26, 32
Bonds of the Congregation, 44, 84–5, 102, 121, 124, 143
Book of Discipline, First, 107, 109–10, 115, 118–19, 132, 135, 137–8, 140; *Second*, 128
Borthwick, Agnes, widow of Mr William Strang, minister at Irvine, 135
—, Mr David, advocate, 55
—, Sir John, 55–6
Boswell, sir William, vicar of Straiton, 125
Boyd, 5th Lord, Robert, 33–4, 94, 99, 108, 110, 123
— of Trochrig, Mr John, archbishop of Glasgow, 129
—, sir George, chaplain, exhorter at Dalry, 110
—, sir Thomas, chaplain, reader at Riccarton and Beith, 110, 111
Brounside, sir George, vicar of Perceton, 131
Brown, Alison, wife of Gavin Naismith, reader (later minister) at Dreghorn, 133, 135
—, sir Gavin, curate of West Kilbride, 32
—, Rankin, burgess of Irvine, 16
—, Thomas, excommunicate priest, 32
Bryce, John, monk of Crossraguel, 126
Buchanan, Mr George, 55
Bunch, William, abbot of Kilwinning, 45
burials, protestant, 139
Burn, Robert, prior of the Irvine Carmelites, reader at Dundonald, 111

Campbell of Bargour, Charles, 68
— of Cessnock, George (Lollard), 40, 42–4
— — —, —, (fl.1560), 36, 46, 94, 99, 105,
— of Kinzeancleuch, Hugh, 67
— — —, Robert, 67, 80–1, 85, 94, 96, 98, 105, 116, 121, 123–4, 140–1, 142
— of Loudoun, Sir Hugh, sheriff of Ayr, 9, 13, 18–19, 62–3, 67, 90, 94, 98
— — —, Sir Matthew, — — —, 7, 81, 99, 121, 123
— of Newmilns, John, 40, 42–3, 46
— of Skerrington, Charles, 69
—, Mr Alexander, minister at Ardrossan, 125
—, Alison, wife of William Kirkpatrick, minister at Kilwinning, 134–5
—, Charles, bailie of Ayr, 106
—, Donald, abbot of Coupar Angus, 98
—, Elizabeth, wife of Robert Campbell of Kinzeancleuch, 81
—, George, son of George Campbell of Cessnock (fl. 1511), 45
—, Janet, wife of Mr David Mylne, minister at Dundonald, 135–6
—, John, Capuchin friar, 125
—, sir John, chaplain, 15
Carmichael of Balmeddie, Peter, 45
Carnwath (Lanarkshire), 39
Carrick, bailiary, 1–2, 28, 108, 111–12, 114, 120–1
Carrington, Thomas, reader at Symington, 111
Cassillis, 3rd earl of, Gilbert, 9, 55, 58–60, 62–3, 65, 103, 108
—, 4th earl of, Gilbert, 108, 120, 123, 126
—, earls of, 2, 19, 20
Cathcart, 4th Lord, Alan, 2, 10
— of Carlton, Alan, 94
—, sir William, chaplain, 15
Chalmers of Gadgirth, Sir James, 55, 81–2, 86, 99, 105, 108, 112, 121, 140, 142
— — —, Sir John, 81–2
— — —, Mr Robert, 55
—, Helen, lady of Polkellie (Lollard), 40, 46, 81–2
—, Margaret, lady of Cessnock, 40
—, Marion, lady of Stair (Lollard), 40, 81–2
Chapel of Our Lady of Kyle, Monkton, 14, 21
— of Our Lady of Lainshaw, Stewarton, 14
— of St Ninian at Lanfine, Galston, 14
— of St Donan, at Girvan, 29
— of St Wissane, Kilwinning, 14
chapels, in burgh churches, 15–17; rural, 14–15, 28–9
Chase-About-Raid, The, 123
Chatelherault, James (Hamilton), duke of, formerly 2nd earl of Arran, governor of Scotland, 10, 57, 62, 65, 76, 101
Chisholm, Mr James, parson of Tarbolton, 30
—, William, bishop of Dunblane, 74

Index

church, pre-Reformation, appointments in, 11–12, 23–6; laity's attitude to, 11, 33–4, 136; provincial councils of, 72–6, *passim*, 92, 136

clergy, post-Reformation, appointments in, 110–13;.effectiveness of, 136–8; financial support of, 113, 115–16, 118; manses and glebes for, 130–2; marriage and families of, 132–6; provision of, 109–19, 127; social background of, 114–15, 133–4

—, pre-Reformation, attitude to the Reformation, 109–12, 125–6; benefice system, 23–6; chaplains, 15–17, 26–8; concubinage, 72–3, 132; curates, 22, 27–33,; effectiveness of, 136–8; laity's attitude to, 33–4; recusants, 120–1, 125–6; training, 26, 109

Clerk, Leonard, minister at Dalmellington, reader at Kirkmichael, 112

Cochrane, George, commissioner for Ayr, 3

—, —, organist and master of the song school, Ayr, reader at St Quivox, 81, 91, 111

—, Janet, wife of James Dalrymple, minister at Ayr, 134–5

Cocklaw (or Gibson), Thomas, canon of Cambuskenneth, 53

collegiate churches, 14

Colmonell, church and parish, 25, 28–30, 96, 112

commendators, 17–19

Confession of Faith, The (1560), 106–7, 124

Congregation, Lords of The, 84, 87, 93–4, 99–104, 105–6, 109, 143; of Cunninghame and Kyle, 94, 96, 98, 101; of Angus and Mearns, 98

congregations, protestant, life of, 136–8, 141–2

Corry of Kelwood, George, 94

Coylton, church and parish, 28–9, 111–12

Craig, John, Dominican friar, later minister at Canongate and Edinburgh, 54

Craigie, church and parish, 28, 30, 98, 111

Crawford of Baidland, William, younger, 26, 32

— of Kerse, David, 94

— of Lefnorris, George, 105, 121

—, Archibald, minister at Kilmaurs, 114

—, Mr Archibald, vicar of West Kilbride, 12, 131

—, Mr James, vicar of West Kilbride, 12

Crichton, David, vicar of Ochiltree, 131

Cromwell, Thomas, English minister of state, 53

Crosbie chapel, 28–9, 45, 110–11

Crossraguel abbey, 1–2, 12, 28, 45, 110, 126; barony, 1

Cumnock, church and parish, 12, 28, 30, 112–13,

Cunningham of Caprington, John, 82, 105, 112, 121

— of Cunninghamhead, William, 98, 105, 108, 121, 123

— of Glengarnock, John, 105

—, Alexander, commendator of Kilwinning, 134

—, Andrew, son of William 3rd earl of Glencairn, 50–2, 62

—, Annabelle, widow of Sir James Chalmers of Gadgirth, 140

—, Florence, wife of sir Alan Porterfield, 125

—, John, minister at Dailly and Ballantrae, 112–15

—, Robert, minister (monastic superior) of Fail, 52, 66, 105

—, Mr Robert, recusant, 124

—, William, bishop of Argyll, 52, 73

Cunninghame, bailiary, 1, 3, 28, 108, 110–11, 114, 125

Curll, sir David, chaplain, reader at Tarbolton, 112

Dailly, church and parish, 28–9, 112, 114, 120

Dalmellington, church and parish, 28–9, 111–14,

Dalry, church and parish, 28–9, 32, 110

Dalrymple of Stair, James, 82, 121

—, James, chorister and later minister at Ayr, 81, 111, 128, 135

Dalrymple church and parish, 28–9, 111–12

Darnley, Henry, Lord, 12, 19, 123

Davidson, Alexander, reader at Maybole and Kirkbride, 112

—, James, minister (exhorter, reader) at Coylton, 112, 114

—, Mr John, regent in St Leonard's college, 116–17, 125, 140
—, sir Rankin, chaplain, exhorter at Loudoun and Galston, 111–12, 114, 137
Denham, Janet, wife of John Hamilton, minister at Dunlop, 133
Dewar, Michael, monk of Crosraguel, 122, 126
discipline, congregational, 137–8
Douglas of Drumlanrig, William (fl. 1417), 37
— of Lochleven, Sir William, 103–4
—, Sir George, brother of 6th earl of Angus, 62
—, John, ex-Carmelite friar, protestant preacher, 85
Dreghorn, church and parish, 21, 28–9, 111
Dumbarton (Dunbartonshire), 8, 62
Dunbar of Blantyre, John, 121
—, Mr George, minister at Ayr, 130
—, Mr John, parson of Cumnock, 12, 125
Dundee, 61, 65, 85,
Dundonald chapel, 45
Dundonald, church and parish, 28–9, 111, 113
Dunlop, sir John, vicar of Dalmellington, 122
—, church and parish, 21, 28, 110
Dunure castle, 123
Durham, Mr Michael, physician, 55
Durie, Andrew, abbot of Melrose, bishop of Galloway, 73

Eccles, sir Thomas, vicar and curate of Colmonell, 125
ecclesiastical estates, management of, 17–19
Edinburgh, 5–7, 86, 105–6; Treaty of, 102
Edward, Prince and later King of England, 57
Eglinton, 2nd earl of, Hugh, 19
—, 3rd earl of, Hugh, 19, 105, 108, 121, 123–4
—, earls of, 9–10, 51, 96
— castle, 120, 123
Elizabeth I, Queen of England, 88, 101–03
England, influence of, 4, 8, 42, 48, 51, 56–61, *passim*, 62–4, 101–04

Erskine, 6th Lord, John, 18, 107
— of Dun, John, 52, 65, 79, 82, 84–5, 101

Fail, monastery, 2, 28, 52, 110–11, 116
family worship, 140–1
Feane, George, reader at Dalrymple, 112
Fergushill of that Ilk, John, 121
feu-ferme, 21
Finlayston (Renfrewshire), 8, 82
Flanders, 4
Fleming, Malcolm, prior of Whithorn, 120, 122
Fockhart, Janet, Edinburgh merchant and moneylender, 6
— (Folkhart, Folkhird), Quintin, Lollard, 37–8, *passim*, 39
Foggo, John, abbot of Melrose, 38–9
Forrest, David, 79, 85
Forret, Thomas, canon of Inchcolm, vicar of Dollar, 53
France, influence of, 4, 76–7, 87–9, 100–04
Francis, Dauphin, later king of France, 87, 101–02
Fullarton of Dreghorn, John, 46, 94, 121, 123
—, — —, Mr John, 55
—, Adam, Edinburgh merchant, 46
—, Margaret, 96
—, Mr William, minister at Dreghorn, 125
—, family, 21, 100

Galloway, 1, 5
Galston, barony, 8; baptismal register, 137; church and parish, 20, 22, 28–9, 39, 50, 66–7, 80, 111, 116, 137
Gaw, John, Augustinian canon, 53
—, Robert, friar, reader at Barnweil, 127
general assembly, 110–11, 113, 120, 128, 131, 136
Gillem, Thomas, friar, 54, 61
Girvan, church and parish, 21, 29, 112, 120
Glasgow, cathedral, 5, 12, 28, 30, 112, 122; city, 5–6, 7–8, 15, 38; collegiate church of SS Mary and Anne, 28, diocesan authorities, 5–6, 40, 49, 51, 61
Glencairn, 4th earl, Alexander, 6–8, 51, 55, 58–9, 71, 78, 82–4, 90, 94, 98–9, 101, 105, 108, 110, 112, 121, 123

Index

—, 2nd earl of, Cuthbert, 45, 50–1
—, 3rd earl of (formerly Master of Kilmaurs, or Glencairn), William, 8, 10, 51, 58–63, 65, 79
—, 5th earl of (formerly Master of Kilmaurs, or Glencairn), William, 82, 105
—, earls of, 7–9, 51–2, 129
— (Dumfriesshire), barony, 8
Good, George, clerk, 49
Goodman, Mr Christopher, minister at Ayr, 97–8, 111, 115
Gordon of Airds, Alexander, 42
—, William, bishop of Aberdeen, 73–4
Gray, 4th Lord, Patrick, 62
—, Andrew, prebendary of Maybole, reader at Colmonell, 126
Greg, Mr James, (?)vicar of Dunsyre (Lanarkshire), minister at Colmonell, 112, 115

Hamilton of Cambuskeith, 120
— of Finnart, Sir James, 9
— of Sanquhar, Sir William, 9, 14, 58, 105, 138
—, Alexander, abbot of Kilwinning, 19
—, —, exhorter (reader) at Kilbirnie, 110
—, Mr Gavin, commendator of Kilwinning, 19, 74, 105, 134
—, John, abbot of Paisley, archbishop of St Andrews, 8, 44, 69, 74, 85–6, 106, 120–22
—, John (Hans), exhorter (reader), later minister at Dunlop, 110, 114, 133
—, Patrick, burnt for heresy (1528), 48, 52, 55, 76
—, Mr Robert, member of Edinburgh privy kirk, 85
—, — —, minister at Ochiltree, 112, 115
—, — —, vicar of Kilmarnock, 12
—, Mr Thomas, vicar of Kilmarnock, 12
—, William, tutor of Cambuskeith, 122
— family, 8–9, 11, 18
Hamilton's *Catechism*, 74–6, 78, 89
Harlaw, William, protestant preacher, 42, 85
Hay, Mr George, 121
Henderson, Alexander, monk of Kilwinning, exhorter at Ardrossan, reader at Kilmaurs, 110, 126, 134
—, Mr David, minister at Kilmaurs, 134
—, sir Edmund (or Eumonides), curate of Kilwinning, 30–1

Henry VIII, King of England, 51, 53, 56, 58–60, 77
Hepburn, Patrick, bishop of Moray, commendator of Scone, 73
Howie, sir John, vicar of, later reader at, Kilmaurs, 30–1, 111, 114, 116, 134
Hume, sir William, curate of Auchinleck, 33, 125
Hunter of Hunterston, Robert, 121
—, sir Henry, curate of Ayr, 30–2

iconoclasm, 49–50, 68–9
Inglis, Mr James, minister at Dailly, 118
—, Mr John, minister at Ochiltree, 128
Ireland, 3–4, 118
Irvine, burgh, 1–5, 106, 129, 143–4; Carmelite friary, 21, 111; grammar school, 137; presbytery, 128; parish, 20, 28–9, 31, 136–8; St Mary's church, 15–16

James, I, King of Scots, 37
—, IV, — — —, 40
—, V, — — —, 24, 50, 53, 56–7, 73
—, VI, — — —, 127–8
Jerome of Prague, 37
Jesuits, 120, 124
Johnston, Mr William, advocate, 55

Kelso abbey, 28, 37
Kennedy of Bargany, Thomas, younger, 109–10, 112, 123, 128
— of Barskeoch, George, 122
— of Blairquhennachy, Hugh, 122
— of Breckloch, John, 125
— of Girvanmains, Sir Hugh, 6, 139
— of Knockdaw, Thomas, 96
—, David, brother of K. of Brunstane, 122
—, Gilbert, monk of Crossraguel, 122, 126
—, Hugh, reader at Kirkoswald, 112
—, Quintin, abbot of Crossraguel, 12, 18, 44, 58, 93–5, *passim*, 105, 108, 120–1, 125
—, Thomas, tutor of Cassillis, 125
—, Walter, poet, 53
—, (unknown), burnt for heresy (1539), 50–1
—, family, 2, 12
Kerr of Kersland, Robert 121, 123
—, sir Alexander, chaplain, 27, 97

—, Mark, commendator of Newbattle, 107
Kilbirnie, church and parish, 21, 28, 30, 110
Kildominie chapel, 29
Kilmarnock, town, 4; church and parish, 28, 111
Kilmaronock (Dunbartonshire), 8
Kilmaurs, barony, 8; collegiate church, 21, 52; church and parish, 20, 28, 111, 114
Kilwinning, abbey, 3, 8–9, 18, 21, 28, 45, 68, 110, 126; barony, 3; church and parish, 28–9, 110
Kinloss abbey (Morayshire), 74
Kirkbride chapel, 39–40, 112
Kirkcaldy of Grange, Sir James, 55
Kirkcudbright-Innertig, See Ballantrae
Kirkmichael, church and parish, 28, 30, 112, 114, 120
Kirkoswald, church and parish, 28–9, 112, 120, 122
Kirkpatrick, John, merchant, bailie of Ayr, 81, 134
—, William monk and later minister of Kilwinning, 81, 110, 114–15, 126, 134
Knox, John, 17–18, 36, 38, 40, 43, 50, 54, 61, 65, 69, 74, 78–84, 86–7, 90, 95–8, 116, 121–3, 141, 143–4
Kravar (Craw, Crawar), Pavel (Paul), Hussite preacher, 36, 38–9
Kyle, bailiary, 1–2, 27–8, 97, 108, 110–14, 117, 121, 125
—, Lollards of, 36, 39–44, 144
Kylesmure, barony, 2, 9, 17–18, 21, 39–40

laity, role in the Reformation, 141–4
Lanark, 39
Landells, Adam, chaplain, exhorter at Cumnock, Ochiltree and Auchinleck, 112–14, 134–5
landholding, 7–10, 20–1
Largs, church and parish, 28–9, 110
Ledhouse, sir John, curate of Riccarton, 32
Leggat, sir Robert, chaplain, curate of Prestwick, vicar and curate of Ayr, reader at Prestwick, 30–1, 33, 81, 90–1, 98, 111
Leitch, sir John, chaplain, 45
Leith, 101; Convention of, 127–8
Lennox, 3rd earl of, John, 51

—, 4th earl of, Matthew, 10, 19, 62, 65
—, earls of, 8–9, 14
Lennox district of, 5, 8
Lesmahagow (Lanarkshire), barony, 37; parish, 39, 44–6; priory, 37, 39
Levington, Beatrix, wife of Adam Wallace, 70
Lind (Lyn, Lyne), John, friar, 54
—, —, minister at Irvine, 113, 115
—, Laurence, reader at Dreghorn, 115
Lindsay, 5th Lord, John, 107
literacy, 55–6
Lockhart of Bar, John, 55, 64–9, 79, 94, 99, 105, 108, 121, 123, 128, 142
Lockhart, Alexander, burgess of Ayr, 99
—, Mr George, 96
—, Helen, wife of Mr Robert Wilkie, minister at Kilmarnock, 133
—, John, bailie of Ayr, 81
—, —, recusant, 125
—, Mr Robert, 64, 66, 70, 79, 85
Lockharts of Bar, 8
Logie, Gavin, principal at St Leonard's college, 53
lollardy, 36–47, passim, 64, 144
Lorne, Lord, 8, 79, 84
Loudoun, church and parish, 28–9, 39, 50, 111
Lumsden, sir Alexander, curate of Stewarton, 31, 111
—, James, reader at Stewarton, 110–11
Lundie of that Ilk, Walter, 107
Luther, Martin, 42–3, 48, 132

MacAlpine, John, friar, 54
MacBrair, John, monk of Glenluce, 43, 69
MacLelland, sir Duncan, curate of Maybole, 125
McCartnay, Donald, monk of Glenluce, 69
MacNeill, sir Rolland, vicar of Girvan, 125
McConnel, John, reader at Dalmellington, 113
McCormyll, Andrew, vicar of Straiton, 17
McDowall, John, friar, 54, 69
McQuhorne, John, exhorter, later minister at Straiton, 112, 114
Maitland of Lethington, William, younger, 79, 101, 106–7
Marischal, 4th earl, William, 64–6, 82, 107

Index 191

Marjoribanks, Mr Thomas, vicar of Craigie, 23
Mary of Guise, Queen Dowager, Regent of Scotland, 62, 64, 76–7, 82–3, 86–90, 93, 99–102, 108, 141
—, Queen of Scots, 19, 57, 87, 101–2, 115–16, 120, 122–4
Mason, sir James, vicar and curate of Kilmarnock, 30, 33–4
—, John, recusant, 124
Mauchline, clachan, 2, 9, 18; church and parish, 13, 28–9, 31, 39, 50, 67–8, 112, 138
Maxwell, 5th Lord, Robert, 57, 62
—, Adam, monk of Crossraguel, 122, 126
—, sir John, curate and later minister (exhorter, reader) at West Kilbride, 110, 112, 131
Maybole, collegiate church, 21; church and parish, 28–9, 112
Meikle Cumbrae, chapel on island of, 29
Melrose abbey, 1–2, 17–18, 21, 28, 39–40, 67, 110
Methven, Henry Lord, 65
Mill, Walter, 87
Millar (Miller), sir John, chaplain, vicar of Symington, exhorter at Barnwell, 111
—, sir Richard, curate of Ayr, 81, 90
Mitchell, sir Andrew, curate of Mauchline, 67, 125
—, James, subprior of Kilwinning abbey, 126
—, sir James, curate of Mauchline, 30, 67
—, sir John, curate at Irvine and Ardrossan, 31, 33
Monkland, barony, 1
Monkton, barony, 2, 110; church and parish, 28–9, 31, 110–11
Montgomerie of Giffen, 105
— of Hessilhead, Hugh, 105, 121, 128
— of Lainshaw, 105
—, sir Jasper, chaplain, 124–5
—, Mr Robert, archbishop of Glasgow, 129
—, sir Thomas, vicar of Kirkmichael, 122
Morton, 4th earl of, James, Regent of Scotland, 84, 113, 116, 127–8
Moscrope, Mr John, advocate, 7
Muir (Mure), of Caldwell, 10
— of Rowallan, John, 94, 105
—, sir John, chaplain, minister at Kilmarnock, 111–12, 115

—, sir John, recusant, 124
—, William, acolyte, 26
Muirkirk, church and parish, 29
music, in protestant worship, 138

Naismith, sir Gavin, exhorter, later minister, at Dreghorn and Kilmaurs, 111, 114, 133, 135
Neill, sir David, curate of Largs and Monkton, exhorter at Largs, 33, 110
Nisbet, Murdoch, 36, 42–3, 46–7, 51, 55
Niven of Monkredding, Andrew, 121
North Berwick, nunnery, 28

Ochiltree, 1st Lord, Andrew, 2, 46, 49
—, 2nd Lord, —, 46, 50, 65, 69, 81, 94, 99, 101, 105, 110, 112, 121, 123–4, 131
Ochiltree, church and parish, 21, 28–9, 112
Oldcastle, Sir John, 37
Oliphant, Mr Andrew, vicar of Ballantrae, 23
Orr, John, schoolmaster at Ayr, 98, 111

Paisley abbey, 2, 18, 28, 33, 68, 110–11, 120, 122
parish clerk, office of, 13–14
parliament, 'Reformation', 105–07
Perceton, church and parish, 28, 30, 110
Perth, 98–100
piety, protestant, 139–41
Porterfield, sir Alan, vicar of Ardrossan, 12, 125–6
—, Mr John, minister at Kilmaronock, Dumbarton and Ayr, 12, 126, 129, 133, 137
Prague (Bohemia), 37
presbyterianism, 127–30
Preston, Mr John, Edinburgh merchant, 6–7
Prestwick, church and parish, 28–9, 111
Primrose, Mr Peter, minister at Mauchline, 118, 128
privy kirks, 78, 84–5

Ramsay, James, (?)curate, later reader at Alloway, 112
Randolph, Thomas, English ambassador, 106–07
Rankin of Shiel, Laurence, 68
recusancy, Catholic, 120–2, 124–6, 136

Reid of Barskimming, Adam (Lollard), 40, 44
— — —, —, signs Band of Ayr, 121
—, Adam, parish clerk of Mauchline, 13
—, Mr Martin, chancellor of Glasgow, 44
—, Paul, bailie of Ayr, 106
—, Robert, bishop of Orkney, commendator of Kinloss, 71, 74
Reseby, James, (English Lollard), 36–8
Riccarton, church and parish, 28–9, 31, 110, 113
Richardson, Robert, canon of Cambuskenneth, 53
Ritchie, John, Kilmarnock merchant, 4
roads, 5
Rolland, sir Thomas, parson and curate of Ayr, 30–1
Ros, Mr Gavin, chaplain and notary, 27
Rothes, 4th earl of, George, 62, 65
Rough, John, friar, 61, 65, 79, 95
Roxburgh castle, 37
Russell, Jerome, friar, 50–1

St Andrews university, 39
St Quivox, church and parish, 13, 28–9, 91, 111
Sandilands of Calder, Sir James, 79, 82, 86
Scone abbey, 98
Scrymgeour, Mr Alexander, minister at Irvine, 125, 137
Seton, Alexander, friar, 53–4
Shaw of Polkemmet, Andrew, younger, (Lollard), 40
—, William, 40
Shaw of Sornbeg, —, 94, 113
Shearer, Nicholas, chorister, 27
Sinclair, sir John, chaplain, 91
Smith, Henry, friar, reader at Glasserton (Wigtownshire), 127
—, Thomas, in Ochiltree, 138
Smollet, Margaret, wife of Mr John Porterfield, minister at Ayr, 133
Somerville, 5th Lord, James, 62
Sorn, church and parish, 29
Spottiswood, John, elder in Mauchline, 138
Stein, Alan, monk of Kilwinning, 126
Stevenston, church and parish, 28, 110
Stewart of Monkton, Sir William, provost of Ayr, 130

Stewart, Alan, commendator of Crossraguel, 12, 126
—, Lord James, prior of St Andrews, later earl of Moray, Regent of Scotland, 79, 100–01, 107, 123
—, James, commendator of Kelso and Melrose, 17, 40
Stewart, Robert, bishop of Caithness, 74
Stewart, Walter, son of 1st Lord Ochiltree, burnt for heresy, 49–50, 95
Stewarton, church and parish, 13, 28–9, 111
Stirling, 8, 90
Straiton, church and parish, 20, 28, 30
Strang, Mr William, minister at Irvine, 135–6
Sunday observance, 138
superintendents, office of, 127, 131
Symington, church and parish, 28–9, 31, 111, 116

Tait, Thomas, Ayr merchant, 5
Tarbolton, church and parish, 28–9, 112
teinds, 19–20, 113, 115–16, 118
Telfer, sir William, vicar of Cruggleton (Wigtownshire), 122
Thirds of Benefices, 113, 115–17, 135
Thornton, Mr John, precentor of Moray, 24
trade, Ayrshire, coastal, 3–4; European, 4–5
Tran, William, Irvine merchant, 4
Trent, council of, 25, 72
Tunnock, sir William, curate of Ochiltree, 31
'Two-penny Faith, The', 75–6, 89
Tyndale, William, 42–3, 48

Walker, sir (Mr), James, parson of Inchcailoch, vicar of, later minister at Stevenston, 82, 110, 114, 116
Wallace of Carnell, Hugh, 80, 94, 96, 99, 105, 116, 121, 123, 128
— of Craigie, John, 55, 94, 99, 105, 121, 140
— of Dundonald, John, 27
— of Wasford, Mr Michael, provost of Ayr, 55, 81, 106, 121
—, Adam, burnt for heresy, 69–71, 99, 142
—, —, chaplain, exhorter at Crosbie, 111
—, sir Adam, chaplain, 27

Index

—, sir David, chaplain, reader at Craigie, 111
—, George, bailie of Ayr, 22
—, Ninian, parish clerk of St Quivox, 13
—, Paul, parish clerk of Barnweil, 13
—, William, parish clerk of Symington, 13
Welsh, Mr John, minister at Ayr, 130
West Kilbride, church and parish, 28–9, 110
Wilkie, Mr Robert, minister at Kilmarnock, 111, 131–2, 133
Willock, John, friar, protestant preacher, 54, 61, 79, 85–6, 93–7, *passim*, 98–9, 109, 141
wills, protestant, 139–40
Wilson, Helen, widow of Adam Landells, exhorter at Cumnock, Auchinleck, 134–5
Winram, John, subprior of St Andrews, superintendent of Fife, 53, 107
Wishart of Pitarrow, Sir James, 65, 101
—, Mr George, reformer, 61, 63–69, 78–81, 95
worship, protestant, 138
Wreitton, Alexander, minister at Kilwinning, 134
Wycliffe, John, 36, 38, 42
Wylie, sir John, preceptor of the Chapel of Our Lady of Kyle, curate of, later minister at Monkton, 111, 113
Young, Mr James, reader at Girvan, 112
—, Mr John, minister at Beith and Irvine, 125, 128